ACCLAIM FOR
Change-Friendly Leadership

"A truly splendid book ... highly relevant, tremendously insightful, remarkably accessible. Rodger deeply understands the change process and how difficult it is for people and organizations to manage change. This profound understanding gives him an insightful perspective into how to solve it, i.e., 'how to engage people's heads, hearts, and hopes.' Rodger has created a user-friendly implementation guide to help buffer the shock wave that often accompanies change."
- Stephen M. R. Covey
New York Times bestselling author of *The Speed of Trust*

"I am impressed by the utter simplicity and brilliance of *Change-Friendly Leadership*. To borrow a well-worn political phrase, 'It's the relationships, stupid!' All too often businesses and organizations run on rules and regulations, bottom lines or fear. Those are obviously not the best way to get the most from people nor have a company be as productive as possible. The practices taught by Dr. Duncan can turn any organization around and create happier and more successful people at all levels."
- Dr. Laura Schlessinger
Radio host, author of twelve *New York Times* bestsellers

"In laying the groundwork for successfully implementing change in an organization, Dr. Rodger Dean Duncan recognizes the vital human elements of a smooth transition: the power of teamwork, the importance of trust, the value of communication, and why it's critical to regard your people as your business partners. With wisdom and insight, *Change-Friendly Leadership* beautifully brings home the simple truth that people are as important as results."
- Ken Blanchard
Coauthor of *The One Minute Manager®* and *Great Leaders Grow*

"I really like this book. It's full of stimulating thoughts coupled with examples that make them accessible and immediately implementable. *Change-Friendly Leadership* should be read—and used—by managers, consultants, academics, and the general public."

- Dr. Edgar Schein
Professor Emeritus, MIT Sloan School of Management
author of *Organizational Culture and Leadership*

"As a leader in the corporate world for over three decades, I find myself drawn to books which offer enlightened thinking on leadership that stand up to scrutiny from a practitioner's point of view and can be put to work on Monday morning. This is one of those books. I highly recommend it."

- Douglas R. Conant
Retired President and CEO, Campbell Soup Company
New York Times bestselling author of *TouchPoints*

"Dr. Rodger Dean Duncan is a brave and imaginative author. Brave because, without apology, he teaches 'people principles' to which many in business pay only lip service. Imaginative because he so clearly shows how those very principles are the key to successful leadership. The very future of our economy – our civilization, in fact – requires genuinely engaging the ingenuity and aspirations of people affected by change. And that's all of us! *Change-Friendly Leadership* shows the way."

- C. Jackson Grayson
Founder & Chairman, American Productivity & Quality Center

"Few people are as qualified as Dr. Rodger Dean Duncan to take a reader by the hand and chart a wise, proven, and practical course to profound change. *Change-Friendly Leadership* distills decades of experience into an engaging education in how to influence a small team or a global enterprise toward lasting change."

- Joseph Grenny
Coauthor of the *New York Times* bestseller *Crucial Conversations*

"Many books have changed my mind, but few have changed my habits. I cannot think of a single individual, company, or organization that wouldn't benefit from *Change-Friendly Leadership* and its powerful calls to action. If it doesn't inspire you to seek permanent, sustainable change, you weren't paying attention. It's *that* good."

- Jason F. Wright
New York Times, Wall Street Journal, USA Today bestselling author

"Dr. Rodger Dean Duncan has produced a truly engaging guide to leadership – packed with real-world stories that breathe fresh life into timeless principles. *Change-Friendly Leadership* will put new leaders on the right track and accelerate the improvement of those who are already more seasoned."

- Douglas Sterbenz
Executive Vice President & COO, Westar Energy

"Rodger has been instrumental in the success of our company. His book emphasizes all of the attributes that have resulted in effective change: engagement of the team, focusing on the hearts of our employees, and the key behaviors associated with building trust. These practical recommendations will make a huge difference in your organization. I am forever indebted to Rodger's insights, care, and compassion which contributed to the 20 years of excellence at STP."

- Ed Halpin
President & CEO, STP Nuclear Operating Company

"*Change-Friendly Leadership* is a highly engaging book with a powerfully positive message about personal transformation and human performance. Dr. Rodger Dean Duncan has crafted a work of brilliantly memorable models, genuinely compelling stories, and highly practical advice that inspire and energize. It's a work of optimism, compassion, and encouragement in a time when so much of what we hear about change is pessimistic, indifferent, and negative. And the self-assessments throughout the book will enable you to personalize the message and make it your own. It's the kind of book you can put to use immediately. So, do it!"

- Jim Kouzes
Coauthor of *The Leadership Challenge* Dean's Executive Fellow of Leadership, Santa Clara University

"*Change-Friendly Leadership* is a wonderful book, packed with truly valuable advice and many helpful examples. Dr. Rodger Dean Duncan distills the essential wisdom from years of experience in the trenches of corporate change efforts. He emphasizes the powerful impact of fully engaging individuals—and teaches how it's done through innovative tools and real world examples. A truly important book!"

- Sue Hickey
Former Chief Operating Officer, Bonneville Power Administration

"It's exciting to read a book that's useful to so many people in leadership positions, including parents. Every single principle that Dr. Duncan teaches has direct application to parenting. Good parenting is all about change-friendly leadership. This reader-friendly book inspires and teaches how to be the best in all of life's roles, including parent and leader."

- Dr. Nancy S. Buck
President, Peaceful Parenting Inc., author, *Why Do Kids Act That Way?*

"Dr. Rodger Dean Duncan is a masterful writer and storyteller! I love the way he uses stories to illustrate the key principles and practices he advocates. His life's work has been engaging people to help them achieve organizational success. *Change-Friendly Leadership* provides the recipe."

- Dr. Brent D. Peterson
Bestselling coauthor of *Fake Work*

"The title of this book says it all: *Change-Friendly Leadership*. It delivers on that promise. This book is a delight to read and has many change-friendly tools and ideas. I didn't think the world needed another book on change or leadership, but it did—and this is it."

- Norm Smallwood, Founder, the RBL Group

"Nothing is more fun to read than a practical book written by an active consultant who's willing to pass along great ideas that work. That's what *Change-Friendly Leadership* delivers. Not lots of theory, but many ideas you can and will actually use."

- Jack Zenger
CEO of Zenger Folkman and coauthor of the bestselling
The Extraordinary Leader and *The Extraordinary Coach*

"*Change-Friendly Leadership* by Dr. Rodger Dean Duncan is a must read for anyone who wishes to obtain and maintain a competitive edge in their business. The change-friendly protocol provides the practical framework for engaging people's 'heads, hearts, and hopes' in a deliberate and strategic way that can only lead to ultimate success."

- Hyrum Smith, Co-Founder, FranklinCovey

"Dr. Rodger Dean Duncan is a true visionary. This positive, thought-provoking book will lead the way to a more change-friendly world. As Rodger so clearly writes, no one can be left out of the dialogue in the society of the future."

- Nancy Harvey Steorts
Former Chairman, U.S. Consumer Product Safety Commission

"As Dr. Rodger Dean Duncan writes, 'Change is not the enemy. The enemy is poor management of change.' *Change-Friendly Leadership* is an excellent book about managing change through empowerment. That's what most workers want: Clear statements about goals and strategy and then the wisely granted freedoms to implement the change. Rodger tells how to do it."

- Diane Stafford, *The Kansas City Star*

"*Change-Friendly Leadership* connects the dots between engagement and leadership in a way that's both thoughtful and inspiring. Rodger Dean Duncan captures the essence of effective leadership in an environment of change. Embrace the behaviors he advocates and you're sure to get better results yourself."

- Dr. R. Wayne Pace
Founding President of the *Academy of Human Resource Development* and author of 30 books, including *Organizational Dynamism* and *Powerful Leadership*

"Leading through change is tough and, now as never before, necessary. Reading Rodger's book is like having a favorite uncle—wise, funny, and (yes) friendly, to guide you. Through timeless stories and real examples, he helps you understand what your people need most from you in the midst of change, and how to provide it."

- Erika Andersen
Founder and CEO of Proteus International, and author of *Growing Great Employees, Being Strategic,* and *Leading So People Will Follow*

"I loved this book! It provides a practical, tactical guide to making change happen and inspires you along the way. Rodger Dean Duncan breaks down the process of change like nobody else. He removes the fear factor and instead leaves you with a roadmap for success."

- Jodi Glickman
Author, *Great on the Job*

"This book will be treasured by anyone who leads or who is involved in a change initiative. It is highly practical and actionable. More importantly, it is grounded in core values that enable relationships to thrive and people to feel fulfilled, valued, and happy. With that foundation, the likelihood of successful change is greatly enhanced."

- Dr. Donald D. Deshler
Williamson Family Distinguished Professor of Education
Director, Center for Research on Learning, University of Kansas

"Dr. Rodger Dean Duncan is the Jedi Master of safe communications. By using the powerful tools identified in *Change-Friendly Leadership,* organizations can get on the fast track to operational excellence. This is a must-read book for leaders of all organizations."

- John F. Remark, PhD
CEO, Tudocs Nuclear Service Company

"From the moment I started to read *Change-Friendly Leadership,* I knew it would be hard to put down. This book is written in an extremely user-friendly way and will help any individual or organization going through change. And aren't we all? I've read a lot of books and heard hundreds of speakers on the topic of change, but this book gets to the real center of the issue with new and refreshing, usable information. Put it at the top on your list of books to read!"

- Nancy Lauterbach
Former president, International Association of Speakers Bureaus

"*Change-Friendly Leadership* is enormously useful. In addition, it's very wise. The wisdom lies in its simplicity, humanity, and humor. This book will have a permanent place in my library so I can savor it over and over."

- Rostya Gordon-Smith
CEO, People Impact (Czech Republic)

"You may not think 'change' and 'friendly' go together, but this new book shows you how it's not only possible but desirable for leaders to achieve. Dr. Rodger Dean Duncan is your guide to a new way of leading in a world where matters of the heart make a huge difference. You and those you lead will benefit from his insights."

- Mark Sanborn
Acclaimed speaker and bestselling author of *The Fred Factor* and *You Don't Need a Title to be a Leader*

"Many improvement initiatives fail because the human component is underappreciated. Rodger's message and framework are therefore especially welcome and timely. *Change-Friendly Leadership* offers a terrific collection of examples, principles and techniques that help produce positive transformation. And who wouldn't want that?"

- Steve Sashihara
CEO of Princeton Consultants, author of *The Optimization Edge*

"Finally! Someone levels with us about change. It's not easy. It takes work. And it takes ethical leaders who lead to tackle the tough issues we read about each day, the same issues no one wants to touch. Rodger dares to raise them. For example, leadership perks can sabotage change. And those perfunctory performance evaluations based on numbers or rating categories will no longer do. Take this book and use it to change your attitudes, your approaches to management, yourself, and, as a result your organization."

- Marianne M. Jennings
Professor of Ethical Studies, W.P. Carey School of Business, Arizona State University

"In an organization of any size, results rule. This thought-provoking book sheds light on leadership and communication practices that guarantee successful results. An excellent resource for any business professional."

- Dr. Nido Qubein
President, High Point University
Chairman, Great Harvest Bread Company

"After reading this book I felt I had just finished a candid two-hour fireside chat with my favorite wise old uncle. The message is both practical and inspirational for anyone who wants to practice extraordinary leadership."

- Carl E. Parry
President & CEO, Utilities Service Alliance, Inc.

"*Change-Friendly Leadership* rightly focuses on the 'people stuff.' Dr. Rodger Dean Duncan's wealth of experience in organizational culture and communications shows through in his excellent guide to challenging paradigms, conducting honest dialogue, earning and keeping trust, and collaborating in ways that foster enthusiasm, ingenuity and real energy in order to achieve successful change. A thoroughly enjoyable read!"

- Graeme Phipps
Managing Director, CoAlignment Pty Ltd, Melbourne, Australia

"Dr. Rodger Dean Duncan understands the challenges facing leaders today. Better yet, he provides a clear guide to meeting those challenges head on – and getting great results."

- Steve Harrison
Radio-TV Interview Report

"Having literally held Rodger's heart in my hands, I'm elated to see him so robustly 'walk the walk' that he advocates in *Change-Friendly Leadership*. Now the rest of us can continue to benefit from his ongoing brilliance and sage advice. Practice these principles faithfully, and they will be much more than merely an exercise. They will become your way of life!"
- Michael E. Gorton, MD
Cardiothoracic Surgeon

"Change happens. Whether you're a manager on any level in the corporate world, small or large business, a non-profit, the military or government, *Change-Friendly Leadership* will help you be more effective. Most of these pearls also apply to church and community service—and to strengthening your marriage and leading your family."
- Glen C. Griffin, MD
Author of nine books, columnist, founder of CAMIE AWARDS, Inc.

"This insightful book presents a refreshingly positive method for motivating your team (and yourself) through these times of guaranteed change. I love the models and stories you can repeat over and over to energize and get your team moving and embracing Change (with a capital "C"). *Change-Friendly Leadership* will alter how we all feel about the C word! It's truly a performance enhancer, and a must read for all leaders who want to go from great to greater!"
- Ann Rhoades
Former Chief People Officer at Southwest Airlines
Author of *Built on Values*

"A critical step toward organizational effectiveness—especially as it relates to safety issues—is creating and maintaining an environment where people are comfortable raising 'risky' subjects for open and honest discussion. *Change-Friendly Leadership* provides a clear guide in how to do it."
- Peter Rail
Founding President, *National Association of Employee Concerns Professionals*

CHANGE-
friendly
LEADERSHIP

CHANGE-
friendly
LEADERSHIP

**How to Transform
Good Intentions into
Great Performance**

Dr. Rodger Dean Duncan

Maxwell Stone
PUBLISHING

Change-Friendly®, Think-Friendly®, Talk-Friendly®, Trust-Friendly® and Team-Friendly® are registered service marks of Rodger Dean Duncan.

Contact us at Resources@DoctorDuncan.com for information on the following:
- Permission to use quotes from the book that are longer than brief quotes for a review
- Bulk orders of the book, with volume discounts
- Workshops and retreats based on the *Change-Friendly Leadership* content
- Diagnostic tools, including culture assessments, 360-degree feedback, etc.
- Keynote speeches and other presentations by Dr. Rodger Dean Duncan

Library of Congress Cataloging-in-Publication Data

Duncan, Rodger Dean.
Change-friendly leadership: how to transform good intentions into great performance / by Dr. Rodger Dean Duncan. – 1st ed.
p. cm.
Includes index
ISBN 978-0-9852135-0-3 (alk. paper) — eBook ISBN 9780985213510
1. Leadership. 2. Friendship—Sociological aspects. 3. Interpersonal relations. I. Title.
HD57.7.D8486 2012
658.4'092—dc23
2012010480

Published in the United States by Maxwell Stone Publishing
Distributed by Midpoint Trade Books
www.midpointtrade.com

Printed in the United States of America

Jacket, interior design, and graphics by Nancy Newland

TABLE OF CONTENTS

Foreword

By Stephen M.R. Covey
Author of the *New York Times* bestseller *The Speed of Trust*

One of my favorite pastimes has been watching my son play on his high school basketball team. I'll never forget one very crucial game when my son's team was struggling to get ahead with very little time left on the clock. For some reason, the team just wasn't "clicking" the way it had been earlier in the game, even though they had their five best players on the floor. They seemed sluggish and out of energy. Sensing this, the coach called a time-out and made a change, taking out the team's 6' 8" big man and subbing in a smaller 6' 0" guard. At first, most of us parents and fans felt it was the wrong move;

"A robust, 'change-friendly' approach to navigating change provides the focus for this truly remarkable book."

after all, our big man was our leading scorer and the crux of the team. It made us very uncomfortable to see him on the bench where the option to pass to him underneath was gone. But soon an amazing thing began to happen. As a result of the change, the fresh, quick guard began to draw out the defense of the other team, opening up entirely new possibilities to score. The whole nature of the game changed. The team was no longer one-dimensional. They began to click again, and they went on to win! Looking back, it was obvious that "mixing things up" had enabled the team to take a big step forward.

This is often the case with change. Initially, it can feel wrong or unsettling because we're messing with something familiar that maybe works well enough; yet we frequently can't see far enough down the line to recognize the enormous benefit we can gain by "mixing things up." This reality, combined with a robust, "change-friendly" approach to navigating change, provides the focus for this truly splendid book written by my good friend and colleague, Dr. Rodger Dean Duncan.

I am honored to have the opportunity to write this foreword because of what I know of Rodger's character and competence—of who he is and what he can do. Rodger deeply understands the change process and how difficult it is for people and organizations to manage change. This profound understanding gives him an insightful perspective into how to solve it, i.e., "how to engage people's heads, hearts, and hopes." Rodger has created a user-friendly implementation guide to help buffer the shock wave that often accompanies change. But most importantly, he compellingly teaches us not only how to shepherd our own way through change, but also how to engage others along the path.

While there are literally dozens of reasons why I love this book, let me focus on the three reasons I find most salient and compelling. First, this book is highly *relevant*. It deals with what's going on everywhere we turn today. It deals with the reality that "the only constant is change." In contrast to the still, calm, placid lake of yesterday, the metaphor

"There are literally dozens of reasons why I love this book ... it is highly relevant, tremendously insightful, remarkably accessible."

that best describes the nature of the world today is what we might call "permanent whitewater"—a constant churning, shifting, changing environment which, unfortunately, we're not yet good at navigating. This is clearly evidenced by the fact that most change efforts fail to achieve their intended objectives. But Rodger's approach empowers us to effectively confront the challenge of change in a whitewater world.

Second, this book is tremendously *insightful*. Rodger's wise, principled material sinks deep into the reader's mind and heart from the start, primarily because it rings true. He emphatically acknowledges how change often creates feelings of fear, stress, anxiety, and concern. While others may dismiss these feelings as "soft" emotions that have no relevance, Rodger's distinct recognition of these universally human feelings gives us confidence in his understanding and hope in his solution. Rarely do people leave their comfort zone without putting up a fight. The fact that this book speaks so convincingly to the whole person, not just the intellect—adds to the confidence and courage we need to break out. This book also provides excellent insight into what constitutes a great leader. Character, trust, listening, fairness, and respect are all characteristics of what we look for in leaders and what others look for in us. Rodger points out how critical developing these qualities is to creating engagement and wisely reminds us that "you can rent a person's back and hands, but you must earn his head and heart."

Third, this book is remarkably *accessible*. Books in this genre are often abstract and theoretical. But *Change-Friendly Leadership* is precisely what its title suggests: easy-to-read, practical, and engaging. Rodger shares four simple yet profound strategies to navigate change, which he names the "Four Ts." These represent the foundational framework that directs us along the path by teaching us important principles and behaviors that will help us succeed. He follows these up with seven critical action steps that create a tool or compass to enable us to

> *"Rodger's approach allows us to take hold of the reins of change in our own lives and to manage it effectively in our organizations."*

navigate successfully to the change we seek. Rodger's "Trust Builders" help leaders develop "influence rather than authority" and empower teams to work together effectively to accomplish results.

Benjamin Franklin once said, "When you're finished changing, you are finished." I am sure Dr. Rodger Dean Duncan would agree. Change is inevitable. It is the natural progression of life. It is also scary and uncertain at times. By validating our unease and then charting a course to follow, Rodger's approach allows us to take hold of the reins of change in our own lives, and to manage it effectively within our organizations. *Change-Friendly Leadership* provides the vital framework and process that enable us to thrive and accomplish our goals. The results we achieve and the growth we gain will make it well worth the journey.

Preface

If nothing ever changed, there'd be no butterflies.

What object is several times larger than most homes, can comfortably accommodate enough people to populate a small town, weighs more than 400 tons, and can fly? The answer, of course, is a jumbo jet. By employing laws of physics discovered by Newton, Bernoulli, and others, the jet is able to overcome its own mammoth weight and create the lift that allows it to soar.

When it relates to change, the airplane metaphor is apropos. Many change efforts that manage a promising takeoff eventually cough and sputter to a crash. Without something to provide lift, most of them never even get off the ground. The burden of their own weight—inertia, skepticism, resistance—is simply too much to surmount.

Most dictionaries describe lift as carrying or directing from a lower to a higher position, the power available for rising to a new level, or a force opposing the tug of gravity. This book is about creating the lift that allows change efforts to soar. In the same way that aerodynamic lift can transport us above the storms of our planet, the principles of human interaction can elevate us above inertia and resistance to new realms of performance.

This book is not intended for the academic purist or for the organizational development wonk, although it is well grounded in sound academic philosophy and OD principles. This book is written to appeal to and help any individual or organization needing a user-friendly guide to managing change, transition, and implementation issues. This includes:

- Directors, senior executives, and middle-management people of business enterprises of any size in any industry, as well as in non-profit organizations
- Human resources, strategic planning, project management, and corporate development professionals
- People involved at every level of merger and acquisition work on both the buy and sell side
- Training and development personnel
- Management consultants and performance coaches
- Colleges and universities, especially as part of a business curriculum (also applicable to student government)
- Local governments, including city councils, county commissions, and all related entities
- Local school boards, churches, and other community organizations that struggle with change, transition, and implementation issues

Yes, that's a pretty broad audience. But most people—from the corporate boardroom to the local school association—are called upon to grapple with change.

Readers who embrace and follow the principles and practices prescribed in *Change-Friendly Leadership* will be:

- More aware of and committed to the power of character-driven change;
- More able to build a compelling case for action on the changes and transitions they champion;
- More attuned to the nuances of resistance, and how to use resistance as a positive force that actually fosters change and transition;
- Better equipped to build a solid network of cascading Sponsors, as well as focused Champions, effective Agents, and receptive Targets;
- More skilled in the subtleties of strategic alignment—

ensuring that change plans are in sync with and take advantage of critical cultural elements;

- More proficient in formulating and using communication and reinforcement strategies and tactics;
- More confident and more competent in dealing with change holistically, avoiding the traps of linear thinking; and
- More effective in every element of principle-centered leadership.

The self-assessments at the end of each chapter are intended to provide good mental gymnastics as well as behavioral reinforcement.

I also encourage you to log on to **www.DoctorDuncan.com** where you'll find a wealth of free resources to help you make the "friendly factor" a key element of your own change efforts. And of course we'd love to have you use our Change-Friendly® diagnostic tools and training workshops in your organization.

Building a critical mass of Change-Friendly people greatly enhances the likelihood of your success.

Dr. Rodger Dean Duncan
Liberty, Missouri

◄ Smart Phone Link
DoctorDuncan.com

SECTION ONE

What's the Big Deal About Change?

When our children were very young, my wife and I took the family on a cross-country trip. Several days in the close quarters of a car can be challenging, especially so when many of the conversations begin with the question "Are we there yet?" So we carefully planned every detail of the journey.

For each of our various stops along the way, we reserved a room at a Howard Johnson hotel. We knew that all across the country these hotels were decorated with exactly the same wall colors, lamps, and bedspreads. To help our children feel more "at home" each night, we even specified that each room must have the beds on the right and the TV on the left. Sameness, we reasoned, would be comforting.

The trip seemed to be going well. The children were patient and the parents were still relatively sane. Then on the third night we checked into yet another Howard Johnson hotel. As soon as we walked into our room—which was identical to the others we'd slept in that week—our four-year-old son threw up his hands and with a tone of utter despair said, "We've been driving forever and we keep coming back to the same room!"

That's exactly what change can feel like. Despite your best efforts, some people will continue to ask "Are we there yet?" Some won't mind taking a trip, just not in the direction you're headed. Others will resist getting in the car at all.

For most people, change really is a big deal. Change can involve the adoption of new technologies, reengineering, mergers and acquisitions, restructuring, culture blending, or any of a number of other forms. Change is a big deal because it often requires leaving our comfort zones. Change is a big deal because it touches on our sentiments and devotions, some of which may not be apparent even to us.

The big deal about change is usually not about strategy or structure or systems. All of those things are of course important. But the core of it all is *feelings*. In the world of human commerce, nothing changes unless and until people's behaviors change. And the kind of behavior change that results in lasting (sustainable) change must accommodate people's *feelings*—feelings that involve trust, confidence, passion, and all those other intangible but very real things that make us human.

You can rent a man's back and hands, but you must *earn* his head and heart.

Change really is a big deal. Work hard to accommodate people's feelings—their heads, hearts, and hopes—and your change effort can be one of the success stories.

All one has to do is hit the right keys at the right time and the instrument plays itself.
Johann Sebastian Bach

You have brains in your head. You have feet in your shoes. You can steer yourself any direction you choose.
Dr. Seuss

If you think you're too small to have an impact, try going to bed with a mosquito.
Anita Roddick

Just when the caterpillar thought life was over, it became a butterfly.
Anonymous

Chapter

The High Cost of Belly Flop:
A Case for Engagement

Losing good people is costly. But the number one most expensive thing that can happen to your organization is for your best and most capable people to quit and stay.

In the sweltering Oklahoma summers of my youth, a favorite pastime was swimming in Mr. Colby's pond. In place of a diving board, we used the horizontal branch of a large elm tree that hung about 10 feet over the water. The pond was too shallow for deep diving, but we didn't have the skill for anything fancy anyway. So the favorite launch protocol—after all, teenage boys like to make loud noises and big splashes—was the belly flop. In exchange for congratulatory whoops and hollers, we often paid a painful price. What the belly flop lacks in grace and elegance it makes up for in the raw force of fundamental physics. It hurts. Sometimes a lot.

Many so-called change efforts seem to employ the launch protocol of the belly flop. Lots of noise, big splashes, a few congratulatory whoops and hollers. But then the pain sets in. Sometimes a lot of pain.

Every time an implementation fails to achieve its stated objectives on time and on budget, there are costs. The costs are both short-term and long-term, both direct and indirect.

Short-term, direct costs of an implementation belly flop include the waste of valuable resources like money, time, and people. And of course the business objective is not achieved—the service is delivered late, the customer is dissatisfied with quality, the organization remains stuck in a weak market position, or hopes for an energized workforce are not realized.

Another common short-term, direct casualty of implementation failure is the job security of the people charged with making the change work. Fair? Maybe not. But it's a reality.

A short-term, indirect cost of implementation belly flop often involves a decline in morale. Our culture studies in a wide range of industries show that a common ingredient in low morale is the belief that "we have trouble finishing anything right around here." A disheartened employee is a disengaged employee.

> "A disheartened employee is a disengaged employee."

The most familiar long-term, direct cost of implementation belly flop is simply that strategic goals are not accomplished. For example, the merger fails to produce its intended synergies, managers fail to make the transition from command and control to a more facilitative style, the organization misses the mark on a range of evolutions that would make it more competitive.

And then there are the long-term, indirect costs of an implementation belly flop. They are often the most painful of all, and they affect the organization's ability even to survive. These costs can include diminished confidence in leadership, increased resistance to change, and an even higher likelihood that the next change effort will fail.

But of course change is inevitable. Change is relentless. Change is ever-present. In fact, as Army General Eric Shinseki put it, "If you don't like change, you'll like irrelevance even less."

Trouble is, as our family obstetrician used to say, for most folks it's easier to conceive than to deliver. That truism applies not just to making babies. It also applies to dealing with change. By nearly every account, the majority of leadership strategies aimed at creating change are doomed for failure.

The Association for Corporate Growth, a top player in the merger and acquisition arena, says only 20% of deals live up to original expectations.

ASTD, the world's leading group of workplace learning and performance professionals, says employers are spending record amounts on training. Yet *Quality Magazine* reports that less than 30% of all training is being used on the job a month later.

At a time of widespread agreement that improving education is critical to America's future, the National School Board Foundation says systemic reform nearly always breaks down because of poor implementation.

How challenging are effective change and implementation? Consider this analogy from the chief operating officer of a large corporation, quoted in the *Harvard Business Review*:

> *"It's like the company is undergoing four medical procedures at the same time. One person is in charge of a root canal, someone else is setting the broken foot, another person is working on a displaced shoulder, and still another is getting rid of a gallstone. Each operation is a success, but the patient dies of shock."* [1]

Change takes us out of our comfort zones and produces stress. It's often the stress that people resist, not the change itself. Even positive change produces stress. Just ask anyone who's planned a wedding.

Another reason for resistance is that change tends to be cumulative, as indicated by the previous quote from the chief operating officer. Simply put, there's a lot of simultaneous activity going on in most organizations—a lot of competition for time, budget, and other resources. Even when we find smart people doing smart things, we often find a lack of integration. The result is what I call *fragmented focus*. It's very frustrating to good people—sort of the way you'd feel if you spent your day trying to push water uphill with a rake: lots of activity but only marginal results.

"It's often the stress that people resist, not the change itself."

Every day's headlines report yet another plan, another reorganization, another big idea that has fallen flat. Tall dreams. Tall talk. Short results. Inertia is winning by a wide margin.

Change can take many avenues. Change can move an organization and the people in it to an exciting new future. Change can seduce people into a limbo of change for change's sake. And change can suck organizations and people into oblivion.

As with many things in our world—like the notions of "culture" and "accountability"—change management has become trivialized and diluted by a multitude of sometimes conflicting and often damaging definitions. Regardless of definition, change is not the enemy. The enemy is poor management of change.

THE FRIENDLY FACTOR

During the years I contemplated writing this book I struggled with many titles. An early idea was ChangeSmarts, connoting the skills needed to "make change happen." But "smarts" can strike some people as a bit arrogant, presumptuous, or self-important.

ChangeWise was another possibility. Wise is better than Smarts because it implies an experienced, even sage-like approach. But wise can also connote sassiness, as in "wise guy."

Then it dawned on me. Many of the failed change efforts I've seen over the past 40 years certainly had the best of smarts and wisdom. Some of them, with their endless charts and graphs and to-do lists, were monuments to planning procedures. What they lacked was ease of use.

> *"Change-by-announcement, change-by-slogan, and certainly change-by-executive-decree are doomed to failure."*

They lacked humanness. They lacked approachability. They lacked . . . well, they lacked *friendliness.*

Change-Friendly Leadership: How to Transform Good Intentions into Great Performance is a simple affirmation that successful organizational change involves—*requires* in fact—the active, willful participation of the people affected by the change.

Change-by-announcement, change-by-slogan, and certainly change-by-executive-decree are doomed to failure.

Effective change requires genuinely engaging the brains of the people expected to embrace and even champion the new state of affairs.

Effective change requires engaging people's feelings—not merely making a business case for action, but making a compelling psychological case for action.

Effective change requires engaging people's earnest hopes.

In this context, *hope* is not used as the verbal equivalent of crossing your fingers—"I hope my team wins the game." In this book, *hope* is used to denote people's heartfelt aspirations, their dreams, even their sense of self. Any

> *If at first the idea is not absurd, there is no hope for it.*
> **Albert Einstein**

change effort that ignores or pays mere lip service to that kind of engagement is destined for disappointment.

In the change approach prescribed here, the Friendly Factor is not just a play on words. It is the very foundation for effectively engaging people's heads, hearts, and hopes. Think-Friendly®, Talk-Friendly®, Trust-Friendly®, and Team-Friendly® form a relationship framework or operating system that brings out the best in people.

WHY ENGAGEMENT MATTERS

Let's define engagement. In our Change-Friendly context we use the concept of engagement to mean the harnessing of people's energy, ingenuity, and allegiance to their work roles. In our view, a person is "engaged" when he feels positive emotions toward his work, when he regards his work as personally meaningful, when he considers his workload to be manageable, and when he has positive expectations (hope) about the future of his work.

When Duncan Worldwide studies an organization's culture, we examine people's behaviors, their attitudes, and their assumptions. Then we examine the conditioning that reinforces those behaviors, attitudes, and assumptions. One of the first dimensions we inspect is something we call "psychological ownership." We want to understand the extent to which people feel they "own" their work. This has nothing to do with entitlement or privilege. It has everything to do with engagement, with feeling a personal connection and commitment to the work.

Engagement is one of the things we listen for when conducting interviews in a culture assessment.

Here's what engagement often "sounds" like:

- *Physical component* – "When I'm at work I seem to bubble over with energy." (Engaged people enjoy vigor and vitality.)
- *Emotional component* – "Our work is important, and I'm glad to be a part of it." (Engaged people feel positively connected to their work.)
- *Cognitive component* – "I get so immersed in my work I lose track of time." (Engaged people are positively absorbed in their work.)

Engagement is not just some soft feel-good factor. It has serious consequences that should be mindfully tended to by anyone who's serious about productivity, effective change, and good business results.

With the job insecurity of an economic downturn, one might assume that people would focus even more on their jobs and be more engaged than ever. But in a time of "psychological recession,"[2] as one expert calls it, many workers are less engaged than ever. Having witnessed years of eroding corporate loyalties, organizational downsizing, job losses to globalization, unstable employment, and fragile trust, many workers adopt a pessimistic view. They invest growing amounts of psychic energy in telling themselves victim, villain, and helpless stories. In times of instability, others try to stay off the "cut" list by working harder and longer to demonstrate their value. But even that noble effort can produce unintended negative consequences such a job burnout, quality deficits, and health problems like chronic fatigue, sleep disorders, stress, anxiety, and depression. In some work environments, these conditions contribute directly to safety problems.

> *Do, or do not. There is no try.*
> **Yoda, *The Empire Strikes Back***

Without doubt, creating and maintaining a work environment that fosters engagement is important at any time. In times of economic stress, it is doubly so.

So, how many workers are engaged in their work? Research studies across a wide spectrum of organizations indicate this general trend:

- 20% of employees can be described as genuinely engaged. They find meaning in their work, feel connected to their organization's purpose, and see how their work contributes to that purpose. These are the people who provide the highest levels of initiative, ingenuity, and vitality so critical to organizational success.

- 55% of employees demonstrate a moderate level of engagement. They show up, they do their jobs, but without much personal investment.
- 25% of employees are actively disengaged, just going through the motions. Except for picking up their paychecks, they have pretty much checked out. In this group we find a lot of ROAD Warriors (Retired on Active Duty).

The numbers vary from place to place, but they seem to be directionally similar everywhere. We've done culture assessments in a wide assortment of organizations, ranging from banks, pharmaceutical companies, and engineering firms to hospitals, manufacturers, and nuclear power plants. Our own studies show that the greatest opportunity for performance improvement usually lies in the middle group, people who are not yet actively disengaged but

> *Results are obtained by exploiting opportunities, not by solving problems.*
> **Peter Drucker**

who have lost (or perhaps never had) the connectedness of the truly engaged workers. Making positive strides with this "show me" group does two things. First, it dramatically boosts overall organizational performance. Second, it makes the ROAD Warriors even more obvious and tends to "call them out" on their behavior. Performance accountability is simply easier to manage when the poor performers are more clearly differentiated from their coworkers.

A 2010 Global Workforce Study by Towers Watson involved more than 20,000 employees in 22 markets around the world.[3] It provides a comprehensive analysis of employee mindset in a struggling world economy.

- The social contract, or "deal," between employer and employee is changing. "Perform well, stay with us, and we'll reward you fairly and help you grow" is evolving into something far more elastic and conditional. The demands of an ever-changing business environment play a huge role in that interdependency.

- In today's super competitive business climate, there's a growing gap between what employees want and expect from the shifting relationship, and what employers can afford to deliver. This widening relationship gap could compromise employers' ability to retain top talent.
- Organizations have a unique opportunity to define a new and more sustainable relationship with their people.

All of this has change and engagement implications. With that backdrop, the Towers Watson study provides other insights relevant to a Change-Friendly work environment:

- Confidence in leaders and managers is dangerously low, especially in terms of the interpersonal or "relational" (versus operational) aspects of their roles. People hunger for an emotional connection to their management teams, and they feel that connection is conspicuously absent.
- Only 38% think their leaders have a sincere interest in their well-being.
- Only 47% regard their leaders as trustworthy.
- Just 42% say their leaders inspire and engage them.
- 61% question how well managers deal with poor performers.

All of these findings are consistent with what we find in our culture audits and performance assessments.

In an age when the desire for security trumps everything else, it's especially critical (and realistic) for organizations to draw a bright line between the old-style "passive" security (the "take care of me" variety) and a more "active" security that enables employees to take

> *He who has a why can bear almost any how.*
> **Friedrich Nietzsche**

care of themselves. Equipping people to secure their own futures is a proven way to retain and engage. A welcome by-product is that engaged employees are less stressed and more productive.

DISCRETIONARY EFFORT

By definition, a Change-Friendly work environment engages people's heads, hearts, and hopes. True engagement is a function of *discretionary effort*. People don't become engaged because they've been ordered or compelled to. They become engaged because they deliberately *choose* to invest their energy, enthusiasm, ingenuity, and passion in a cause that has meaning and value for *them*. An "engagement gap," then, is the difference between the level of discretionary effort needed to produce desired results and the level of discretionary effort actually expended.

LEVELS OF ENGAGEMENT

In our work with culture and performance issues, we notice that people connect to the organization across three dimensions:

- *Rational* – the "thinking" part of the relationship dynamic. How well do people understand their roles and responsibilities? To what extent do they really understand the contribution they make and how it "fits" with the work of others?
- *Emotional* – the "feeling" part. How much passion and energy do people bring to their work? How much do they really care about the organization's success? To what extent are they vested in what's best for the organization's stakeholders?
- *Motivational* – the "acting" part of the relationship. How well do people perform their roles? How much effort do they put into personal improvement?

Based on responses to our questions (as well as our observations of their actual behavior), people are clustered into four groups:

- *Engaged* – These people are giving full discretionary effort. They have high scores on all three dimensions (Rational, Emotional, and Motivational).
- *Enrolled* – These people are partially engaged. They typically score well on the Rational and Motivational dimensions, but are less connected on the Emotional dimension.

- *Disenchanted* – These people are partly disengaged. They have lower scores on all three dimensions of engagement, especially the Emotional connection.
- *Disengaged* – These people have disconnected on all three dimensions. They do not contribute to organizational success, and they are often a noticeable drag.

As you might expect, there can be migration within and between these clusters. With the right mix of opportunity, coaching, and encouragement, Enrolled people can become fully Engaged. If they perceive opportunity to be diminishing, and absent the right coaching and encouragement, Enrolled people can become Disenchanted.

> *The vision is really about empowering workers, giving them all the information about what's going on so they can do a lot more than they've done in the past.*
> **Bill Gates**

In turn, Disenchanted people can become fully Disengaged if they go extended periods without an emotional connection to their work.

With appropriate diagnostic tools, it's possible to get a fairly clear reading on where people are operating on the engagement continuum. This is not just interesting information. It's critical data in creating and maintaining an environment that engages people's heads, hearts, and hopes.

"THE PEOPLE STUFF"

In some organizations the pace of change is so frenetic and the people feel so out of control that the workplace resembles a cast party for *Return of the Zombies*. In this kind of atmosphere, resistance, cynicism, and fatigue come not so much from a particular change effort but from the cumulative enormity of what people are asked to do.

The question is not whether to change. Change is a constant, and it's not going away. If it seems as though the status quo is the status quo for only about 20 minutes, it's because that's simply the world in which we live. Standing still means being left behind. Success hinges on choosing what to change and then implementing the change with appropriate timing and speed while tending to the "people stuff" that can make all the difference.

Of course "the people stuff" is often the biggest challenge.

Here's a true story about a baggage handler who was a walking metaphor for what ails many change efforts.

My Delta Airlines flight had just landed in Fort Myers, Florida. The flight was an hour late and I was especially eager to stay on schedule for a client meeting. This particular plane was a smaller aircraft (with only about 50 seats), so we had to check luggage at the gate. Upon arrival, we were told to wait for our bags to be unloaded and then carted to the jetway.

I watched the baggage handler carefully. He had his left hand in his pants pocket and reached into the belly of the plane with his right hand to retrieve each bag. Even with the heavier bags, which he lifted only with great effort, he used only his right hand. Naturally, this slowed the process considerably. Being an experienced traveler, I quickly did the math. This one-armed baggage handling method was going to take at least ten minutes longer than normal. About 30 passengers were waiting for their luggage. That's 300 minutes—five hours!—of unnecessary waiting.

> *"Of course 'the people stuff' is often the biggest challenge."*

An airline gate agent was standing nearby, so I started a conversation.

Rodger: *Do you notice that the baggage handler is using only one hand?*

Agent: *Yeah. He keeps his left hand in his pocket.*

Rodger: *Is he injured?*

Agent: *No. He's lost a lot of weight and he keeps one hand in a pocket so he can hold his pants up.*

Rodger: *Are you serious?*

Agent: *Yeah. He's planning to lose about 20 more pounds and he doesn't want to buy new pants until he reaches his target weight.*

Rodger: *Why doesn't he cinch up his belt?*

Agent: *It's already on the tightest notch and he doesn't want to buy a new belt until he's finished losing weight.*

Rodger: *I wonder if he knows that he could punch more holes in his belt. Or he could hold his pants up with suspenders, or even a piece of rope.*

Agent: *He's apparently not thought of that.*

Rodger: *I wonder if he realizes he could burn more calories and lose weight faster if he used both arms to handle the luggage.*

Really, I'm not making this up.

Here was a man who was clearly not engaged in his work (and apparently his supervisor wasn't either). In fact, it could be argued that he wasn't fully engaged in his own weight loss program.

Being Change-Friendly is about engaging people's heads, hearts, and hopes in the causes they serve. It's about helping people "connect the dots" between their own values and aspirations and the strategic goals and purposes of their organizations. Unlike the baggage handler who kept customers waiting rather than hold his britches up with a tighter belt (or even a piece of rope), Change-Friendly people see the big picture. They understand strategic imperatives. They understand the tactics needed to translate good intentions into great results.

Then they make it happen.

---

[1] Jeanie Daniel Duck, "Managing Change: The Art of Balancing," *Harvard Business Review*, November-December 1993, 1.

[2] Bardwick, J.M. (2007). *The Psychological Recession: Why your people don't seem all that excited about coming to work these days.* New York: The Conference Board. Accessed online May 18, 2010 from www.conference-board.org/articles/atb_article.cfm?id=444.

[3] *The New Employment Deal: How Far, How Fast and How Enduring.* New York: Towers Watson. Accessed online May 18, 2010 from www.towerswatson.com/global-workforce-study.

*Nobody can go back and start a new
beginning, but anyone can start today and
make a new ending.*
Maria Robinson

*Life is change. Growth is optional.
Choose wisely.*
Karen Kaiser Clark

*God grant me the serenity to accept the people
I cannot change, the courage to change the
one I can, and the wisdom to know it's me.*
Anonymous

*The reasonable man adapts himself to the
world; the unreasonable one persists in trying
to adapt the world to himself. Therefore, all
progress depends on the unreasonable man.*
George Bernard Shaw

*Continuity gives us roots; change gives us
branches, letting us stretch and grow and
reach new heights.*
Pauline R. Kezer

Chapter

Change-Friendly: Its Rhyme and Reason

Changes and transitions need not have a fingernail-on-the-chalkboard quality. When handled well, they can be at once energizing and comforting.

What's so friendly about change?

Often not much. And that's the point.

As I said earlier, change moves us out of our comfort zone. The resulting discomfort then produces stress. Stress often manifests itself as resistance. Resistance in the face of change is like having one foot on the brake while the other foot presses the gas pedal.

In the words of psychiatrist R. D. Laing, we live in a moment of history where change is so fast-paced that we "begin to see the present only when it is already disappearing." Change is not just faster. It's also exploding in quantity and magnitude. Experts say we can expect more change in our lifetimes than has occurred since the beginning of civilization more than ten millennia ago. Trying to keep up with change can feel like getting trapped on a runaway treadmill. *Managing* it can be even harder.

Why is change so difficult? It's not for lack of time or money or consultants. Those resources are in rich supply. It's not lack of effort. The marketplace of ideas has an abundance of hard workers. Intelligence isn't the issue. Smart, eager people are all around us. And I don't believe change is so hard because would-be practitioners fail to "organize" properly. Most of the scores of organizations I've worked

"Success with change is less like engineering an event and more like navigating a journey."

with over the past three decades have some sort of "change planning" system or procedure or protocol. Microsoft Project and dozens of other tools are commonplace. Flow charts are as ubiquitous as Blackberrys and iPhones.

One challenge of dealing effectively with change is that it's too often regarded as a linear sequence when it's in fact more of an organic process.

In short, success with change is less like installing an air conditioner and more like growing a garden. Success with change is less like engineering an event and more like navigating a journey. Success with change does require skill with "organizational" things like adjustment of priorities and redeployment of resources. But even more importantly, success with change requires skill with the "people stuff" – challenging paradigms, conducting honest dialogue, earning and keeping trust, and collaborating in ways that foster enthusiasm, ingenuity, and real synergy.

The "people stuff" is what Change-Friendly is all about. In this context, "friendly" is not intended to connote coddling or laissez faire. And it certainly is not intended to imply a warm and fuzzy, hands-off approach to serious issues. Change-Friendly is a behavioral protocol. It produces successful change by acknowledging the sentiments and leveraging the individual gifts of people affected by the change, whether as Champions, Agents, Sponsors, or Targets. Being Change-Friendly may occasionally entail tough love, but it always operates from a platform of respect and caring, not intimidation and contention.

Change-Friendly is also about leadership. Not leadership by title and certainly not leadership by command or control. Change-Friendly is about leadership that engages the heads, hearts, and hopes of the people whose genuine "buy in" is critical to the success of the change.

Leading effectively is a challenge under the best of circumstances. It's especially so in an environment of change and transition. People are unsure about the future, and this ambiguity feeds the aversion to risk. In such an atmosphere, people need a shepherd, not a sheep herder. They need comfort and confident direction, not a drill sergeant.

COMPLIANCE OR COMMITMENT

This brings us to the issue of compliance versus commitment. We'll address this in more depth later, but it's worthy of an introduction here.

Compliance and commitment are sometimes viewed as "opposites." In reality, they work best when combined.

I delivered a seminar to the executive leadership team at the U.S. Nuclear Regulatory Commission. If there were ever an organization whose reason for being is compliance, it would be the NRC. The agency's role is to formulate policies and develop regulations to ensure safe use of radioactive materials. This is very serious business. And a critical component of the desired outcome of the NRC's work is strict *compliance* with policies and regulations designed to protect the public.

> *We all have big changes in our lives that are more or less a second chance.*
> **Harrison Ford**

But let's consider another paradigm that's every bit as important to the work and mission of the NRC. That's the paradigm of *commitment*.

Obviously, we want everyone in the nuclear industry to *comply* with policies and regulations that ensure safety. That is doing the right thing.

At the same time, we want them to operate in compliance—not just because they want to avoid getting written up—but because they understand and agree with the rationale behind policies, regulations, and stacks and stacks of rules.

That involves commitment.

That involves doing the right thing for the right reasons.

Not long ago I was discussing this very subject with a bright young manager at a nuclear power plant. He clearly understood the importance of compliance, but seemed to be struggling with the role of commitment. "What difference does it make?" he asked. "As long as people are doing what they're told to do, why does it matter what their motivation is?"

I noticed in his office he had photos of his young family. I engaged him in conversation about his sons, aged three and five.

"Do you have seatbelt laws in your state?" I asked.

"Yes, we do. And they're well enforced," the young father told me.

"Do you buckle up your boys?"

"Absolutely. They have the best car seats money can buy and I always crawl into the back seat to ensure that they're strapped in correctly."

"So you invest that effort to avoid getting a citation from the police?" I asked.

"Why, no. That never occurred to me," he said. "I buckle up my boys because I love them and want to keep them safe."

"Ah, ha," I said. "*That* is commitment. You're doing the right thing for the right reasons. You're not motivated by fear, you're motivated by love – which is a much higher purpose."

Yes, I know. "Love" is not a word we often hear in the workplace. But we certainly hear a lot of synonyms: "He really has a *passion* for excellent service." "Our team gets *excited* every time we land a new client." "Customer *care* is our first priority."

It's possible for people to operate out of compliance while they have very little commitment. But the opposite is virtually impossible. If one is truly committed, compliance is rarely an issue. The young father is genuinely committed to the safety of his little boys, so his compliance with safety laws is automatic.

> *Change always comes bearing gifts.*
> **Price Pritchett**

With well-placed modeling, a good leader can instill this distinction in others. In the early 1970s Dr. Henry Kissinger was the U.S. Secretary of State. One day he asked a couple of the bright young guys on his staff to draft a white paper for him. In that context, a white paper is a document that describes an important issue, then outlines the options available to the decision maker. The document also includes an analysis of the implications associated with each decision option.

The young staffers drafted the white paper and sent it upstairs to the Secretary of State. The next morning Kissinger summoned the two guys to his office.

"Is this the best work you can do?" Kissinger asked.

"Well, actually, Mr. Secretary, we could provide a bit more data on this section, and we could do a little more research on that section," came the reply.

"Well, then, please do it," Kissinger said.

After the second draft came upstairs, Kissinger summoned the two guys again.

"Is this the best work you can do?" Kissinger asked again.

"Actually, Mr. Secretary, there are a couple of ambassadors we could consult, and there are some data points from another agency we could include," came the response.

"Well, then, please do it," Kissinger said.

After the third draft arrived, Kissinger again sent for the young staffers. By now they were probably feeling like truants called to the school principal's office.

"Now, is this the best work you can do?" Kissinger asked again.

"Yes, sir, it is," came the reply. "We've exhausted every resource available to us. We've carefully scoured intelligence briefings, ambassador communiqués and every other piece of pertinent data. This is definitely the best white paper we can produce."

"Thank you," Kissinger said. "*This time* I will read it!"

Henry Kissinger knew the importance of expecting only the best, and he understood the difference between compliance and commitment. It's a sure bet that from that day forward his two young staffers were committed to the excellence he had a right to demand. Because they feared him? No. Because

> *He who rejects change is the architect of decay. The only human institution that rejects progress is the cemetery.*
> **Harold Wilson**

he helped them understand the importance of their work and the necessity of getting it right.

As any Change-Friendly leader knows, people may perform temporarily in a certain way because they *feel the heat*. But the change becomes permanent only when they *see the light*.

TRANSACTIONAL OR TRANSFORMATIONAL LEADERSHIP

Another balancing act the Change-Friendly leader must perform involves transactional leadership and transformational leadership. In my consulting role I have the opportunity to work with hundreds of leaders. Most of them have an abundance of good *transactional* skills. What they often need is more *transformational* skills—the ability to create a psychological case for action as well as a technical and business case for action.

Transactional leadership helps foster a culture of compliance.

Transformational leadership helps foster a culture of commitment.

Every organization needs both to move to the next level of performance.

So, what's the difference?

A *transactional* leader focuses on routine and regimented activities. He invests most of his energy in making sure meetings run on time, that administrative details are properly handled, and that completed tasks are noted on check lists.

A *transformational* leader focuses primarily on initiating and "managing" change. He influences people to improve, to stretch, and to redefine what's possible.

While every thriving enterprise needs both kinds of leaders, it is the transformational leader who is most influential in bringing about performance improvement in people.

At a nuclear power station, for example, a good plant manager will certainly ensure (mostly by delegating to other capable people) that appropriate information is gathered and accurate reports are generated, that all operational matters

> *"A transformational leader influences people to improve, to stretch, and to redefine what's possible."*

are planned, organized, and correctly executed. These are *transactional* matters that must be done properly.

It could be argued that the plant manager's primary responsibility, however, is to be a transformational leader—to be a primary catalyst in fostering excellence and continuous improvement in the performance of his people. He does this not just through cheerleading, but by developing a vision, by teaching correct principles, by giving encouragement, and by holding people personally accountable for results.

In most every organization it's of course critical that appropriate transactional things are done properly. But transformational leadership is also critical. Transactional things involve making sure the train runs on time. Transformational things involve ensuring that the train is on the right track, that it's headed in the right direction, and that everyone who wants to make the trip has a ticket.

> *Simplicity, clarity, singleness: These are the attributes that give our lives power and vividness and joy.*
> **Richard Holloway**

In a change or implementation effort, your *transformational* leadership is likely the most important role you can play. It's in that role that you articulate a vision that captures the imagination of your followers. It's in that role that you model the values you're asking others to embrace. It's in the transformational role that you reinforce the new behaviors that will produce the results you want.

THE ELEGANCE OF SIMPLICITY

Our friend Jeri finally found a house that suited her needs. It was in a quiet, friendly neighborhood with lots of trees and little traffic.

One thing Jeri liked most about this house was the front entry, a large door surrounded by nine small windows. Trouble was, the previous owner—apparently for the sake of privacy—had glued plastic beads, the kind you'd buy at a craft store, to the inside glass of all nine of the windows.

Removing the plastic beads was to be the first of Jeri's refurbishing projects. But it turned out to be more challenging than she anticipated. She tried chipping. She tried prying. She tried harsh chemicals. She even tried Goof Off, a product that some consumers refer to as a chain-saw-in-a-can. No luck. So she tried a hot air gun, hoping to "relax" the glue enough to make it easier to pry off the beads. Still no luck.

A friend suggested spritzing the windows with a light mist of hot water. Jeri had nothing to lose, so she tried it. She walked away from the windows. Moments later, she heard plink, plink, plink. The hot water apparently softened the glue just enough to release the plastic beads, which then fell harmlessly to the floor. Wiping the windows with another coating of hot water rendered them, well, as clear as glass.

> *Time is a dressmaker specializing in alterations.*
> **Faith Baldwin**

Sometimes we make jobs more difficult than they need to be. Simplicity can be the key to breakthroughs. The change approach prescribed in this book is deliberately simple. And it works.

CHANGE-FRIENDLY STEPS

Regardless of your title or the placement of your "box" on the organization chart, the authenticity of your personal leadership has a profound impact on your effectiveness. This is especially true as you navigate the Change-Friendly steps explained in this book:

- *Validate the Journey* – In addition to making a solid business case for change, you must make a compelling psychological case for change. Everyone listens to the same station: WIIFM ("What's in it for me?"). You'll get little traction by merely telling people what to do. That feels like force. But you can make significant headway when you understand and appeal to their agenda. That feels like influence, and it requires authentic leadership.

- *Scan for Speed Bumps* – New ideas often fail, not on their relative merits, but on how well resistance is handled. A Change-Friendly leader knows how to neutralize or convert resistance. This requires trust. This requires authenticity.

- *Chart the Course* – A Change-Friendly leader appreciates the value of compliance and understands the advantages of commitment. Earning commitment requires the systematic creation and reinforcement of behavioral norms based on trust and transparency, integrity, empathy, and healthful relationships. This requires authenticity.

- *Build a Coalition* – Critical to any successful change effort is the way you deal with the CAST of Characters (Champions, Agents, Sponsors, Targets). A Change-Friendly leader knows that synergy it not created by merely *adding* things together. Synergy comes from *bonding* things together *differently*.
- *Ford the Streams* – Fording the streams is about ensuring that the change and/or transition fits comfortably with your organization's pertinent cultural elements. The authentic leader acts as an emotional guide in helping people navigate the white water of resistance.
- *Stay on Message* – Honest communication is the lubricant of all good relationships. The authentic leader is adept at using symbols and metaphors to reinforce desired behaviors. As Gandhi counseled, "become the change you seek in others."
- *Mind the Gap* – Change-Friendly leaders make constant course corrections. They know that resistance is like a savings bond—it doesn't go away, it just matures with interest. So they deal with resistance early and often. They know that many sponsors don't buy into change, they just rent. Change-Friendly leaders work hard to maintain strong and meaningful sponsorship. They calibrate for results to ensure that the gap between the current state and the desired state is constantly shrinking.

In working with change, you notice that a recurring challenge is dealing with resistance. Inherently, resistance is neither good nor bad. As we will explore later, managing—and even welcoming—resistance is a key ingredient of effective leadership. Some of the best ideas in the dialogue can come from people who are resisting a change. Opposition to change forces sponsors and change agents to examine even more carefully the gap between the current state and the desired future state. In fact, well-managed opposition can create a healthful tension between the old and the new and can help everyone monitor and improve the change.

Effective leaders help people feel safe in expressing their resistance. Even the person who strongly resists a change may not fully understand his own resistance. He simply knows he's not happy or comfortable with the proposed adjustment to his world. Making it safe for him to explore and express his own feelings is a critical first step toward three possible outcomes, and all of them are good: (1) he will discover that his fears are unfounded or that his concerns are being addressed, (2) his resistance will be neutralized or he will be converted into a supporter of the change, or (3) you and other change agents will learn something from the resistor and will make appropriate adjustments in the change effort.

> *"Managing—and even welcoming—resistance is a key ingredient of effective leadership."*

In his breakthrough book *The Fifth Discipline*, Peter M. Senge writes of this reluctance to change:

> *"Whenever there is 'resistance to change,' you can count on there being one or more 'hidden' balancing processes. Resistance to change is neither capricious nor mysterious. It almost always arises from threats to traditional norms and ways of doing things. Often these norms are woven into the fabric of established power relationships. The norm is entrenched because the distribution of authority and control is entrenched. Rather than pushing harder to overcome resistance to change, artful leaders discern the source of the resistance. They focus directly on the implicit norms and power relationships within which the norms are embedded."* [1]

In short, Change-Friendly leaders work honestly and openly in partnership with the targets of change to reduce the resistance, change the change, or help the targets cope with their resistance.

As one change expert points out, "managing change" does not mean some narrow, lock-step regimen that tightly controls all the variables. "Managing change means setting boundaries around the chaos, challenging the changes, and providing a process for continuing examination and redefinition within the framework of the vision/mission." [2]

Change-Friendly practitioners know that their most important legacy to an organization is not just in orchestrating a single transformation. Their most important legacy is in teaching the organization how to change and perpetually adapt and in helping its people muster the will to do so.

My colleagues and I work with some of the world's best organizations to help them make change (sometimes known as "performance improvement," "accountability management," "culture blending," or any number of other aliases) a source of advantage rather than a source of anxiety.

Our Guiding Principles are the foundation of everything we do. We didn't invent the Principles. They are timeless. If these Principles resonate with you, you're well on your way to being a Change-Friendly practitioner.

Try these on for size.

Keep it Simple. Back to Basics.

The stones in the Jefferson Memorial were deteriorating badly. The initial, knee-jerk plan was to replace the stones with fresh ones hauled up from a quarry in southern Virginia. This would cost a gazillion tax dollars and require closing the memorial to tourists for many months.

So some simple questions were asked: Why were the stones deteriorating? Because they were frequently cleaned with harsh chemicals. Why was this cleaning necessary? Because pigeons were leaving too many calling cards. Why all the pigeons? They fed on the heavy spider population. Why so many spiders? They were attracted by a huge moth population. Why all the moths? The moths were attracted by the monument's lights during their twilight swarming frenzy.

Solution: Turn on the lights one hour later.

This is *systems thinking*, examining the big picture to reveal the multiplicity of causes and effects. Smart organizations use it to find simple and cost-effective solutions to a wide range of performance issues. They sort through the loops and links. They ask the right questions. They avoid asking the wrong questions. They diagnose before they prescribe.

Make Results, Not Excuses. Get Real.

Denial can cost you a fortune at the auto shop if you postpone that oil change too long. Denial can choke the life out of a marriage when one partner refuses to make small adjustments to accommodate the other. Denial can kill airplane passengers when pilots ignore the warning signals of their navigation systems.

Denial does damage in organizations, too.

When marginal performance is only marginally differentiated (if at all) from excellence, there's damage. When people invest energy in assigning blame rather than in solving problems, there's damage. When rank weighs more than a good idea, there's damage. When assumptions go unchallenged, there's damage. When opinions go untested, there's damage. When feedback goes unheeded, there's damage.

> *It is not the strongest of the species that survive, nor the most intelligent, but the one most responsive to change.*
> **Charles Darwin**

Denial causes smart people to do dumb things because they prefer not to see, or simply can't see, a warning signal. It's sometimes described as *selective amnesia* or *blinders*. In most cases it's not a character flaw. It's simply a part of being human. Then results hoped for are replaced by excuses and blame. It can render even the best business strategy totally impotent.

Worried about symptoms? Get real. Rush to the root causes. Create results, not excuses.

Control the Journey. Draw Your Own Map.

Seasoned hikers wouldn't dream of heading off into the wilderness without a map and a compass. But organizations do it every day.

Two years after the breakthrough book *In Search of Excellence* reported on 43 of the "best run" companies in America, 14 of the 43 firms were in financial trouble. The reason, according to a *Businessweek* study: their failure to deal effectively with change.

In other words, they lost their bearings.

Every organization is perfectly aligned to get the results it's getting. Unsatisfied with results? Check your map and compass.

Strategic alignment is every bit as critical for organizations as it is for hikers. Call it pathfinding. Call it navigating to true north. Call it mission and vision. Call it taking responsibility for shaping events.

Call it good leadership. Call it smart business. It's not a destination, it's a journey. Take charge.

Want to Lead? Be a Gardener. Go for Growth.

A first tendency of many business people is to fix things. After all, they're paid to solve problems, so the metaphor of the mechanic seems natural.

But successful leaders invest energy in *growing* rather than *fixing*. They know the organization is a living organism with many inter-related elements, capable of extinction or growth. Successful leaders are gardeners. They don't rely on chance. They create a nurturing environment—or culture—and they cultivate with care.

Successful gardeners need reliable tools. Consider using customizable diagnostic tools and services to analyze your organization's strengths and vulnerabilities, to address root causes, and to nurture your people so you can enjoy a continuous harvest of strong performance.

Be a leader. Be a gardener.

Lead the Whole Person. Lift Your People.

Some managers seem to regard people as *stomachs*. They try to mo-tivate only with salary and benefits. It's the old notion of *just be grateful you have a job*. In today's economy, such a parochial (some would say inhumane) view is a fast ticket to low performance and high turnover.

Successful organizations use a different approach. They lead the whole person.

People have heads. They want to grow and develop intellectu-ally. They want to learn. Give them a good reason and they'll even stretch their own comfort zones.

People have hearts. They want to be treated with kindness, respect, and dignity. They want good relationships. They want to feel appreciated.

People have spirits. They want meaning in life. They want con-text. They want to be inspired. And they want to know that what they contribute really matters, that they *fit*.

Is all this warm and fuzzy, touchy-feely stuff for soft people? Not at all. It's the key to the hard realities of high performance in the tough and fast-moving world in which we will live for the rest of our lives.

Believe it. Practice it. It makes all the difference.
Be Change-Friendly.

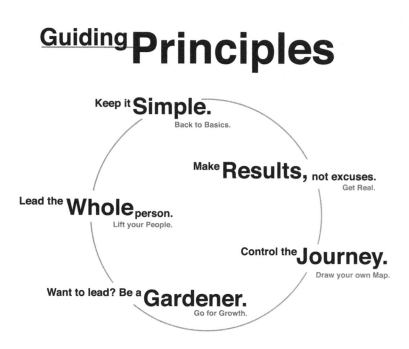

[1] Peter M. Senge, *The Fifth Discipline: The Art and Practice of the Learning Organization* (New York: Doubleday Currency, 1990), 88.

[2] Jeanenne LaMarsh, *Changing the Way We Change: Gaining Control of Major Operational Change* (Reading, Massachusetts: Addison-Wesley Publishing Company, 1995), 23.

Good leaders must first become good servants.
Robert Greenleaf

Being a leader is like being a lady. If you have to remind people you are, you aren't.
Margaret Thatcher

Great leaders conceive and articulate goals that lift people out of their petty preoccupations and unite them in pursuit of objectives worthy of their best efforts.
John Gardner

A dangerous leadership myth is that leaders are born, that there is a genetic factor to leadership. This myth asserts that people simply either have certain charismatic qualities or not. That's nonsense. Leaders are made rather than born.
Warren G. Bennis

Chapter

You Make a Lousy Somebody Else: Authentic Leadership

As you participate in or lead change, what you do is of course important. But of even greater importance is who you are.

Jim Rainey was a man with a mission.

As the first outsider to be appointed president and CEO of Farmland Industries, he was charged with the task of returning this agribusiness giant to profitability.

Resuscitating a giant is always a mammoth undertaking, and this would be an especially tough challenge. Farmland's business units—ranging from fertilizer and pork processing to grain, petroleum refining, and ag chemicals—were test enough. But the nature of Farmland's federated structure was a mixed blessing: the company was owned by more than 2,000 local associations or "co-ops" in 19 states. Because these same 2,000 local co-ops were also Farmland's primary customers, a natural conflict of interest ensued. As owners, the co-ops wanted high profits. As customers, they wanted low prices.

Farmland was hemorrhaging from operating losses—$374 million for the previous five years. Within 12 months of taking over as Farmland's CEO, Jim Rainey injected a proactive, collaborative spirit into the corporate culture, inspired the workforce and their constituencies to accomplish things never before dreamed, and returned the company to profitability. The impressive turnaround is now a case study at the Harvard Business School.

The most pertinent point here, though, is not *what* Jim Rainey helped his people accomplish. The most pertinent point is *how* he did it.

He did it with integrity, trust, and respect.

He did it with tough-minded focus on business detail, coupled with genuine caring for the human element of organizational change.

He did it with authentic leadership.

A couple of stories illustrate Jim Rainey's approach to leadership. A few days after joining Farmland he walked into an early morning strategic planning meeting. You can imagine the attentiveness of all the eager beavers trying to impress the new boss. When he first entered the room, Jim overheard a young man mention that his wife was in the hospital. Jim inquired about the woman's health, and the man said his wife was expecting a baby which was likely to be delivered that day.

> *They must often change, who would be constant in happiness or wisdom.*
> **Confucius**

"Let me make a deal with you," Jim told the young father-to-be. "I promise to give you a personal briefing on the outcome of this meeting if you'll rush over to the hospital where you belong. You'll get only one chance to witness the birth of your baby, and you don't want to miss it."

On the surface that may seem like no more than a nice gesture. But it's that very kind of thoughtfulness that earns trust and loyalty.

"Walking the talk" is another way to earn trust and loyalty.

During Jim's first day on the job, the head of Farmland's motor pool asked what car he wanted for his personal use. Jim requested a simple Chevrolet with standard options. Then the conversation went like this:

> **Jim:** *When the car arrives, just give me the invoice and I'll write out a personal check.*
>
> **Motor pool guy:** *Oh, you don't understand, Mr. Rainey. You get a free company car.*
>
> **Jim:** *No, **you** don't understand. This company lost tens of millions of dollars last year. I've been asked to turn things around and, beginning today, **nobody** gets a free car.*

Jim immediately told me about the conversation and asked that I check to see how long it took the word to reach employees a thousand miles from headquarters. What would you guess? Two days? One day? It took less than 10 minutes for people several states away to get word of the new CEO's policy on executive privilege. (This was before the use of email.)

For the next several years I watched Jim Rainey demonstrate integrity, trust, and respect in hundreds of private acts that quickly (almost instantly, in some cases) became part of his leadership legacy.

I see other leaders badly erode their credibility by ignoring or miscalculating the power of example. Somehow they assume that either nobody notices or nobody cares if they are petty or thoughtless in dealing with subordinates and colleagues. Oh, how dangerously wrong they are.

The issue here is not gossip. It's the natural tendency to pass along information (perceptions) about the way people are treated—which is one of the most important determinants of loyalty, commitment, and return business.

> *"Leaders badly erode their credibility by ignoring or miscalculating the power of example."*

Hmmm. That sounds a lot like what the experts say about *customers*, doesn't it?

Why the similarity? Because people's feelings cannot be neatly compartmentalized. People have many of the same needs in every one of life's roles.

You return again and again to a first-rate retailer like Lands' End or L.L. Bean or Nordstrom because you're confident you'll have a positive experience. You know you'll be treated with dignity, you'll be listened to, your needs will be met. And you reward the retailer with your loyalty and lots of return business which, by many metrics, is the best kind of business.

YOUR LEADERSHIP LEGACY

The great leaders I know honor the same principles with their own people. They treat them with dignity. They listen to them. They meet their needs. And they're rewarded with loyal workers who are passionate about strong performance and great results.

> *Action and reaction, ebb and flow, trial and error, change— this is the rhythm of living. Out of our over-confidence, fear; out of our fear, clearer vision, fresh hope. And out of hope, progress.*
> **Bruce Barton**

For smart leaders, this has very little "Ah-ha" factor. They understand and practice the principle almost instinctively. For others, the notion of employee-as-customer seems foreign and counterintuitive. They are the ones whose competitive advantage is slipping or nonexistent.

If you're one of the former, my hat's off to you. If you're one of the latter, I simply say "get with the program." You should be treating your employees at least as well as you treat your very best customer.

Either way, you're building your leadership legacy.

This is a book about change. It's also a book about leadership. Why the dual focus? Because effective change *is* about effective leadership.

Unfortunately, much of today's psychobabble about leadership has the wrong focus. A lot of the training and development in our corporations focuses on learning about *things*. People learn *what* to think, not *how* to think. They learn *what to do,* not *how to be.* They learn *what* to achieve, not *how* to achieve. They learn all about *things*, but very little about the *nature of things*.

Popular definitions of leadership also tend to be externalized. Many of the definitions focus on the outer manifestations of leadership—such as vision, judgment, creativity, drive, charisma, podium presence, etc.—rather than getting to the essence of leadership itself.

This external pattern continues at the organizational level. People often receive recognition for their external mastery. Success is often measured in terms of revenue, profit, new product breakthroughs, cost containment, market share, and many other familiar metrics. Clearly there's value in achieving and measuring external results. But that's not the real issue. The more relevant issues are (1) "What produces the external results?" and (2) "What enables the sustaining of good external results?"

The answer to the first question is *leadership*.

The answer to the second question is *great leadership*, the *authentic* variety.

Authentic leadership is a product of *honesty*. Honesty about putting the needs of others ahead of your own. Honesty in communicating information, both positive and negative. Honesty in accepting—welcoming—viewpoints different from yours. Honesty in integrating the values you profess with the behaviors you exhibit (sounds a lot like "integrity," doesn't it?).

Authentic leadership is also a product of *clarity*. Clarity in what you stand for, and what you will not stand for. Clarity in your navigation through the sea of limitless choices, using the "True North" of your values to keep you constantly on the right path and enabling you to make the necessary course corrections when you temporarily stray.

We *become* what we want to *be* by *being* what we want to *become*.

In pre-Revolutionary Russia a priest was confronted by a soldier as he walked down a road. Aiming his rifle at the priest, the soldier demanded, "Who are you? Where are you going? Why are you going there?" Unfazed by the sudden interrogation, the priest replied with a question of his own: "How much do they pay you?" Somewhat surprised, the sol-

> *Know what's weird? Day by day, nothing seems to change, but pretty soon... everything's different.*
> **Calvin from Calvin and Hobbes**

dier answered, "Twenty-five kopecks a month." After a thoughtful pause, the priest said, "I have a proposal for you. I'll pay you fifty kopecks a month if you'll stop me here every day and challenge me to respond to those *same three questions*."

None of us has a "soldier" confronting us each day with life's tough questions. But we can honestly ask the questions of ourselves.

If we choose to, we can issue our own self-challenges to push ourselves not only to do better but to be better.

In his book *The Fifth Discipline*, Peter Senge writes, "People with a high level of personal mastery are acutely aware of their ignorance, their incompetence, their growth areas, and they are deeply self-confident. Paradoxical? Only for those who do not see the journey as the reward."

The word *authenticity* is derived from the same Greek word as *author*. Becoming an *authentic* leader requires day-to-day focus and lifelong commitment to self-discovery. Many executive coaching programs seem to emphasize personality more than character. People are often coached on *how to act* instead of *how to be*. This charm school approach produces only superficial, short-term results. With sufficient stress, all the old patterns usually return.

Authenticity is a matter of choice. We deliberately choose to behave in certain ways under certain circumstances.

Here's an illustration. In the area where we live, my wife Rean served on the board of directors of Habitat for Humanity, the volunteer group that builds homes for poor people. One summer Habitat had a "blitz build"—they built eight homes in ten days. Starting with only concrete slabs, ten days later they had eight completely landscaped, fully inspected homes ready for occupancy. This required the efforts of hundreds of volunteers.

One afternoon I drove over to the construction site to help my wife with something. It was a beehive of activity, and especially colorful because all the volunteers wore brightly-colored T-shirts with the names of their churches printed on the front. I was watching a man installing sheetrock. (Remember, these were not experienced drywallers; they were volunteers.) This guy was really going after it, pounding nails at blazing speed. Then he got out of rhythm and slammed his thumb with his hammer. He dropped the hammer, grabbed his thumb, and yelled "Ouch!"

> **"Authenticity is a matter of choice."**

I walked over to help him staunch the flow of blood, and inquired if I could ask him a couple of questions.

"I notice that when you slammed your thumb with the hammer you said 'Ouch!'"

"Of course I did," the man said. "It hurts!"

"I'll bet it does," I said. "But let me ask you this. Is it possible that you might have reached into your repertoire of responses and said something other than 'Ouch'?"

"Not with my church minister standing three feet away!" he said.

"So you're telling me that in the nanosecond it took the 'hurt' signal to travel from your thumb to your brain you deliberately decided to say 'Ouch' instead of something else?"

"I guess so," the man answered, by now getting a bit irritated by my social science questions.

Do you believe he made that deliberate choice? Of course he did. We've all done it. And we're able to do it because we have "Ouch" in our toolkit. "Ouch" is one of the many response choices available to us. And if "ouch" is not our "default" response, we can deliberately choose it repeatedly enough that it *becomes* our default response.

> *Only in growth, reform, and change, paradoxically enough, is true security to be found.*
> **Anne Morrow Lindbergh**

AUTHENTICITY = TRUST

The same principle applies to authentic leadership. Authentic leadership is not an outside-in thing. It's an inside-out thing. It's a matter of deliberate choice.

Authentic leadership is all about *trust*.

Can our people trust us to tell them the truth?

Can our people trust us to stake out a path that is for the best good of everyone, not just us?

Can our people trust us to accept feedback and even criticism without getting defensive or, worse, engaging in retribution?

Can they trust us to give them the resources they need to do the work we demand?

It was Mahatma Gandhi who said, "The moment there is suspicion about a person's motives, everything he does becomes tainted."

Unlike some people in the public arena, the truly authentic leader does not try to "compartmentalize" his life. For example, no matter how brilliant he may be with business and organizational matters, a man who cheats on his wife jeopardizes his trust with coworkers. In other words, you're either trustworthy or you're not.

My company has conducted culture assessments and individual performance profiles in scores of organizations around the world. We've found that the answer to the simple question *"Do you trust your boss?"* is more predictive of team and organizational performance than any other question we can pose.

A cynic might ask, "So what's the big deal? Isn't trust just a nice-to-have, feel-good quality? Isn't brain power the most important ingredient of success?" In his insightful book *The Speed of Trust,* my friend Stephen M.R. Covey talks about the economics of trust. Trust, he says, always affects two outcomes—speed and cost. When trust goes down, speed will also decline and costs will rise. When trust improves, speed also improves and costs drop.

To illustrate the cost of fragile trust, Stephen cites the Sarbanes-Oxley Act, passed by Congress in response to a spate of corporate scandals. Although the legislation may be having a positive effect on public trust in the markets, it comes with a substantial price. Studies show that the cost of implementing only one section of the regulations is at least $35 billion, more than 28 times the original estimate. "Compliance regulations have become a prosthesis for the lack of trust,"[1] Stephen writes, "and a slow-moving and costly prosthesis at that." To illustrate the value of trust, Stephen tells the story of Warren Buffett—generally regarded as one of the most trusted business people in the world—who completed a $23 billion acquisition with only two hours of discussion and a handshake.

"In the aristocracy of leadership issues, trust is king."

In the aristocracy of leadership issues, trust is king.

For some, trust sounds and feels like a spiritual issue. It is. And even for people who may not regard themselves as "religious," trust is an all-important anchor. As Teilhard de Chardin wrote, "We are not human beings having a spiritual experience. We are spiritual beings having a human experience."

In this age of fierce competition and rapid-fire change, the benefits of trustworthy leadership are well known. The costs of trust-deficient leadership are also well known (think Enron, WorldCom, Tyco, and the numerous other corporate train wrecks caused by dishonest and/or incompetent wannabes masquerading as leaders).

But trust-deficient leadership can be costly in other ways.

Daniel Yankelovich, a leading social scientist, asked thousands of American workers if they agreed or disagreed with a simple statement: "I put in as little energy and effort as I can get away with without getting fired."

Want to take a guess at how many respondents agreed with that statement? 5%? 10%?

A whopping 44% of American workers surveyed agreed with the statement "I put in as little energy and effort as I can get away with without getting fired."

A knee-jerk conclusion might be that American workers are simply lazy and looking for a free ride. My own experience tells me just the opposite. I believe most people want to add value, they want to contribute, they want to feel "connected" to a good cause. I believe most people also want to be appreciated. When they are treated as a dispensable commodity rather than as a treasured asset, many people simply "check out." It's not necessarily a conscious decision, it's merely a natural by-product of a respect deficit.

THE LAW OF THE HOG

On some occasions, of course, a response to bad leadership is a conscious choice. Consider this example:

As part of their Stanford University doctoral programs, my colleagues Kerry Patterson and David Maxfield spent a summer working at a large lumber mill in the Pacific Northwest. When they arrived for their first day of work they noticed an ambulance driving away from the administration building. On a gurney in the back of the ambulance was a man with his faced all bloodied. Kerry and David walked into the building to sign in. They asked about what they assumed was some sort of "accident." "Oh, that was no accident," they were told. "That was Fred. He mouthed off to his supervisor, and his supervisor punched him out."

Kerry and David soon learned some very interesting things about the performance culture at this lumber mill.

Supervisors were notorious for their brutal treatment of employees. It didn't always take the form of a broken nose like Fred's, yet the disrespect and verbal violence were every bit as hurtful.

But the employees were not completely powerless.

"We don't have to take the abuse sitting down," one worker told Kerry and David. "Come out to the back and I'll introduce you to 'The Hog.'"

The man escorted Kerry and David to another building that housed a gargantuan chipping machine with gaping jaws and whirring blades to rival the most terrifying Hollywood monster.

"When a supervisor's behavior gets unbearable, we feed him to 'The Hog,'" the worker said. "In fact, step a little closer and you'll see what we're doing to the supervisor who punched out Fred."

Edging closer to the huge chipping machine, Kerry and David saw other workers tossing large sheets of veneer into the whirring blades. Even to the novice eye, this was obviously not scrap. It was beautiful (and expensive) product—the kind used for upscale woodwork and fine cabinetry.

"You see, supervisors are rewarded on the basis of production," the worker explained. "Production is measured according to a ratio of board feet of good product versus waste. Thanks to 'The Hog,' Fred's supervisor is now toast. He punched our buddy Fred, we feed 'The Hog,' production ratios take a nose dive, and the supervisor either gets demoted or fired. It works every time."

This was of course blatant sabotage, triggered (not justified, but *triggered*) by poor leadership. For obvious reasons, Kerry and David now refer to this practice as "The Law of the Hog."

For every incident of poor leadership, a hog gets fed. This may not be in the form of blatant sabotage or deliberate destruction of property, but the costs are enormous nevertheless.

I believe that the second most expensive thing that can happen to your organization is for your best and most capable people to quit and leave. Studies show that replacing a good employee can cost up to 150% of that person's annual salary and benefits package.

Losing good people is costly. But I believe the number one most expensive thing that can happen to your organization is for your best and most capable people to quit and *stay*.

Disengaged people are enormously expensive. Engagement flows out of trust, and trust flows out of confidence. They are mutually reinforcing.

Studies by the Gallup organization show that 96% of engaged employees trust their leaders, while only 46% of *dis*engaged employees trust their leaders. Gallup puts a conservative price tag of $300 billion per year on disengagement in the United States alone.

So which comes first, the fragile trust or the disengagement? Both. And that's the point. Trust affects everything. Even when people have difficulty articulating their dissatisfaction in the workplace, we find that fragile trust in leadership is nearly always at the core of the dissatisfaction.

Think about it. Study after study shows that poor leadership is a primary reason smart people leave one organization and move to another. This brain drain is terribly expensive. The "ROAD Warriors" (Retired On Active Duty) in your organization are affecting (infecting?) everything they touch. Their lack of engagement has a negative ripple effect throughout the organization.

> *Change means movement.*
> *Movement means friction.*
> *Only in the frictionless vacuum of*
> *a nonexistent abstract world can*
> *movement or change occur without*
> *that abrasive friction of conflict.*
> **Saul Alinsky**

THE POWER OF NATURAL CONSEQUENCES

Great leaders don't rely on title or tenure or any other accoutrement of office to get things done. And they don't need to use power or authority. Great leaders rely on *influence*. They know the difference between imposed consequences and natural consequences.

My friend Joseph Grenny tells the story of a frustrated high school janitor. The girls in the school made a game of blotting their lipstick on the restroom mirrors. This produced a greasy mess that was very hard to clean up.

The janitor appealed to higher authority. He asked the school principal to help him out. The principal, who had the *imposed* consequence mentality, announced on the school intercom that anyone caught blotting her lipstick on a restroom mirror would be sent to after-school detention. Guess what? The problem immediately worsened. Apparently it had never occurred to a lot of the girls to blot their lips on a mirror. But thanks to the principal's suggestion, they now participated in a new game that was sort of fun.

Now the janitor had an even bigger mess than before. But he had the *natural* consequence mentality. So he asked the principal to invite ten of the school's most popular girls (opinion leaders) to join them for a demonstration in the rest room. The janitor started the show-and-tell by saying "Look at this mess, girls. Lipstick is greasy and it's very hard to clean off the mirrors. In fact, none of my regular solvents seems to work. I've found only one way to clean the mirrors, and it requires a lot of effort. Let me show you." The janitor took a long-handled brush, opened the door of a toilet stall, and swished the brush around in the toilet water. Then he took the dripping brush over to the mirror and started scrubbing. To the horror of ten gagging girls, he repeated this process three times before the mirror was finally clean.

Do you think lipstick on mirrors was ever again a problem at that school? Of course not. And the good result did not come through the threat of *imposed* consequences. The good result was spawned by an honest appeal to *natural* consequences. The janitor was Change-Friendly.

WHY PEOPLE FOLLOW

In today's world it's easy to be confused about a term like "leader." Sometimes the title may be applied when it's not really accurate. Some people may have authority to act, but they are not necessarily "leaders."

Occasionally in a coaching session with a group of clients I show a PowerPoint slide with a simple message:

> "We are facing a serious problem! I need you to give everything you have over the next several weeks to help us solve it. I'm afraid you won't sleep much or be able to spend much time with your family until things are back to normal."

After they've had a chance to ponder the message, I ask the people in the room: "Would you follow this person?"

Naturally, they want to know who it is. So I put a face on the request. The next slide shows photos of a wide range of people — Ronald Reagan, Pope John Paul II, Mikhail Gorbachev, Tony Blair, Martha Stewart.

"Which of *these* people would you follow enthusiastically?" I ask. Then, "Which of *these*?" and I show a third slide with even more people – Arnold Schwarzenegger, Meg Whitman, Nelson Mandela, Jack Welch, Mother Teresa, George Bush, Steve Jobs, Hillary Clinton, Yasser Arafat, Condoleezza Rice, John Kerry, Saddam Hussein, Nancy Pelosi, Donald Trump.

I point out that each of the people has (or had) a formal leadership position. But you would not want to follow them—or anyone else – unless and until you had confidence in three things:

Character – the person's integrity, motives, principles, values. Character is what a leader is.

Competence – the person's skills, gifts, talents, ability to deliver on promises. Competence is what a leader does.

Cause – the person's reason for leading, his vision, goals, his "end game." Cause is what most often motivates and inspires. Cause is the why of noble and compelling leadership.

After some lively discussion about character, competence, and cause, I then ask the people in the room: "What about *you*? What are you doing to inspire confidence in *your* character, in *your* competence, and in *your* cause?"

> *"Great leadership the result of deliberate effort and attention to detail."*

Great leadership is no accident. It's the result of deliberate effort and attention to detail. This involves managing values, the "core doctrine" of what you profess to stand for. In managing values, Change-Friendly leaders practice something I call CPR.

For lifeguards and other rescue personnel, "CPR" stands for Cardio-Pulmonary Resuscitation, a method for breathing life into a suffocating person. In this instance, CPR stands for *Converse, Practice* and *Reinforce*—a way to breathe life and vitality into an organization.

In a typical business, people are pretty good at the *Converse* part. They can rattle off a list of values or valued behaviors they claim to embrace. Things like Accountability, Innovation, Integrity, Quality, Respect, Teamwork.

The *Practice* part is a bit more challenging. This involves actually doing what you say you value. A critical part of trustworthy lead-

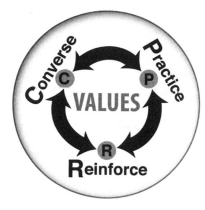

ership is the degree to which what you profess and what you practice are in alignment.

The *Reinforce* part requires even more effort. Reinforcement involves specific and deliberate application of affirmation, encouragement, and "rewards" for positive behavior. It also involves specific, deliberate, and friendly correction of negative behaviors.

SYMBOLS AND METAPHORS

Symbols and metaphors can play an important role in the way you perform CPR.

Here's an example, another Jim Rainey story. As the new CEO of a multi-billion-dollar service company, Jim was hired to reverse a serious decline in the business. He was concerned about turf protection and other forms of in-fighting that had become a cancer to the corporate culture. Shortly after coming on board, Jim grabbed a can of spray paint and walked into the executive parking lot (knowing full well that hundreds of employees could see him from their windows in the headquarters building). Executive parking symbolized the "privilege of rank" that was a sore spot with many workers. Jim went to each parking space and methodically sprayed paint over the name of the executive on the sign in front of the car. Then he walked inside and got on the intercom system that previously was used only for fire drills.

"Good morning, ladies and gentlemen," he said. "Some of you were watching me out in the parking lot. You were probably wondering 'What's that guy doing out there? Is he firing all the executives?' No, I'm not firing our senior executive team. I just want to emphasize that we're all in this boat together and we need to row in unison. Last year this company lost $156 million. We need to invest our collective energy in working together for solutions, not fussing about silly things like parking places and the size of office furniture. So starting tomorrow, anybody can park anywhere. If you work in the mail room and you get here early, the best spot in the lot can be yours. If you're a senior executive and you come in late, you may get rained on. Have a nice day."

Gamesmanship? Not really, especially since Jim followed up with countless other genuine acts to emphasize accountability and performance over rank and title.

It's estimated that 15% of a leader's effectiveness comes from the *Converse* part of CPR (what the leader says and teaches). About 35% of a leader's effectiveness comes from the *Practice* part (the actual behaviors the leader personally models). And a whopping 50% of a leader's effectiveness comes from the *Reinforce* part (how the leader encourages positive performance and corrects negative performance).

> *Leadership is the art of getting someone else to do something you want done because he wants to do it.*
> **Dwight D. Eisenhower**

Reinforcement is really not complicated. You might ask, "Should I reinforce my people for their little day-to-day successes, or should I save up my strokes for when they accomplish something really major?"

The answer to that question lies in the way most volunteers get their work done. (Yes, your people *are* volunteers. Remember that you can rent their backs and hands, but you must earn their heads and hearts.) The simple fact is that, for most of your people, work is not a string of dazzling successes that they produce one right after another. Instead, the majority of their work consists of somewhat routine activities. They perform most of these quietly and without fanfare.

You'll do well to stay aware and appreciative of the "behind the scenes" effort expended by your people. Then you'll be in a position to follow the first rule of positive reinforcement: "Make a big deal about little things." In fact, giving frequent, specific, and genuine reinforcement on positive behavior tends to crowd out negative behavior.

In addition to values, the performance environment you establish consists of behaviors and "unwritten rules" at play in your organization. To get the positive performance you want, the unwritten rules must be consistent with the professed values. Your own CPR efforts affect the way values are perceived and acted on. The "acted on" part is the behavior of the people you lead. And their behavior is affected by the unwritten rules they observe. Then behavior *becomes* the unwritten rules or "the way things really work around here."

One national retailer made a big deal of touting teamwork and collaboration. All the company's sales training emphasized team building and partnering among the sales associates. But the annual awards bash at Disney World featured extravagant prizes and recognition for *individual* sales performance. Wrong message, wrong reinforcement. (More details on this in Chapter 7).

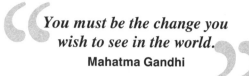

> *You must be the change you wish to see in the world.*
> **Mahatma Gandhi**

Your leadership effectiveness is closely associated with how well you perform CPR. It can be the breath of life.

Every step in the Change-Friendly framework requires authentic, trustworthy leadership. Remember: trustworthy leadership is as much of a competitive advantage as brand equity or proprietary technology.

In this world of constant change, what could be more valuable than the ability to align smart people behind a mutual purpose in an atmosphere of candor and honesty?

---

[1] Stephen M.R. Covey, *The Speed of Trust* (New York: Free Press, 2006), 14.

Section ONE

BONUS•POINTS

To enrich your use of the Change-Friendly methodology, check out our **Bonus Point** material after reading each section of this book. Additional material is posted on the Doctor Duncan website.

All the material is free to readers of the book (you!), and we'll be adding to it periodically. The Bonus Point material includes thought pieces, White Papers, free diagnostic tools, interviews, videos, and other items.

To access the Bonus Points, simply scan this QR code with your smart phone and let your browser take you directly to the content. Alternatively, go to www.DoctorDuncan.com/BonusPoints

See you there!

◄ Smart Phone Link
DoctorDuncan.com/BonusPoints

SECTION

The Power of Four Ts

M any years ago the editor of a national news magazine asked
me to write an article exploring the current state of American
education. This was at a time when many people were demanding more "relevance" in their book learning. At dozens of colleges,
teachers of non-required courses were either advertising their cur-
riculums with an eye toward current moods or lecturing to half-
empty classrooms. At the University of Massachusetts in Amherst,
for example, the English department was trying to lure students into
the classics—Aeschylus' *Agamemnon* and Shakespeare's *Macbeth*—
by adding movies like *The Godfather* to the assignment and calling
the course "The Gangster in Film and Literature."

To get a taste of the day's thinking, I interviewed more than
twenty prominent Americans. I asked each of them a single question: "What's the mark of an educated person?" Their views varied,
but their responses reflected some common themes.

Norman Rockwell, the illustrator-artist, told me: "You aren't really educated unless you can honestly evaluate opinions contrary to
your own. To do that, you must give the other idea a fair trial. We
often say we've changed our minds when we're merely rearranged
our prejudices. Nobody is so charitable that he'll go bankrupt making allowances for others. And, of course, an attitude of tolerance affects your entire relationship with others. You'll never meet a broad-
minded person with a swelled head."

Anthropologist Margaret Mead said: "An educated person has a sense of time, of sequence and simultaneity of events; a sense of place, where he is in relation to the rest of the world; and a sense of comparative values. He is cosmopolitan enough to know that there are and have been value systems other than his own."

Ara Parseghian, former football coach at the University of Notre Dame: "There are three kinds of people—those who make things happen, those who watch things happen, and those who don't even know what's happening. An educated person finds himself more often in the first category than the second, and never in the third."

Psychologist and author Joyce Brothers: "The educated person is distinguished by his treatment of all others, whether they are above or below him in stature or ability. He has an inquiring mind and sincerely believes he can learn something from every person he meets."

In all of the interviews I conducted, not a single respondent mentioned time in the classroom as the mark of an educated person. In fact, it seemed that they went to great lengths emphasizing that the real mark of an educated person is about behaviors and relationships, not about degrees or certificates.

That same orientation—behaviors and relationships in place of titles and stature—is the foundation of the Change-Friendly framework. It's based on what I call the power of Four Ts: Think-Friendly, Talk-Friendly, Trust-Friendly, and Team-Friendly.

The behaviors and skills associated with being *Think-Friendly* include adopting a growth mindset that you are indeed capable of solving problems in fresh ways. It includes exercising curiosity by asking smart questions to explore and discover. It includes challenging your own conclusions to ensure that your assumptions are valid. And it includes making appropriate connections that lead to breakthrough ideas.

Being *Talk-Friendly* is about the behaviors and skills of collaborative dialogue and appreciative inquiry. It's about listening to learn and understand rather than to rebut and overpower. It's about exercising influence rather than authority. It's about willingness to be influenced rather than assuming that the views of others should always be subservient to yours.

A person is *Trust-Friendly* when his behaviors consistently enable him to earn trust, extend trust, and *be* trust. Effective change leaders know how to make trust first in order to make it last.

Finally, the effective change leader must be *Team-Friendly*. This involves working with people in ways that foster genuine collaboration and engage their heads, hearts, and hopes.

These Four Ts, then, inform all the behaviors in the Change-Friendly protocol.

Overall, the Change-Friendly protocol is seven steps. But don't think of it as linear. Although it's tightly organized for purposes of manageability, it's fluid enough that the steps overlap. The protocol is designed to be your servant, not your master.

The greatest obstacle to discovery is not ignorance—it's the illusion of knowledge.
Daniel J. Boorstin

We usually see only the things we are looking for—so much so that we sometimes see them where they are not.
Eric Hoffer

All organizations are perfectly designed to get the results they get.
Arthur W. Jones

If you don't like something change it; if you can't change it, change the way you think about it.
Mary Engelbreit

Chapter

Think-Friendly:
See the World Through a Fresh Lens

*It's not the challenges that give meaning
to your life, but the meaning you give to
the challenges.*

You may not recognize the name Arthur Fry, but there's a better than even chance you've benefitted from his ingenuity. Art was a scientist at the 3M company. One of his coworkers developed an adhesive with an unusual molecular structure, yielding a glue strong enough to cling to objects but forgiving enough to peel off without doing harm. No one at 3M had yet figured a way to use this sticky-but-not-too-sticky substance.

Art sang in his local church choir. He used slips of paper to mark the pages in his hymnal. When the book opened, these makeshift bookmarks either moved around or fell out altogether. One Sunday it occurred to Art that his colleague's adhesive might be useful in solving this problem: if it could be coated on paper, it would hold a bookmark in place without damaging the page on which it was placed. The next day, Art went to the 3M lab and requested a sample of the sticky-but-not-too-sticky adhesive. He began a series of experiments, using these "test runs" to write notes to his boss and others in the company. Art Fry's experimentation—his sound thinking – resulted in the ubiquitous Post-it® Note, one of the best-selling products in 3M's century-long history.

Twenty years ago I worked with a client named Bart Withers. Bart was the senior executive at a nuclear power plant. He was smart and savvy and a practical leader. But Bart had a problem. A couple of vice presidents on his team were engaged in a childish feud: they literally wouldn't talk to each other. Ordinarily this would be only annoying and inconvenient, but in this instance it had far-reaching implications. Most everyone at the plant knew of the feud. Many people had taken sides. The silo mentality between departments was deepened. Worse yet, the workforce was not enjoying the benefit of the brainpower of these two otherwise capable men.

I asked Bart if he could do without either of these guys. No, he said, both of them had unique skills and no other candidates were on the horizon. Both of the men had been "coached" on the feud issue, and each projected all the blame to the other. In essence, they were holding their boss and everyone else hostage. I told Bart I could give him some suggestions but it would be best for him and his organization if he figured it out for himself. I would be back in two weeks, and I challenged him to consider all the nuances of the situation and come up with a solution.

When I saw Bart two weeks later he had excitement in his eyes. "I've got it!" he said. "I know how to put these two guys on the road to recovery. I'm going to have them switch jobs!"

Switch jobs? Yes, switch jobs. Both positions were absolutely critical to the operation of the nuclear plant. By switching jobs, these two men would *have* to talk to each other. And they did. Oh, they never became fishing buddies, but that wasn't the goal. The goal was simply to get them to communicate with each other. At first, it sounded like: "Help me understand why this process works in this way." Or, "Why is this procedure done before that one?"

> *Most of the change we think we see in life is due to truths being in and out of favor.*
> **Robert Frost**

Or, "What's the history behind this protocol?" Quickly the basic communication evolved to coordination. Then the coordination evolved to cooperation. Then the cooperation evolved to collaboration. Trust began to be restored, and finally the two former combatants worked together with no signs of their previous grudge match. The sound thinking of their boss helped transform their relationship from a public feud into productive teamwork.

Then there's Tom Pulliam. For many years, Tom worked as a manager at a food manufacturing company in Oklahoma City. In his off-hours he liked to do crossword puzzles. He got good at it, *very* good at it. So good, in fact, that when he ran out of puzzles to solve he started creating his own. Then he got so skilled at creating new puzzles that he began to sell them. That was two decades ago. Today, if you want the best book on the subject, pick up a copy of *The New York Times Crossword Puzzle Dictionary*—by Thomas H. Pulliam. Oh, yes, Tom also made a name (and a fortune) for himself as an actor, doing voiceovers for a wide range of TV and radio commercials. Tom would insist that he was no smarter than the next guy. Maybe not, but he definitely took a cue from Albert Einstein, who advised that we should live out of our imagination rather than out of our memory. Tom's sound thinking enabled him to discover opportunities that enriched both his life and his bank account.

> *"Sound thinking is at the center of every effective change effort."*

Sound thinking is at the center of every effective change effort. It doesn't necessarily have to be *brilliant* thinking, although that never hurts. It doesn't even have to be innovative or breakthrough thinking, although an occasional dose of that can certainly help. But it does need to be *sound* thinking—thinking that raises the right questions and elicits a range of reasonable answers. It needs to be thinking that challenges the status quo, thinking that bumps up against existing norms, thinking that either spawns new ideas or welcomes fresh application of old ideas. Thinking that expands possibilities.

In this context, sound thinking is not really a function of IQ scores and is certainly not a function of formal education. It is more a function of behavior and habits. Happily, through mindful practice and deliberate repetition, behavior and habits can be strengthened. In other words, by proactively exercising our sound thinking, we can get better at it.

The Change-Friendly practitioner is alert to four dimensions of sound thinking:
- Capacity
- Curiosity
- Conclusions
- Connections

CAPACITY – WHY MINDSET MATTERS

Legions of writers—from Dale Carnegie to Napoleon Hill to Norman Vincent Peale to Anthony Robbins—have touted the value of positive mental attitude. Scores of rah-rah speakers evangelize on the doctrine of believing in ourselves. All of that is important, but sound thinking requires more than a rosy outlook and a dose of self esteem. Sound thinking requires a mindset—or orientation—that's both receptive to fresh (even contrary) ideas and accepting of the notion that most of us can be more creative than we've ever dreamed.

When Carol Dweck was a sixth-grader at P.S. 153 in Brooklyn, New York, she experienced something that motivated her to explore why some people view intelligence as a fixed trait while others embrace it as a quality that can be developed and expanded. Young Carol's teacher seated the students around the classroom according to their IQ scores. The boys and girls who didn't have the highest IQs were not trusted to carry the flag during school assemblies. They weren't even allowed to clap erasers or wash the chalkboard or take a note to the principal.

"Our teacher let it be known that IQ for her was the ultimate measure of your intelligence and your character," Carol says. "So the students who had the best seats were always scared of taking another test and not being at the top anymore. It was an uncomfortable thing because you were only as good as your last test score. I think it had just as negative an effect on the kids at the top [as those at the bottom] who were defining themselves in those terms."

Today Carol Dweck is a professor of psychology at Stanford University, having previously taught at Yale, Columbia, and Harvard. Her special interest is in people's self-theories about intelligence and the profound influence such theories have on the motivation to learn. She says people who hold a "fixed" theory are mainly concerned with how smart they are (or are perceived to be). They prefer tasks they can already do well and they tend to avoid tasks on which they may make mistakes and jeopardize their "smart" image. By contrast, Dr. Dweck says, people who believe in an "expandable" or "growth" theory of intelligence thrive on challenging themselves to increase their abilities, even if they fail at first.[1]

This and related research on intelligence and motivation highlights the role of personal *capacity* in becoming Think-Friendly.

Why was Art Fry able to imagine a new use for the sticky-but-not-too-sticky adhesive? Because he was more concerned about solving a problem than about adhering to an arbitrary "that's-not-my-area-of-expertise" paradigm. He believed the adage

> *Things alter for the worse spontaneously, if they be not altered for the better designedly.*
> **Francis Bacon**

that necessity is the mother of invention, he believed he could cook up some workable ideas, and that expansive self-image enabled him to invent Post-it Notes.

How did Bart Withers devise a creative way to arbitrate a feud between two senior managers? He rejected the "I'm-an-engineer-so-I-can't-cope-with-this-people-stuff" mentality. His "growth" mindset enabled him to imagine a situation that *required* the feuders to replace the silent treatment with conversation, then coordination, then cooperation, and finally collaboration.

What empowered Tom Pulliam to add "successful actor" and "bestselling author" to his resume? Did he have more brain cells than his colleagues at the food manufacturing plant? Tom would insist he was surrounded by smart people, and he was. Sure, Tom had obvious gifts (like a great voice and a romance with words). But what really set him apart was his refusal to be hamstrung by a "fixed" mindset. He knew that most opportunities don't just fall into our laps, we must create them. So he did.

While some people talk about "thinking outside the box," folks like Art Fry, Bart Withers, and Tom Pulliam would ask "*What* box?"

Half a century ago Maxwell Maltz aroused the minds of millions with his book *Psycho-Cybernetics*. His primary premise was that many people are trapped in self images that limit them, while others have self images that open the door to a cornucopia of possibilities. Dr. Maltz said that in the human brain there's a sort of motion picture projector, and the "self movie" is played over and over and over again. If a child is told (especially by a parent, teacher, or other trusted authority figure) that she's clumsy and awkward, there's a good chance she'll regard herself as clumsy and awkward the rest of her life. In fact,

> *"The view we adopt for ourselves profoundly affects the way we lead our lives."*

she'll likely go out of her way to prove it. If we learn to believe that we're not good at math, that we can't speak with confidence in public, or that we're not comfortable making new friends, all of that will likely be true. In short, the view we adopt for ourselves profoundly affects the way we lead our lives. But the good news is that we can deliberately *choose* to project a different "self movie" on the motion picture screen in our brains. Just like the heroine in the classic children's book *The Little Engine That Could*, we can tell ourselves "I think I can, I think I can, I think I can." And then there's a good chance that, indeed, we *can*.

This does not mean, of course, that a middle-aged couch potato can employ mental gymnastics to transform himself into a professional basketball star. Nor does it mean that a card-carrying pessimist can change the world by merely thinking positive thoughts, or that a tone deaf piano novice can "will" himself to be the next Beethoven. What it does mean is that our intelligence—our mental *capacity*—is not carved in stone.

By rejecting the "fixed" mindset and adopting the "growth" mindset we can cultivate and expand our abilities to develop skills and solve problems that heretofore would have stumped us.

In 1954 Roger Bannister adopted the "growth" mindset to be the first person ever to run a four-minute mile, rebuffing the conventional wisdom that such a feat was anatomically impossible. With the myth shattered, 16 other runners also cracked the four-minute mile over the next three years.

When my son Baylor was nine, his teachers told my wife and me that Baylor was a nice little boy but not really capable of excelling in school. (His grades at the time seemed to reinforce that view.) We thought otherwise. We believed Baylor was simply bored and under-challenged. So we asked the teachers to give him extra assignments. In addition to keeping our boy busier, the extra assignments apparently sent him the message "You're smart, so here's some additional work to stretch your mind." Baylor began to thrive. His confidence —and his grades—soared. Throughout high school and two university degrees he earned nearly all "A" grades. He now speaks several languages, is a world traveler, and is a diplomat for the U.S. Department of State. The turning point was when he jettisoned the "fixed" mindset and adopted the "growth" mindset.

This deliberate and proactive expansion of one's own mental *capacity* is a critical step toward being Think-Friendly.

CURIOSITY—THE POWER OF THOUGHTFUL QUESTIONS

Egyptian novelist Naguib Mahfouz said it best: "You can tell whether a man is clever by his answers. You can tell whether a man is wise by his questions."

Decades of diagnostic work—survey research, interviews, etc.— have taught me a lot about the value of thoughtful questions. I can distill it into two salient points. First, you must ask the right questions. Well of course, you say. That's obvious. Yes, but the second point may not be quite so obvious: You must carefully avoid asking the wrong questions. Why? Because asking the wrong questions will still get you data, and then you'll chase the wrong rabbits. Asking the wrong questions is a dangerous and common mistake. It can result in massive reports and beautiful PowerPoint presentations that take unwitting detours to conclusions that shouldn't be reached and decisions that shouldn't be made.

In some ways, we live in the age of the reluctant thinker. Original thinking is not always rewarded. Despite a lot of lip service about the value (and necessity) of strategic change, many corporate cultures cling tenaciously to the status quo. People who question "the way things have always been done" risk being branded as mavericks or even troublemakers rather than as innovators.

A good case study, mentioned in Chapter 2, is the story about cleaning the stones at the Jefferson Memorial. It illustrates the power of *systems thinking*, examining the big picture to reveal the multiplicity of causes and effects. Smart organizations use it to find simple and cost-effective solutions to a wide range of performance issues. They sort through the loops and links. They ask the right questions. They avoid asking the wrong questions. They diagnose before they prescribe.

In our "just do it" society, thinking is often viewed as unproductive. When economic times get tough, training budgets are often among the first to be slashed. Good training involves good questions and good answers, which lead to good thinking, which leads to productive people. But many short-sighted managers don't have the big picture. So they cut the training and development, then wonder why their people seem stuck in the old ruts. It's sort of like "I don't have time to stop and get gas because I'm too busy driving!" Asking thoughtful questions—which can be strengthened with good training and development—is a core competency that pays huge dividends.

Let's consider six dividends of Think-Friendly questions.

(1) *Think-Friendly questions stimulate exploration (and even serendipity)*. When we get stuck in a particular pattern of thinking, it's often because we keep asking ourselves the same questions. Change the question and you're more likely to come up with a more practical answer.

Sixty years ago, Edwin Land was walking along the beach with his young daughter. He stopped to snap a few photos with his Brownie camera. Impatient for the results, his little girl asked an intriguing question: "Daddy, why can't we see the pictures right now?" It was a problem in search of a solution, and from that innocent question came the development of the Polaroid Land camera and the ability to see a completed photograph only seconds after it was taken. Art Fry's role in the development of the Post-it Note was an example of a solution in search of a problem. The sticky-but-not-too-sticky adhesive concocted by his colleague was just the answer to Fry's question "How can I make a bookmark that will stick to the page but won't tear the paper when I move it somewhere else?"

(2) *Think-Friendly questions lead to valuable information*. Change-Friendly people tend to be questioning detectives. Remem-

ber Columbo, the television cop who always solved the crime by asking (in his famously offhand manner) just one more question? We should be more like Columbo, asking that extra question to probe and clarify until we're sure we understand what we need to know or do.

Good journalists, good detectives, good *thinkers* focus on five Ws and an H—Who, What When, Where, Why, and How. They ask questions that march them down the path to the information or understanding they seek. They know that not everyone volunteers information, so they ask. They know that

> *Not everything that is faced can be changed, but nothing can be changed until it is faced.*
> **James A. Baldwin**

some people speak in generalities, so they ask for specifics. They know that assumptions can be faulty, so they question assumptions —beginning with their own. They know that effects have many disguises, so they dig for root causes. They know that words and phrases can mean different things to different people, so they seek clarity and common ground.

Even in this age of Internet search engines and other means of instant information, we can never know everything. And even when we do find answers, we only generate more questions. For generations, scientists struggled with the question "How can we prolong life?" Today we have the technology to keep people alive long after their bodies cease to function on their own. So now one of the questions has become "*Should* we prolong life?"

(3) *Think-Friendly questions help us gain control.* Just like there's bad cholesterol and good cholesterol, there's bad control and good control. The bad kind of control has to do with manipulation of others or smothering their initiative. The good kind of control has to do with managing situations and, especially, managing ourselves.

We can help manage our own physical vitality by asking the right kind of questions of our doctors, dentists, pharmacists, and other health care providers. We can manage our own financial health by asking the right questions of our brokers, accountants, attorneys, insurance people, and financial planners. We can manage our own home maintenance by asking the right questions of the plumber, the electrician, the landscaper, and the guy at the hardware store.

Change-Friendly people tend to be good conversationalists. And the best conversationalists are usually people who ask good questions. They don't interrogate, they simply ask meaningful questions that other people are willing to answer. People who seem to do best in job interviews are those who come prepared with questions of their own. People who are really good at engaging the heads, hearts, and hopes of others tend to ask questions that evoke that engagement.

Good questions, coupled with genuine listening, enable us to be in control without appearing to be controlling, to be assertive without being aggressive. (Good listening will receive more attention in subsequent chapters.)

Although effective communication usually has a spontaneous feel to it, a bit of planning is often in order. Lewis Carroll's book *Alice in Wonderland* offers some pertinent lessons. You may recall the exchange between Alice and the Cheshire Cat about the importance of setting goals. Consider this passage in which Alice asks the Cheshire Cat for advice on which direction to go.

> "Would you tell me, please, which way I ought to go from here?"
> "That depends a good deal on where you want to go," said the Cat.
> "I don't much care where—" said Alice .
> "Then it doesn't matter which way you go," said the Cat. "—so long as I get *somewhere*," Alice added as an explanation.
> "Oh, you're sure to do that," said the Cat, "if you only walk long enough."

It really takes no effort to get *somewhere*. Just do nothing, and you're there. If you want to get somewhere *meaningful*, however, you must know where you want to go. Then you need to make plans on *how* to get there. Think-Friendly questions can help provide a good roadmap.

(4) *Think-Friendly questions stir people to open up.* Ask routine questions and you'll likely get routine, minimalist responses.

"How was your day?

"Fine."

"Was the traffic any better?"

"About the same."

"Did your presentation go okay?"

"Pretty much."

I practice my questioning habits with my young grandchildren. Why? Because they're among my all-time favorite people and because their answers usually lead to delightful, self-revealing conversations. The questions that jump-start these great dialogues are designed to provoke thought and are not conducive to routine answers. One of them doesn't even end with a question mark.

"What was the funniest thing that happened to you today?"

"What part of today would you like to happen again tomorrow?"

"Tell me how that spelling bee can help you in other school subjects."

"What important thing have you learned since we last talked?"

"How can you help me be smarter?"

"In what ways were you a good friend today?"

"Who are the characters in the book you're reading? What do you like about them?"

Of course I delight in the innocent questions of my grandchildren, too. Questions like:

"What color is thunder?"

"Do cows get bored? Do they care?"

"Does the Fairy Princess know she's not real?"

"How old is dirt?"

"Who came before God?"

There's really nothing complicated about thought-provoking questions. They simply require thought—your thought in asking them, and the respondent's thought in answering them. And they are appropriate in any venue.

Rather than ask a client to tell me generally what's going on in his company, I may ask "What kind of day-to-day business situation has the power to keep you awake at night?" Or "If you could wave a magic wand over your business, what would you change? Why?" Or, "Whose leadership style do you most admire? How is your own style different or similar?"

While good questions can stir others to open up, it's our own genuine listening that helps persuade them to *stay* open with us. A comic once said that authentic communication is 50% sincerity, and then you just fake the rest of it. That line may get a chuckle, but it's a dangerous practice. Genuine listening is much, much more

> *"Genuine listening involves connecting heart to heart and working to understand the other person's viewpoint even if you don't agree with it."*

than eye contact and an occasional "uh-huh." Genuine listening involves connecting heart to heart and working to understand the other person's viewpoint even if you don't agree with it. Good questions can pave the way.

(5) *Think-Friendly questions influence people to persuade themselves.* A secret to persuasion is to encourage or enable people to come up with their own solutions to problems. Said another way, we can persuade others by helping them persuade themselves.

It's a fact of human nature that many people have more confidence in what *they* say than in what *you* say. When people come up with their own answers and when they say something in their own voice, they're much more likely to take ownership of the idea.

The best coaches I know—athletic coaches, speech coaches, music coaches, business coaches—invest most of their time and effort in asking pertinent questions that result in focused feedback.

For example, let's say a speech coach is helping a business executive prepare for an important presentation to employees. Rather than simply prescribe a step-by-step approach to drafting and rehearsing the presentation, the coach is likely to ask a series of targeted, Think-Friendly questions:

> *"Specifically who are your audience members?"*
>
> *"Based on the feedback you receive, what seems to be their view of your own work performance? What is your credibility with them?"*
>
> *"In what ways can you help your people 'catch the vision' of the organization's possibilities?"*

"How can you genuinely differentiate your business from your competitors?"

"What kind of data will meet the information needs of your audience, and how can you package the data in a fresh, compelling way?"

"How can you show your audience the linkage between the company's success and their own personal best interests?"

"How can your presentation come across as a friend-to-friend chat on subjects of mutual interest rather than as a hollow pronouncement from the big guy in the corner office?"

These are pertinent questions, and the answers have a lot more influence when they come from the person being coached.

(6) *Think-Friendly questions foster self coaching.* Self coaching requires the willingness to seek honest feedback from others and the discipline to translate that feedback into deliberate improvement. Unfortunately, many people have fallen into the "been there, done that" rut. They forget that self criticism—when it's honest and balanced—is a critical ingredient in personal improvement.

Change-Friendly people tend to ask themselves questions like these:

"What went well yesterday that's worth repeating today? How can I make it happen?"

"How can I prepare for this meeting so my participation will add real value?"

"This interesting solution doesn't quite fit the problem. Can it be applied to another problem?" (Remember the story of the Post-it Notes.)

"What things are my colleagues genuinely interested in? What questions are most likely to trigger an interesting conversation?"

"What specific activities—right now—are most likely

to advance me toward my goal?" (Yard by yard it's hard, but inch by inch it's a cinch.)

"What have I learned from a recent mistake or missed opportunity? How can I put that learning to good use?"

Remember to ask questions from the perspective of the "learner" rather than as a "judger." Acting as a judger can influence us to look for blame rather than solutions. In the learner mode, you use questions to probe the dilemma gently, without bias. Learners tend to ask open-ended, information-gathering questions. If you find yourself in the judger

> *"Remember to ask questions from the perspective of the 'learner' rather than as a 'judger.'"*

mode, you can change the character of your inquiry by using your mental "switching lane" and asking learner questions. For example, instead of thinking "Why is this person such a jerk?" you can "switch lanes" and ask "What is this person looking for?" or "What is this person *really* concerned about?" Learner questions, posed in a Think-Friendly way, help create a safe environment that influences people to explore their own motivations honestly and openly.

Think-Friendly questions are not complicated. In fact, they're deceptively simple. And using smart questions to make yourself even smarter is a practice that's – well, it's as old as dirt.

CONCLUSIONS – CHALLENGE THE STORIES YOU TELL YOURSELF

Bob is a big car guy. He loves horsepower. The rumble of a classic glasspack muffler is like a symphony to his ears. He has a buddy who owns a mint condition 1968 Corvette Roadster, cherry red. Bob has salivated over that car for years. Suddenly the car is for sale and Bob had better move fast because his friend is already getting feelers from other car enthusiasts. Bob quickly goes to his broker and pulls $20,000 from his already eroded retirement fund. He buys the car of his dreams and is sure this is the happiest day of his life.

Bob takes the Corvette out for its first road test. It's a beautiful day. Wind blows in his face as he races down a country highway.

Bob isn't sure what he's enjoying most, the noise and vibration of all that horsepower he's riding or the surge of testosterone through his body.

Then, out of nowhere, a young boy appears and throws a rock smack into the side of Bob's dream car. Wham!

Bob's immediate thought goes something like "Hmm, let's see. In this jurisdiction would what I'm about to do constitute cold-blooded murder or would it simply be justifiable homicide?" Well, something like that. Let's just say that Bob instantly shifts gears from being a gratified automobile enthusiast to being a raving maniac in the grasp of a serious case of road rage. He slams on the brakes, throws the Corvette in reverse, and burns rubber all fifty yards back to where the rock-thrower is standing. But instead of finding a boy with a look of terror on his face, he discovers a boy with a look of pleading, even supplication. "Mister, I'm so sorry about hitting your car with a rock. But I've tried to flag down other people and nobody will stop. My little brother is over there in the tall grass. He's had a seizure and we've lost his medicine. Can you *please* help us?"

How does Bob feel now? How do *you* feel now?

In an instant, Bob is transformed from a raging hothead ready to do damage to a child a fraction of his age ... to a compassionate and empathic grownup willing to provide grownup help to someone in need.

Why the quick turnaround? With a fresh set of data (a boy taking a risk to help his little brother versus a punk kid doing vandalism), Bob changed his "story." With a fresh story came a new set of feelings. And with a new set of feelings came a very different kind of action: help rather than harm.

That's the power of the stories we tell ourselves.

On a drive along California's central coast I noticed an interesting bumper sticker on the vehicle in front of me: "Don't believe everything you think."

Unlike most bumper stickers, this one caused me to ponder the layers of meaning and even to challenge—well, to challenge my own thinking.

Everything we do is a product of our thinking. Every single act is rooted in a thought. Our thoughts may be subtle or even unconscious, but they nevertheless are at the root of our behavior.

Here's how it works. Let's say you're with a group of people and they laugh at you. Based on that observation, you instantly tell yourself a story. It goes something like "They're mocking me. They're ridiculing me. They're belittling my ideas." That story then spawns a feeling, which could range from hurt to anger. You then act on that feeling. Maybe you defend yourself, or go silent, or even get up and leave.

Here's another scenario. You're with a group of people and they laugh at you. Based on that observation, you instantly tell yourself a story. It goes something like "It's really fun to be with my friends. That's why we decided to hold this Super Bowl party. They're not laughing at me out of ridicule, but out of friendship and camaraderie." That story then spawns feelings that could range from amusement to outright joy. You then act on that feeling. Maybe you join in the laughter, maybe you poke fun at the other guy. You enjoy the moment.

Do you see the difference? In both instances, people laughed at you. But your path to action produced vastly different behaviors, and the critical variable was the story you told yourself. The difference was your thinking.

At one time or another, most of us have claimed that our emotions—our feelings—are imposed on us, that we have no control. Have you ever said something like "He makes me so mad!"? The reality, tough though it may be to swallow, is that nobody can *make* us be mad, or glad, or sad, or anything else. We *choose* our feelings based on the stories we tell ourselves. Then our feelings lead to actions that produce results. If we don't like our results we can challenge our own thinking, because what we *think* is what launches us on our path to action that produces our results.

> **The absence of evidence is not evidence of absence.**
> **Dr. Carl Sagan**

At first blush, this idea may come across as a touchy-feely mind game. It's not. The ability to improve our results by challenging our own thinking is one of the most powerful skills we can develop. It can unlock our true potential by freeing us from the constraints of the stories we often tell ourselves.

Let's see how this can work.

Your brain has a mind of its own. No kidding. On its own accord, the brain tends to act more out of self-preservation than out of rationality. We have a natural tendency to tell ourselves stories that justify what we're doing or failing to do. We have a natural tendency to allow our stories to masquerade as facts. We have a natural tendency to seek information that reinforces our view and to filter out or ignore information that contradicts our view. When we're not careful, some of us can jump to conclusions faster than an Olympian can do a back flip. This isn't a character flaw, it's just part of being human. But these natural tendencies can be crippling. The good news is that we can teach ourselves a new set of behaviors that serve us better.

> *"We have a natural tendency to allow our stories to masquerade as facts."*

Here's an approach to challenging our own conclusions that I've discovered to be helpful. I've given it a name: FIND-IT, which stands for Focus, Inquire, Notice, Discern—Integrate, Translate.

First, let's examine the nuances of each of these action verbs.

To Focus is to clarify, to concentrate, to more carefully define.

To Inquire is to investigate, to seek information by questioning. Effective inquiry requires an openness, a willingness to discover and accept information that differs from our first impressions or preconceived notions. Appreciative inquiry involves searching for solutions or explanations that may already exist and looking for the good and reasonable. That's not to suggest that we wear blinders that prevent our seeing what's dangerous or harmful. It's to suggest that we honestly consider the possibility of bright sunshine obscured by the dark clouds.

To Notice is to pay mindful attention to details, to become more aware of the individual parts that comprise the whole. I recall an art gallery that I visited with my grandchildren. A major exhibit featured the playful work of Walter Wick, the photographer whose *I SPY* and *Can You See What I See* books for children are longtime bestsellers. With careful examination, I was able to notice things in Wick's work that were completely missed in my initial, cursory look. In some situations there may be less than meets the eye. In others, there is definitely more than meets the eye. The only way to know is to notice mindfully.

To Discern is to distinguish, to recognize as distinct or different. True discernment also involves wisdom. Do you remember the Naguib Mahfouz quote? "You can tell whether a man is clever by his answers. You can tell whether a man is wise by his questions." Discernment is an outgrowth of honest inquiry and mindful noticing.

To Integrate involves incorporating parts into a whole, giving fair consideration to the possible interdependency of the individual pieces. A related word is *integral*, which denotes something that is necessary to complete the whole. Another related word is *integrity*, which denotes a state of being that's whole or complete, and, of course, soundness of moral character. All of these are essential to Think-Friendly behavior.

To Translate is to change something's form, nature, or condition or to explain it in terms that are more easily understood and more appropriately dealt with.

To illustrate the utility of the FIND-IT model, let's consider Stephen Covey's classic story of his experience on a subway. At one station stop a man stepped onto the subway along with several children. The man sat down, stared blankly at the floor, the train lurched forward, and the children went nuts. They pushed and shoved each other, wrestled over sitting space,

> *Myth: Something that never was, and always will be.*

and generally made a loud nuisance of themselves. One little boy, barely able to toddle, tripped over the feet of other passengers and seemed oblivious to the possible danger. Stephen, who's the father of nine children, found himself irritated with the man. His conclusion was that the man was rude and uncaring and simply wouldn't be bothered with managing his unruly children. So Stephen stepped across the aisle, sat down beside the man, and asked a couple of simple questions:

"Sir, are these your children?"

"Oh, yes they are."

"They seem anxious about something. Are you concerned that this littlest guy might get hurt in the crowd?"

Inside, Stephen was frankly annoyed by the children's behavior. Most of all he was annoyed by the man's apparent indifference to the situation. But then he got a response that changed everything.

"Oh, yeah, I realize the children are out of hand. You see, we just left the hospital. My wife has been gravely ill for several weeks. She died about an hour ago. I've told the children that their mother is gone and I'm afraid they're kind of in shock. I certainly am. I don't know how I'm going to live without my wife."

With that fresh insight, Stephen's paradigm—his "story" or frame of reference—changed instantly. Instead of viewing the man as rude and uncaring, he now saw him for what he was—a fellow human swallowed by grief and shock. And when Stephen's viewpoint changed, his behavior changed. His urge to judge and lecture was replaced by the urge to comfort and help. He offered to cancel his appointments and help the man, a total stranger who was suddenly humanized by more complete—and more accurate—information.

When we sincerely Focus on a situation, we begin to see things that were not at first apparent.

When we respectfully Inquire—not for the purpose of playing "gotcha" but rather for the purpose of discovering possibilities we had not considered—we are often surprised by what we learn.

When we mindfully Notice the details of a situation we begin to see and appreciate the individual pixels that comprise the landscape.

When we carefully Discern what's going on in a situation, we honestly distinguish between the facts (verifiable data) and our assumptions (the unsubstantiated stories we tell ourselves).

When we Integrate what we've noticed and discerned, we're well on our path to appropriate and useful conclusions, decisions, and behaviors.

Finally, we're able to Translate it all in a way that leads us to productive outcomes.

The next time you're struggling for a useful approach to a situation, be Think-Friendly. FIND-IT.

CONNECTIONS – PRIMING THE IDEA PUMP

If you've ever studied semantics, organizational behavior, or even history and politics, you've likely heard some variation of this:

> There are *known knowns*. These are things we know we
> know. There are *known unknowns*. These are things we
> know we don't know. There are *unknown unknowns*.
> These are things we don't know we don't know. And
> there are *unknown knowns*. These are things we know,
> but don't realize we know them.

There's a lot of wisdom in that tongue-twister. In any change effort (in fact, in life itself) we must constantly juggle what we know with confidence, what we'd like to know but don't yet know, what we don't even know we don't know, and what we unknowingly already know.

As we exchange intellectual currency—ideas—with our friends and colleagues, we must be alert to the four dimensions of sound thinking. The Capacity dimension underscores the value of a "growth" mindset that can open up whole new worlds of creative thinking. The Curiosity dimension emphasizes thoughtful questions that can take us down paths we didn't even imagine. The Conclusions dimension is where we suspend judgment, challenge our own stories, and double-check the validity of our assumptions.

These first three dimensions of sound thinking inform and culminate in the fourth dimension: Connections. Let me illustrate with an example.

As a young businessman in the early 1980s I headed worldwide communication for Campbell Soup Company. My department was in charge of things like the annual report, stockholder relations, working with the news media, and reinforcing the company's vast marketing operations. Campbell owned about 80% of the condensed soup market, but we also had a wide range of other popular brands —Vlasic, Godiva, Pepperidge Farm, Prego, Swanson, V-8, and many others. Although I enjoyed walking over to the Campbell test kitchens for an afternoon visit and snack with the company food scientists, my expertise was in communication, not product development. But on some occasions I was asked to step out of my comfort zone.

I enjoyed a good rapport with Campbell president Gordon Mc-

Govern. One day he walked into my office and asked: "What do you think of Swanson fried chicken?" I told him I hadn't eaten any Swanson products for a while, but my recollection was that the fried chicken tasted like spiced cardboard. "You're my man!" Gordon said with excitement. "And the fact that you know nothing about product development helps qualify you for this assignment." I took that as a compliment because I knew Gordon wasn't questioning my intelligence, he was merely acknowledging that I had no preconceived notions about *what* to do about the Swanson product but I was pretty good about asking what he called "naïve questions" (remember the Columbo analogy?).

Gordon turned me loose on the project. My assignment was to discover why our Swanson fried chicken product was so far behind its competition, then to suggest improvements that would lead to better market position. It frankly never occurred to me that I was unqualified for the task—not because I think I'm smarter

> *Everyone thinks of changing the world, but no one thinks of changing himself.*
> **Tolstoy**

than other people (there's ample evidence to the contrary), but because my work as a journalist, university professor, and consultant had given me lots of experience with the four dimensions of sound thinking: Capacity, Curiosity, Conclusions, and Connections.

With what my family called "the chicken project," I started with information-gathering. I talked with people who had conducted focus groups that agreed with my "spiced cardboard" assessment (some of them had even less flattering descriptions of the product). I consulted with people in the marketing department. I interviewed grocery store managers. I talked with product development specialists and nutritionists. I even flew to Arkansas to tour the production plant and to visit with people in charge of processing the actual product.

These conversations helped me identify a surprising root cause of the product's failure in the marketplace. An unintended consequence of the company's bonus system was that senior managers were incented to cut expenses in ways that actually hurt the company. In this case, a senior vice president received a quarterly bonus based on a formula that factored in marketing, product development, and processing costs. The marketing staff told me they were using consumer data four and five years old—virtually worthless in the fast-moving world of food merchandising. The production people told me they were using out-dated processing equipment that simply couldn't keep pace with the consumer's demand for frozen fried chicken that cooked up as a moist, appetizing dish. Every time they got the newer equipment in the budget it was jerked at the last minute—just in time to plump up the senior executive's quarterly bonus.

With this validated conclusion we quickly made the right connections.

The bonus system was retooled to reward ingenuity that benefitted the company rather than people's self-serving and short-term personal interests. The marketing staff got their fresh consumer data. The processing people got their new equipment.

> *"The best thinking often has a strong element of serendipity."*

We launched a new "Plump and Juicy" fried chicken product that performed much better than its predecessor.

The best thinking often has a strong element of serendipity. You're energized by the prospect of a difficult challenge. You suspend judgment. You ask a lot of questions, many of them seemingly naïve and unrelated. You double-check your data and challenge your assumptions. You discover things you weren't even looking for. Then you have a solution—not necessarily the *only* solution, but one that works—that you never imagined.

Regardless of your official title, in your role as a Change-Friendly team player you'll likely be called on for big-picture thinking. Look beyond your parochial agenda and consider how your decisions and actions may affect others.

When the situation calls for *creative* thinking, seek opportunities in ambiguity and non-conformity. Regard failure as a natural part of exploring what works and what doesn't (again, remember the Post-it Note). Be prepared to connect seemingly unrelated ideas and thoughts.

When *strategic* thinking is needed, be clear about the direction you want to take and the reasons for doing so, then evaluate the pros and cons of ideas. With strategic thinking, planning is a priority. Ask questions to break issues down into manageable parts.

With *possibility* thinking, dream new dreams with no barriers or limitations. (Just a few short years ago only a handful of people dared to dream of a powerful communication device like an iPhone that could be carried in your shirt pocket.)

When *reflective* thinking is the order of the moment, look back and learn from what you and others have done. Past experience can be very instructive, as long as we avoid getting stuck in the "we've always done it that way" trap. Reflective thinking can help you put issues into perspective, reveal the big picture, evaluate issues logically without emotions of the moment, and provide insight for future situations.

Not every thought you have will be (or can be) original. As satirist Ambrose Bierce said, "there is nothing new under the sun, but there are lots of old things we don't know." *Shared* thinking is often a combination of several other forms. With this, you can combine two or more ideas or embellish the thinking of others. Virtually all technological advances are the result of such shared thinking.

> *When our first parents were driven out of Paradise, Adam is believed to have remarked to Eve: "My dear, we live in an age of transition."*
> **William Inge**

We can be prisoners of our thinking or be can be liberated and propelled by our thinking. Viktor Frankl, an Austrian psychiatrist, endured the atrocities of several Nazi concentration camps by redirecting his thinking from the suffering around him to the meaning of his existence. He embodied the truism that although we cannot control our circumstances we can control our response to them. Compared to Frankl's situation, the typical change or transformation effort is a walk in the park.

So you want to have a positive impact in your organization? You want to help incubate ideas and innovations that really make a difference? You want to influence people to embrace change rather than resist it? Then resolve not to behave like the *Saints*, the *Ain'ts*, and the *Complaints* we see in many organizations.

The *Saints* are people who regard themselves as martyrs. They believe they are victimized by systems, processes, or other people. Their woe-is-me demeanor seems to feed on itself, stifling creativity and smothering any hint of personal accountability. The cure: Let go of any victim stories you may be telling yourself. Confront the reality that your own behavior or constraining paradigms may be part of the problem. Honestly ask yourself the question, "What am I doing, or failing to do, that could be contributing to this predicament?"

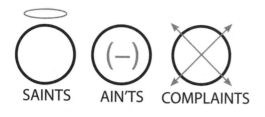

SAINTS   AIN'TS   COMPLAINTS

The *Ain'ts* are people who play the blame game. Their negative outlook is focused on what they perceive others to be doing or failing to do. They sometimes play the double role of Saint and Ain't. After all, if you're a victim doesn't there need to be a villain somewhere in the story? The cure: Seriously challenge any villain stories you may be telling yourself or others. Such stories are often ill-founded and they serve no productive purpose even if true. Honestly ask yourself the question, "Why might they (other people) be doing what they're doing?" Consider that the same data (your observations) could reasonably lead to a wide range of conclusions.

The *Complaints* are people who lament most anything and everything around them. Just about anything can be a target of their condemnation and criticism. Naturally, if the real problem is "out there" somewhere, they can absolve themselves of responsibility. The cure: If you find yourself in the Complaint mode, jettison any helpless stories you may be telling yourself or broadcasting to others. Honestly ask yourself the question, "What can *I* do at this moment that could help produce a better outcome?" If re-focused thinking can enable Viktor Frankl to triumph over the Holocaust, you can surely succeed with the change effort on your plate.

An excellent launching pad can be the four dimensions of sound thinking: Capacity, Curiosity, Conclusions, and Connections.

It's a critical part of being Change-Friendly.

THINK-FRIENDLY SELF-ASSESSMENT

Instructions: *Read each statement and decide how accurately it describes your use of the Think-Friendly behaviors described in this chapter:*

    a. Never or rarely engage in this behavior (0 points)

    b. Sometimes engage in this behavior (1 point)

    c. Regularly engage in this behavior (2 points)

    d. Always or almost always engage in this behavior (3 points)

Place the point value of your response choice beside each statement.

_____ I think in ways that challenge the status quo, that challenge existing norms, and that clearly expand possibilities.

_____ I ask smart questions ("smart" in the sense that they explore fresh territory and help uncover information that other people may have missed).

_____ I carefully challenge my own stories to ensure that they're based on facts rather than on assumptions.

_____ I constantly look for the root causes of things that affect my change effort, not just the superficial symptoms.

_____ When faced with difficulty, I ask myself "What am I doing, or failing to do, that could be contributing to this predicament?"

_____ Total Number of Points

Interpreting Your Scores

0-5: You're missing opportunities to expand your thinking and are likely mired in a rather ho-hum change effort. It's not uncommon for smart people to assume they can simply "wing it" through a change effort without paying the price of deliberate and strategic thinking. Does that describe you? Ratchet up your thinking habits with the behaviors outlined in this chapter and you'll enjoy a noticeable improvement in your results.

6-10: You're making better-than-average use of good thinking behaviors, but you're still not operating at the level for which you should strive. Continue to ask a lot of smart questions—always from the perspective of the "learner" rather than from the "judger"—and you'll be pleased by the progress you make.

11-15: Congratulations, your thinking behaviors are definitely the ones that will produce superior results. But don't get complacent. Because change by its very nature is a fluid process, Think-Friendly behaviors are a critical ingredient at every stage of every change effort.

---

[1] See *Mindset: The Psychology of Success* by Carol S. Dweck (New York: Ballantine Books, 2006)

*We must love them both, those whose opinions
we share and those whose opinions we reject.
For both have labored in the search for truth
and both have helped us in the finding of it.*
Thomas Aquinas

*Wise men talk because they have something to
say; fools, because they have to say something.*
Plato

*Know how to listen, and you will profit even
from those who talk badly.*
Plutarch

*If you talk to a man in a language he understands,
that goes to his head. If you talk to him in his
language, that goes to his heart.*
Nelson Mandela

Chapter

Talk-Friendly:
Put Your Best Voice Forward

People serious about engaging others in change know how important it is to revive the lost art of meaning-full conversation.

As a young boy I enjoyed spending hours with my grandmother working on jigsaw puzzles. She especially liked puzzles of outdoor scenes. These were particularly challenging because the colors and textures of nature often merge without clear lines of demarcation. My initial childish inclination was to try to "win" at solving the puzzles. But when I tried to argue or debate, I missed opportunities for progress. I discovered that my piece of a puzzle was both valid and limited. It was not the whole picture. When I became curious and started to inquire about other puzzle pieces (my grandmother's perspective), I began to see a fuller picture and was better able to collaborate in solving the puzzle.

Effective conversation is a lot like collaborating on a jigsaw puzzle. Each person's perspective adds to the whole. This is made possible by dialogue. The Greek roots of the word are *dia* (through) and *logos* (meaning). Although this definition may seem a bit academic, we should remember that it's through the *meanings* we share that we form the very basis for understanding each other at all. It's through shared meaning that we form religious congregations. It's through shared meaning that we form communities. It's through shared meaning that we are able to *engage* people we wish to influence and by whom we are willing to be influenced. It's through shared meaning that we form any *meaningful* relationship.

Dialogue does not consist of two competing monologues. Genuine dialogue involves the free flow of clear meaning toward a shared purpose in an atmosphere of mutual respect.

Notice that I didn't say free flow of *information*. I said free flow of *meaning*.

Putting your piece of the puzzle (information) on the table is not enough. Your perspective on how that piece fits (meaning) is also important. "Oh, you think turning the piece upside down helps? Ah, yes, it does. Now it contributes to the whole."

Of all the things you do as a leader of change, talking is among the most visible and certainly among the most influential. Think about it. You don't add your greatest value by virtue of your skill in manipulating project management software or flipping switches or turning valves. You add your greatest value by interacting with other human beings, and you do that primarily by talking. It's amazing how many books have been written on the subject of talking—*Fierce Conversations, Difficult Conversations, Crucial Conversations, Powerful Conversations, Authentic Conversations, The Art of Focused Conversation, How to Talk To Anyone*, etc. They all contribute to the discussion, but their essence can be summed up simply: We are most effective when we talk so other people will listen and when we listen so other people will talk. And not necessarily in that order.

> *"We are most effective when we talk so other people will listen and when we listen so other people will talk."*

Here's an example. A nuclear power plant was in the middle of a planned outage. That's when the plant is temporarily shut down for routine maintenance. During an outage, a nuclear plant is of course not generating electricity and is therefore not making money. It's *spending* money, lots of it. So it's important to complete the outage safely and as quickly as possible. In my role as a leadership consultant I was observing the beehive of activity in the outage control center, a large room with dozens of computers and closed-circuit TV screens for monitoring the work being done in the plant. The plant vice president walked into the room with a concerned expression on his face.

"What's going on?" I asked.

"We've got a problem."

"Is it a safety issue?" I inquired.

"No, it's not a safety issue."

At this point I realized he was probably using the word "safety" in reference to *physical* safety concerns like a radiation leak or an industrial accident. I, on the other hand, was talking about *psychological* safety. But I just let the conversation unfold. The vice president explained that a crew had entered a room in the plant, set up scaffolding, and started dismantling equipment for inspection and, if needed, replacement. The first crew finished its shift, and the second crew entered the room to continue the work. At the end of the second shift a third crew came in and one of its workers immediately said, "Hey, this is the wrong room. We're not scheduled to work on this equipment until the next outage twelve months from now."

Oops.

I asked the vice president how this mistake would affect the schedule for this outage. He said it would delay the outage by at least 18 to 24 hours. In addition, there would be a ripple effect on the hundreds of supplemental workers who had been hired to help with the outage.

"What's your company's selling price for electricity these days?" I asked.

"About $50 per megawatt."

"Okay," I said. "This nuclear plant features a 1,000-megawatt reactor. A thousand megawatts multiplied by $50 is $50,000 per hour. Multiply that by 24 hours and you get $1.2 million of lost income. Add to that the expense of keeping several hundred supplemental workers on site for an extra day and the cost jumps to well beyond $2 million."

My friend didn't like the explicit math, but he knew it was accurate.

"But you say it wasn't a safety issue?" I asked again.

"No, it had nothing to do with safety. It ..." He paused, and then he got it. "Oh, yeah, it *was* a safety issue."

"Tell me about it," I invited.

The vice president explained that the first work team was led by a take-no-prisoners crew chief whose command-and-control style was feared by all. He made it clear that people should simply do what he told them and not ask any questions. A couple of guys on his team knew this was the wrong room and the wrong equipment, but they didn't dare speak up. A similar situation existed with the second team—some people knew it was the wrong room and equipment, but their boss had long ago intimidated them into silence.

> *A good listener is a good talker with a sore throat.*
> **Katharine Whitehorn**

The third crew was different. The crew chief could read the organization chart. He knew he was the boss, but he didn't feel the need to remind people. His orientation toward his work mates went something like this: "Our job on this team is to help each other work smarter. The only way to do that is to challenge each other's thinking. I'll challenge your thinking and I expect you to challenge mine." So in that kind of environment it was easy for a member of this crew to say "Hey, this is the wrong room!"

Not every instance of conversational silence has a $2 million price tag. But the cumulative effect of such silence—reluctance or outright refusal to speak freely—adds up quickly. Let's say you have ten smart people at a table and three of them don't feel "safe" in speaking up. Not only do you not benefit from the "smarts" of the silent three, I suggest that you don't have the full benefit of the other seven.

A national study by VitalSmarts and The Concourse Group showed 85% of high-stakes business initiatives fail when people avoid discussing five critical issues. The study involved more than 1,000 executives and project management professionals across 40 companies in a wide range of industries. The findings pointed to five "undiscussable" issues that are the most prevalent and most costly barriers to project success:

- *Fact-free planning* – a project is put on a trajectory to failure when deadlines or resource limits are set with little consideration for reality (a flaw that's often not discussed effectively).
- *AWOL (absent without leave) sponsors* – sponsors fail to provide adequate leadership, political clout, time, energy, or other reinforcement to see a project through to completion, and no one effectively addresses the sponsors' anemic "assistance."
- *Skirting* – people simply work around the priority-setting process and nobody holds them accountable.
- *Project chicken* – team leaders and team members fail to admit when problems occur and instead just wait for someone else to speak up first.
- *Team failures* – team members perpetuate dysfunction when they're unwilling or unable to support the project, then they're reluctant to discuss their failure candidly.

Other key findings were that 90% of business leaders interviewed routinely experienced one or more of the five common issues, but fewer than 14% reported being able to get their concerns heard or understood.

The good news? Business leaders who successfully address one or more of the five issues are 50% to 70% more likely to fully achieve project objectives.

Clearly, the presence of these five problems is *not* a death sentence for projects. What typically dooms a project is the failure of participants to resolve problems by *talking* about them openly and effectively. In the language of our context, Change-Friendly leaders don't just understand and discuss reasons for failure with high stakes initiatives, they are skilled in practices that help *prevent* failure.

> *"Ours is a debate culture. Radio and television 'talk shows' are little more than gladiators with microphones."*

That's what being Talk-Friendly is all about.

Communication is at the center of our culture as human beings, yet in today's society we rarely make time for true communication.

People waste literally years of their lives emailing, texting, and Twittering rather than engaging in real conversation. And when people finally do talk face-to-face they often engage in most anything but real dialogue. Ours is a debate culture. Radio and television "talk shows" are little more than gladiators with microphones. Apparently loud and obnoxious combine for good ratings. Be-

> *"True dialogue is the antidote to the poisonous 'discussion' and debate tactics that characterize so many interactions in so many organizations."*

havior seen in corporate meetings rooms is often not much better —the same old patterns of competition, one-upmanship, I'm-right-and-you're-wrong power plays that smother any hope of real teamwork. Oh, I know, civility and even collegial warmth are the superficial norms in many organizational cultures, but the unwritten rules that lurk beneath the surface are more about turf protection and going for the jugular than about honestly seeking the best ideas.

That's where real dialogue—being Talk-Friendly—can make all the difference.

Let me explain what dialogue is *not*. Dialogue is not pie-in-the-sky, let's-all-hold-hands-and-sing stuff. Neither is it a touchy-feely, warm-and-fuzzy, soft-headed approach to thinking and interacting.

True dialogue dates back to Aristotle, Socrates, Plato and others who discovered its power in helping people build deeper and deeper layers of trust and understanding. True dialogue is the preferred communication model of some of the toughest-minded—and most successful – modern business practitioners I know. (Jim Rainey, introduced to you in Chapter 3, is an example.) True dialogue enables people to blend and synchronize their ingenuity and work in ways not otherwise possible. True dialogue is the antidote to the poisonous "discussion" and debate tactics that characterize so many interactions in so many organizations.

In a nutshell, here's what you must do to practice true dialogue:

- **Relinquish Power.**
- **Defer Judgment.**
- **Tame the Elephants.**

- **Listen with Empathy.**
- **Inquire to Discover.**
- **Advocate with Respect.**
- **Pool the Meaning.**

Let's consider each of these in turn. You'll notice that each one is supported and reinforced by the four dimensions of sound thinking discussed in the previous chapter: Capacity, Curiosity, Conclusions, Connections.

Relinquish Power

Simply put, true dialogue cannot occur in an atmosphere where anyone is inclined to exert power over another. Command-and-control is the antithesis of an open and honest sharing of meaning. Of course outside the context of dialogue there may be significant status differences. Asking people to check their titles at the door does not erase the reality that they have different titles, different levels of authority, and different power bases. But during dialogue itself, equality must reign supreme. For the occasion, participants must remove their badges of status and resist any temptation to pull rank. Before participants can open up honestly with each other, mutual trust must be present. And an atmosphere of mutual trust is impossible to establish if any of the participants are perceived to be holding their power ready for an ambush.

We've all seen the same scenario. The big guy organizes an executive retreat for the purpose of discussing strategic planning, an acquisition, a new training initiative, or something else that will impact the life of every person on the team. He invites his people to dress casually for the occasion. At the beginning of the meeting he reminds everyone that he expects straight talk with no holds barred. He says all the right things. But somewhere lurking in the shadows is his "boss" persona, ready to pounce at the first idea that's at variance with his. And lame attempts to lighten the

> *You can't talk your way out of what you've behaved yourself into.*
> **Stephen R. Covey**

91

moment—I actually heard one CEO ask his team, "Does anyone care to make any career-limiting comments?"—can make dialogue even less likely. Inviting people to dress casually and to talk candidly are empty gestures if not accompanied by a genuine (albeit temporary) relinquishing of power.

In the movie *First Knight*, King Arthur is portrayed as a person of truly noble character. He proudly displays his Round Table, which he says is designed so it lacks a special place of privilege for him. Yet it is Arthur who either makes or disproportionately influences every decision reached at the table. Despite the furniture arrangement, there's no ambiguity about who's the boss.

During a visit with one of my clients in the nuclear power business I was invited to observe a meeting of about twenty people. The participants were from several different levels on the organization chart. They were planning for an upcoming outage during which a multi-million-dollar piece of equipment was to be replaced. Schedules were tight. Budgets were sacrosanct. Reputations, and even careers, were on the line. These

> *"Dialogue cannot pay rich dividends if its currency is shrouded in preconceived notions and untested conclusions."*

were the perfect ingredients for self-indulgent power plays. But after an hour of observing the interchange, I still couldn't tell who the top dogs were in the room. In fact, when I later discovered the "official" pecking order, I was pleasantly surprised. The "head man" turned out to be the most deferential person in the room. During the meeting he was the one who most frequently said things like "How do you see it?" "Oh, I hadn't considered that," "I wonder if we might combine a couple of ideas that have been offered." He talked tentatively—not at all in the sense of weak confidence, but rather in a way that made it safe for people to continue the open dialogue.

Defer Judgment

Deferring judgment doesn't mean that you'll never reach a conclusion. Of course you will. But you'll serve yourself and others best if you delay, postpone, or hold off on your judgments until you have sufficient data to proceed with justifiable confidence. Dialogue cannot pay rich dividends if its currency is shrouded in preconceived notions and untested conclusions.

Several forms of premature judging act as barriers to dialogue. Here are five.

Allness. This a dogmatic, unqualified, categorical attitude that we know all there is to know about something.

Have you ever met a guy who's a nut on sports statistics? He knows everything there is to be known about ice-age batting averages and ancient football scores. If you don't believe it, just ask him. And if you're looking for an argument, try contradicting him. He's never wrong. There's something about the tone of finality and absoluteness of some people that is irritating to the point of pain. When they speak it's almost as though they're telling you, "What I'm saying is all there is to know about this subject.

> **The only man I know who behaves sensibly is my tailor; he takes my measurements anew each time he sees me. The rest go on with their old measurements and expect me to fit them.**
> **George Bernard Shaw**

There's nothing more." And this absoluteness is hardly confined to the characters on C-SPAN. Right now in thousands of barber shops and beauty salons the intricate problems of politics, disease, war, economics, climate change, and who's the top talent on *American Idol* are being neatly and conclusively solved.

»*Corrective Action 1:* If you have an intolerance of other viewpoints, you won't be very popular in many places and you certainly can't be successful with dialogue. Be wary of building up an "all wall" that separates you from the reality of what you actually know. Look out for those moments when you risk being viewed as too self-assured, just too certain. Self-confidence is wonderful, but make sure you don't lead with it or you'll smother dialogue and be offensive to boot. Practice saying four simple words: "I didn't know that." It's amazing how a generous, self-administered dose of genuine humility can cure a conversation—or a relationship—of hostility. Apply the humility early and often.

Hardening of the Categories. This is a failure of differentiation. Most of us are in the habit of categorizing. When we meet a person for the first time we have a natural tendency to place him in a pigeonhole. "How's he classified?" we unconsciously ask ourselves. "I can see that he's short and pudgy, but what does he do for a living? Is he a political conservative or liberal? Is he a Catholic, Jew, Protestant, sun worshipper, or atheist? What kind of education does he have? Is his wife attractive? What neighborhood does he live in?" Of course categorizing is not inherently undesirable. But when our personality pigeonholes become unyielding, they short-circuit further investigation of people, and that's harmful to relationships.

»Corrective Action 2: The real difficulty in treating a case of hardened categories is that the sufferer is often unaware that his stereotypes affect his behavior and hamper his communication. To heal this breach, one must accept the premise of uniqueness. In other words, come to the realization that an individual member of any group (or category) is just that – an individual. No two people are quite alike. Just ask anyone who has a so-called identical twin. There's really no such thing as a "typical" Italian, a "typical" New Yorker, a "typical" politician, or a "typical" engineer.

> *No one would talk much in society if they knew how often they misunderstood others.*
> **Goethe**

Frozen Evaluation. This is another kind of problem with differentiation. It occurs most frequently when we assume that people don't develop and change. For example, a father may refuse to let his son use the family car because three years ago the boy dinged a fender at the supermarket parking lot. The father is assuming that his son is no more reliable or mature after three years than he was then, and therefore can't be trusted. But if the son hasn't given any other demonstration of irresponsibility (or simple carelessness), his father's distrust based on this one incident in the past is sure to produce a lack of communication and a widening of the generation gap. A man I know, after a decade of exemplary work for his employer, made a costly mistake on a budget projection. It was four years before his boss gave him a chance to redeem himself with similar assignments. Some people are quick to condemn but slow to forgive. (See the next chapter that focuses on being Trust-Friendly.)

»*Corrective Action 3:* Frozen evaluation is a communication problem with a relatively easy cure. Simply accept the premise of change. Have you ever made a mistake? Of course you have, thousands of them. But this doesn't mean you'll continue to make the same mistakes the rest of your life. (Okay, now, resist the temptation to list the people you think are exceptions to the rule.) If people thought of us only in the context of our past errors, none of us could be trusted in any circumstance. The so-called "when index" helps here, too. Right after a fender-bender you might be reluctant to lend the family car to your teenaged son until he gets a little more practice driving close to home. But applying the 16-year-old profile to a 19-year-old's situation is unreasonable.

Inference-Observation Confusion. This is a pattern of communication mix-up that's had us all in hot water at one time or another. This occurs when you infer more than you've actually seen or heard about a situation. Suppose you arrive at work one morning and see standing alone in your manager's office a woman you don't recognize. Answer the following questions by saying "true," "false," or "don't know":

(a) You have a new manager.

(b) A woman you don't recognize is standing alone in your manager's office.

(c) The woman is your manager's sister, visiting from out of town.

(d) There is no one in your manager's office.

(e) The woman standing in your manager's office is from the finance department and she's conducting a surprise audit.

If you think item (b) is true, item (d) is false, and you don't know about the others, you get the idea about distinguishing statements based on inferences. But if you think items (a), (c), and (e) are true, consider other possibilities. Suppose the woman is a job applicant who's arrived early for an interview. Suppose the woman is a homeless lady who's sneaked into the building and has decided to camp out in your manager's office. The possibilities beyond what you actually observe are endless. Clearly, items (a), (c), and (e) are based on inferences. You cannot say with a high degree of confidence whether they are true or false.

»*Corrective Action 4:* Be mindfully aware when you're inferring as opposed to observing, then calculate the degree of probability that your inferences are correct. Lever Brothers mailed out more than 50 million samples of its new Sunlight dishwashing detergent. Despite the fact that the label stated "Caution: Harmful If Swallowed," more than 1,000 consumers used the product on salads and in drinks. They incorrectly inferred from the product's scent, the picture of lemons on the label, and the word "real lemon juice" that it was a food product. "Read the label carefully" is good advice for our communication as well as for our use of consumer products.

I once gave a presentation to several hundred people. It was a controversial topic and I was eager to "connect" with the audience. In the back of the room I noticed a woman with her arms folded and what seemed to be a scowl on her face. I interpreted this body language as skepticism or even anger. When the meeting was finished I made my way to the back of the room. I asked the woman if she had any questions. She said she was satisfied with the information I provided. I asked if she wanted me to elaborate on any particular issue. Again, she said she was satisfied with what I'd already said. Then she inquired why I had sought her out in the crowd. I admitted that I'd noticed her body language (folded arms and what appeared to be a scowl) and assumed she was doubtful about something in my presentation. "Oh, don't worry about that," she said with a smile. "My arms were folded because this room is chilly, and I was frowning because I've misplaced my glasses and I was struggling to read your slides on the screen."

The lesson? Don't jump to conclusions. Beware of inferring too much from what you actually observe.

Bypassing. This is a communication failure that many of us create more or less intentionally. We are bypassing when we listen selectively. For instance, a man's wife may tell him she has tickets to the symphony the following Thursday night. When Thursday rolls around, however, the husband has scheduled a bowling date which he then claims simply can't be broken. Since attending the symphony is not his idea of a fun evening, he didn't really hear his wife tell him about the tickets. Oh, he heard her talking, alright; but because of the subject matter he subconsciously tuned her out and the message was never actually received. Youngsters often fall into the same habit ("Oh, I didn't hear you tell me that, Mom!"). Bypassing also occurs when we attribute different meanings to the same word. Remember: meanings reside in people, not in messages or individual words. In my Oklahoma youth the word "puny" was used to denote sickly or weak, as in "The runt in that litter of pigs looks kind of puny." When I later worked on Wall Street I heard my Eastern-born colleagues use the same word to denote unimportant or unnecessary, as in "That fourth document is puny, so let's kill it." Although one might argue that these uses of the word are directionally similar, the differences are certainly ripe for confusion.

»*Corrective Action 5:* Old-fashioned specificity is the best remedy for bypassing. If you aren't sure what someone means when he's talking to you, simply ask for clarification. Paraphrasing the other person's words can also help: "When you say you'd like the report by the end of the month, is the 31st okay or do you expect it sooner?" Specificity also helps when you're on the sending end of the message.

> *"A natural consequence of undiscussables in a culture is that fresh viewpoints get deflected, or even smothered."*

My wife was in charge of a church pot luck dinner. She assigned a dozen other ladies to bring "a salad" for the meal. I'm not sure what the statistical odds are for this, but to her surprise she got exactly twelve red gelatin salads. She learned a lesson. In the future she will specify tossed green salad, fruit salad, vegetable salad, or some other particular variety.

Another way to avoid bypassing is to ask open-ended questions that invite further dialogue: "*What* have I said that we should talk about more?" "*Which* points could use more clarity?" "*How* can we set this up so we both understand each other?" Asked sincerely and with an encouraging tone, such open-ended questions are very important. Close-ended questions such as "Do you understand?" or "Are there any questions?" may be met with silence, especially in a group setting. People sometimes won't admit their confusion or misunderstanding because they don't want to appear dense or incompetent.

Tame the Elephants

Because it requires honesty and clarity, true dialogue can be uncomfortable. And because people like to avoid discomfort, it's tempting to allow some topics to remain unaddressed—sort of like leaving a splinter in your finger even though logic tells you the temporary pain of digging it out is not nearly as bad as the likely infection from leaving it in.

Most of us have been in situations where there's a relevant issue that nobody seems willing to talk about. We might even say to ourselves, "There's an elephant in this room, and I sure wish someone else would tame that animal." Well, to tame an elephant—an "undiscussable"—you must first acknowledge its existence.

A natural consequence of undiscussables in a culture is that fresh viewpoints get deflected, or even smothered. That's contrary to the whole purpose of dialogue, and dangerous for any organization interested in vitality and achievement.

Our recent (as well as remote) history is replete with examples of intolerance for facts that disturb the status quo. At NASA, insulation foam falling off fuel tanks and hitting space shuttles became an undiscussable. For Detroit automakers, the marketplace surge of Japanese cars was an undiscussable. At IBM, Apple was an undiscussable. At American Airlines, cross-state rival Southwest Airlines was an undiscussable. At Kodak, digital photography was an undiscussable. In the music industry, MP3 file-sharing was an undiscussable. Among Michael Jackson's entourage of hangers-on, the pop star's drug dependence was an undiscussable. You can make your own list. Some organizations harbor veritable herds of unnamed, untamed elephants.

> *A bore is a fellow talking who can change the subject back to his topic of conversation faster than you can change it back to yours.*
> **Laurence J. Peter**

After completing a culture assessment for a major corporation I was doing my "What? So what? and Now what?" presentation to the senior management team. That's where I describe the results, point out the implications of the findings, and make recommendations for change. One of the find-ings was that the CEO had a shoot-the-messen-ger reputation that was stifling open dialogue on key operational issues. In

> *Thinking is the talking of the soul with itself.*
>
> **Plato**

sharing some of the open-ended comments from the survey, I put up a slide with a direct quote from one of the anonymous respondents: "I would love to share my ideas with [the CEO], but it's not safe to speak your mind around here. All he seems to want is a bunch of yes-men." Within a nanosecond of reading that comment the CEO slammed his fist on the table and shouted "That's ridiculous! Find out who said that and usher him out the door! We don't have room in this organization for people who are too weak-kneed to speak up." All the other executives sort of cowered in silence at this display of fury. Then I simply said: "I. Rest. My. Case." After a long pause the CEO smiled, then chuckled, then broke into a hearty laugh. The elephant in the room (the CEO's bullying style) had been identified, and now the CEO and his team (and later others) were ready to discuss the undiscussable. They were finally on their way to taming the elephant. And taming that elephant led to identifying and tam-ing others.

Talk-Friendly practitioners understand the difference between *implicit* and *explicit* communication. The elephant—an undiscuss-able subject—is implicit. It's latent, tacit, undeclared, unexpressed. People talk *around* the elephant without acknowledging that it's in the room and affecting everything that's going on. But until the elephant's presence is made explicit—plain, clear, straightforward, obvious—the quality of true dialogue is limited. Naming and tam-ing the elephant is a metaphor for making implicit issues explicit.

Let's consider another metaphor that reinforces the point. In his now famous parable entitled "The Abilene Paradox," Dr. Jerry Harvey describes an interesting variation on the reluctance to speak up. In blazing hot west Texas his family was trying to survive an uncomfortable afternoon by playing Dominoes on the front porch. Then someone suggested, "Let's get in the car and go to Abilene and have dinner at the cafeteria." Driving 53 miles in an unairconditioned 1958 Buick sounded miserable, but nobody spoke up. Everyone piled into the car, they trekked to the cafeteria for a meal worthy of an antacid commercial, then braved the brutal heat for the return trip. Four hours and 106 miles later the family was again on the front porch playing Dominoes. Jerry dishonestly said, "It was a great trip, wasn't it?" Nobody responded. Finally his mother-in-law said with unconcealed irritation that she didn't enjoy the trip at all and wouldn't have gone if the others hadn't been so enthusiastic. In the ensuing conversation the family discovered that nobody—including the one who made the initial suggestion—wanted to leave the front porch. But in a paradoxical display of group dynamics they all did exactly what they didn't want to do.

The Abilene Paradox is at play in every stratum of our society. It has a role in countless personal tragedies like divorce and family break-ups. It has a role in corporate fiascoes like Enron. It's a factor even in national tragedies like the Watergate scandal. Travel the road to Abilene and you'll arrive at a place where logic and reasonableness fall victim to a misguided "go along to get along" mentality. It can be a bumpy ride, culminating in costly outcomes and blame. But you can skip the trip if you know how to read the road signs.

In practicing dialogue, we must be constantly alert to clues that someone may be passively accepting an idea or decision without communicating his true feelings about it. This requires focus. In our natural tendency to avoid resistance, we sometimes hear what we *want* to hear. In reality, we can often learn as much from what is *not* said as from what *is*. Some people hesitate in speaking up to avoid being ostracized or being viewed as "not a team player." An individual's private apprehension at being regarded as different is often more influential on his behavior than actual group pressure.

Undiscussables can easily become the fabric of individual relationships and organizational culture. It works something like this:

(1) People craft messages (expressed in words and/or behaviors) that contain inconsistencies. For example, "integrity" and "accountability" may be professed

values, yet team members frequently miss production deadlines and nobody raises an eyebrow.

(2) Team members act as if the messages are not inconsistent.

(3) Team members treat the ambiguity and inconsistency as undiscussable.

(4) Team members make the undiscussability of the undiscussable also undiscussable.

Taming elephants is a three-part process.

First, identify the elephant. A Chinese proverb says that the beginning of wisdom is to call things by their right names. Although you always want to be respectful, identifying the elephant is not the time to mince words. Call the elephant what it is. In the case of the CEO with the "my way or the highway" leadership approach, referring to his style as merely "tough minded" would have missed the mark and might even have been accepted as a compliment. I told him he was widely regarded as a bully and that his style was having the unintended consequence of shutting down the very kind of straight talk he said he expected of his people.

> *"Make it safe to talk openly about the elephant."*

Second, uncover the underlying assumptions that people have about the elephant. In a spirit of genuine curiosity and discovery, talk openly about your view of the "elephant" and invite the other dialogue participants to share their perspectives. You will be enlightened, and possibly even surprised, by the ways people have constructed their versions of "reality."

Third, make it safe to talk openly about the elephant. Peo-

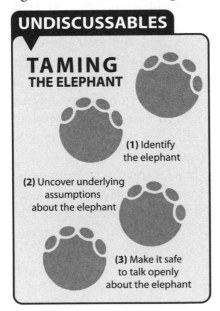

UNDISCUSSABLES

TAMING THE ELEPHANT

(1) Identify the elephant

(2) Uncover underlying assumptions about the elephant

(3) Make it safe to talk openly about the elephant

ple are afraid of elephants because they don't want to get stomped on. Good dialogue skills like listening with empathy and inquiring to discover can help create an atmosphere of acceptance so people can deal openly with their concerns. Underscore the mutual interests you share with the other players. This is also an important time for participants to relinquish power. Position and status differences have a major effect on people's readiness to explore different points of view honestly. When I called out the CEO on his bullying tactics, he was mature and professional enough to accept the blunt assessment gracefully. He invited his team to give him examples of where his style had stymied open discussion, assured them his request was genuine, and promised there would no recrimination. This opened the floodgates of some breakthrough feedback and set the stage for candid dialogue on future occasions as well.

Listen with Empathy

Some people seem to operate under the misconception that to "listen" is merely to allow the other person to talk while you prepare your response. Real dialogue requires much more.

First, some important points on "empathy." Empathy is not the same as sympathy. Sympathy involves commiseration, agreement, or a shared feeling. *Empathy* is more about appreciation and understanding. Understanding between and among the participants is a critical goal of dialogue. People engaged in true dialogue may or may not come to agreement. Their primary goal is mutual understanding. It's a difference worth noting. (After all, if agreement is going to be reached, it must be preceded by understanding.)

> *I just wish my mouth had a backspace key.*
> **Anonymous**

Let me illustrate with an example from my early career as a journalist. I was assigned to write a series of articles on prostitution and drug traffic. Naturally, this involved interviews with people who worked in those unsavory rackets. The local crime commission helped me line up sources who had information I needed. (With these kinds of interviews, for safety reasons as well as to protect my reputation, I always had another reporter accompany me.) One of my sources was a young prostitute named Cindy. I interviewed her on several occasions because she helped corroborate (and in some instances contradict) the information I received from other sources. The first two or three times I interviewed Cindy she seemed reticent and even shy, not qualities I'd expect of someone in her line of work. But by our fourth interview she began to open up and talk more freely. Then she turned the tables and asked *me* a question: "Do you notice that I'm more willing to talk with you now?" I acknowledged that I did indeed notice, and asked her why. "Because you finally stopped judging me," she said. "Now you're finally trying to understand me. I don't expect you to agree with what I do, I just want you to try to understand how I arrived where I am." That simple statement from a scared young prostitute taught me as much about true dialogue as anything I later heard in graduate school. I don't think I had been "judging" Cindy in a holier-than-thou way, but I'd certainly felt sorry for her. She didn't want sympathy. She wanted empathy. She was willing to talk openly, but only if I listened to understand rather than to judge.

> *The less you talk, the more you're listened to.*
> **Abigail Van Buren**

Now, another point of education from my early years as a journalist. At *The Dallas Times Herald* my editor was Jim Lehrer, whom you now know as the anchor of PBS's award-winning news broadcast. Jim was an excellent coach, well attuned to the nuances of good communication. One day he walked over to my desk in the newsroom and started a conversation about interviews. Bear in mind, I was an investigative reporter, not the art critic. By definition, investigative reporters ask tough questions, and the people they interview are often—shall we say?—less than eager to chat with reporters.

Jim: *Tell me about your interviews.*

Rodger: *Well, I do a lot of them. Specifically what do you want to know?*

Jim: *How do you prepare?*

Rodger: *When I get an assignment I make a list of likely sources, I prepare a preliminary inventory of questions, then I make appointments to talk with some of the sources and simply show up unannounced to talk with others. I first try to talk with the people I suspect have the most pertinent* *information I'm seeking, then I talk with other people to corroborate or contradict that earlier information. I continue this process until I'm satisfied I have valid data on which to base a story."*

Jim: *Okay, let's say you're in an interview and I'm a fly on the wall. What would I see and hear?*

Rodger: *I'll ask a question. The source will give me an answer. Then I'll ask another question.*

At this point, Jim made a sound like a buzzer going off on a TV game show. "Wait a second," he said, raising his hands in a "time out" gesture. "You said you ask a question. The other person answers. Then you ask another question."

Rodger: *What's the problem with that? The purpose of interviews is to gather information. The only way to get answers is to ask questions.*

Jim: *Don't be too quick to believe that the only way to get answers is to ask questions. Another way is to listen slowly.*

Jim then taught me a behavior that has served me well for the subsequent four decades. He urged me to ask a good question, listen attentively to the answer, *and then count silently to five before asking another question.* At first that suggestion seemed silly. I argued that five seconds would seem like an eternity to wait after someone responds to a question. Then it occurred to me. Of course it would seem like an eternity, because our natural tendency is to fill a void of silence with sound, usually that of our own voice.

Jim: *If you resist the temptation to respond too quickly to the answer, you'll discover something almost magical. The other person will either expand on what he's already said, or he'll go in a different direction. Either way, he's expanding his response and you get a clearer view into his head and heart.*

I was scheduled for a round of interviews that day and Jim asked me to try the silently-count-to-five approach and let him know how it worked for me. Later that evening I returned to the office and Jim motioned me toward his desk. I knew what he wanted, and I was pleased to give him a five-word report: "I never got past three!"

Giving other people sufficient psychological breathing room— even those who weren't very eager to talk with a reporter—seemed to work wonders. When I bridled my natural impatience to "get on with it," they seemed more willing to disclose, explore, and even to be a bit vulnerable. When I treated the interview more as a conversation with a purpose than as a sterile interrogation, the tone of the exchange softened. It was now just two people talking, not a news reporter mining for data like a dentist extracting teeth.

Don't misunderstand. I'm not trying to equate dialogue with a news reporter's interviewing approach. But I am suggesting that listening with empathy requires patience. It requires a willingness to allow the other person to take the conversation in fresh directions (serendipity can pay dividends). It requires letting go of your own needs and focusing on the other person's needs. It requires mindful attention to the subtleties of tone, mood, temperament, and the spirit of the moment. It's all about listening to understand rather than to control or to coerce.

But what if you're talking with someone who simply "doesn't get it"? What if the other person holds a view that seems contrary to everything you stand for? Surely, you may say, this notion of empathy doesn't apply in such situations. Yes it does.

Karen Swallow Prior and Karalyn Schmidt were mortal enemies in the pitched battle over abortion, one of the most polarizing issues of our time. The streets in their home town of Buffalo, New York, seethed with angry protesters. The pro-lifers screamed "babykillers" and blockaded abortion clinics. Defiant abortion-rights advocates broke through the blockades, yelling "religious lunatics" and other insults. Inside a local radio studio Prior and Schmidt squared off for an on-air debate. "The hostility in the room permeated everyone's pores," Prior, president of Feminists for Life, later told the *Philadelphia Inquirer.* "Karalyn embodied my own personal stereotype of the strident, pro-choice misanthrope." The ill feelings were reciprocated. "I could easily have smacked Karen," said Schmidt, then director of the local Planned Parenthood clinic. "I perceived her as, at best, kind of stupid. I could not comprehend how a woman could hold the position she did." But Schmidt did learn to understand Prior, and Prior did learn to understand Schmidt. Once they stopped hurling emotional grenades and started *listening* to each other, they discovered that they actually had mutual interests. Then these once mortal enemies became the unlikeliest of allies.

> *"A common tactic by command-and-control folks is to play the 'Gotcha' game."*

Prior and Schmidt are part of a larger, quiet movement that's gaining momentum across the U.S. It's called the Common Ground Network for Life and Choice, consisting of both pro-life and pro-choice activists who are tired of choking on the noxious air between them. Their goal is not to compromise their principles or to alter the other side's position. Their goal is to redirect the nature of the conversation, to calm things down. Their goal is *dialogue*.

What do these two camps have in common? They've discovered agreement that politicians of every stripe use abortion as a wedge issue, dividing people when unity and understanding are more important than ever. They agree that more should be done to lower the incidence of teen pregnancy. They agree that adoption should receive greater consideration by women faced with unintended pregnancies. And, yes, they agree that the number of abortions should be reduced.

How did they unearth their mutual interests? With help from a non-profit conflict resolution group called Search for Common Ground, thousands of people like Prior and Schmidt are discovering that good things can happen when you replace combat with civility and curiosity. When you listen with empathy.

These same principles apply just as powerfully in the offices, hallways, conference rooms, and factory floors of business. Or at your own kitchen table.

Inquire to Discover

In a typical "discussion," inquiry might come across (and in fact be intended) as interrogation. We've all seen people who ask questions primarily for the purpose of challenging the other person or bolstering their own position. A common tactic by command-and-control folks is to play the "Gotcha" game in which they ask questions designed to convince or win, or even to entrap, attack, or overpower people. Inquiries rooted in these motives, no matter how congenial in tone, quickly begin to feel like a prosecutor's cross-examination. This is absolutely *not* the purpose of authentic inquiry. In the context of true dialogue, we should inquire to learn, to discover, to deepen our understanding. That's not to say we will or necessarily should agree with everything we hear. It's merely to say that inquiring to learn is a natural outgrowth of deferring judgment. A smart person will come to certain judgments about things, but not before an honest investigation of the range of possibilities.

As we dig into the principles associated with inquiry, it will help to provide some connective tissue relating to listening. Inquiry is a natural companion to listening. The two behaviors are—or at least should be—inextricably joined. When we listen mindfully we learn things that whet our appetite for more. Then we inquire to keep the cycle going. And our listening and inquiry should be directed toward ourselves as well as other participants in the dialogue.

The "Ladder of Inference" and the "Left-Hand Column," constructs developed by Harvard professor Chris Argyris and his colleagues, can help us in our quest to become more skilled with our listening and inquiring behaviors.

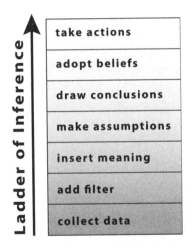

The Ladder of Inference is a metaphor showing how quickly we can leap to conclusions with only a modicum of data and little if any intermediate thought. It's as if we are rapidly climbing up a ladder in our minds.

It works like this. Let's say you're in a meeting and you notice Bob is yawning. This observable data is so self-evident that it could be captured by a video recorder (Bob yawned at the meeting). Within a millisecond you climb the ladder to assumptions (Bob must be bored), then to more general conclusions (Bob doesn't care if this project fails). Because most of these conclusions are never challenged openly, there's no way to verify if they're justifiable or bogus.

In summary, here's what the Ladder of Inference looks like.

- At the bottom rung we find observable *"data"* and experiences. These are things that we, and any dispassionate third party, can see and agree on.
- Then we filter the observation and take the *data* we're willing to use.
- Next, we add *meaning* to the data by putting our own cultural and personal spin on it.

- Based on the meaning we've added, we make *assumptions*.
- From our assumptions we draw *conclusions*.
- Our conclusions lead us to adopt certain *beliefs*.
- Based on our beliefs, we take *actions*.

An Exercise in (Mis)Understanding

(2) LEFT HAND COLUMN	(1) RIGHT HAND COLUMN
· *feelings*	· *dialogue replay*
· *thoughts*	· *actual script*

← LADDER OF INFERENCE

Climbing the ladder is so fast and seems so reasonable that we are relatively unaware of doing it. Let's face it. We live in a world of self-generating beliefs, many of which are mostly unchallenged. Incorporating the "ladder" metaphor into our conversation can provide a safe way to broach and double check the varied interpretations that can block the flow of true dialogue.

Now to the Left-Hand Column. According to this model, there are two "columns" at play in our minds as we deal with situations. We may be unaware of the columns, but they are present nonetheless.

Consider this exercise. It can be very revealing and instructive.

(1) Select a problem or challenge you've dealt with recently. It might have to do with difficulty in resolving an issue with a colleague. It might involve your irritation with a co-worker who's not honoring commitments. It might be a situation where you believe your viewpoint was ignored or discounted. It might be a team member who's resisting a change you're trying to implement.

(2) Write a brief description of the challenge. What's going on? What are you trying to accomplish? Who or what seems to be getting in the way? What are the risks? What are the missed opportunities? What are the consequences?

(3) Now, think of a frustrating conversation you've had regarding this situation. If you haven't had a conversation (perhaps you've avoided it for a variety of reasons), imagine a conversation that you likely would have had if the subject were brought up.

(4) Next, take several pieces of paper and down the middle

of each page draw a vertical line. (If you prefer using a word processor on your computer, simply activate the two-column feature.)

(5) In the right-hand column, write the conversation exactly as you recall it playing out. This is sort of like a movie script—what you said, what the other person said, then what you said, etc. If the conversation didn't actually occur, write down what you're confident *would have* been said. This conversation "script" might go on for several pages. (Meanwhile, leave the left-hand column empty.)

(6) Now, in the left-hand column write down what you were thinking and feeling while the conversation in the right-hand column was being played out. Be perfectly honest, and flesh this out as completely as possible.

(7) Finally—and here's the kicker—carefully and honestly analyze the contents of the left-hand column.

- What really led you to think what you thought and to feel what you felt?
- Were you climbing the ladder of inference to unjustified assumptions about people and their intentions?
- Were you stuck in allness, hardening of the categories, frozen evaluation or any of the other traps discussed earlier?
- Did you feel victimized by the other person?
- Did you attribute less-than-honorable motives to the other person?
- How did your part of the conversation actually contribute to the problem?

Remember, this honest self-appraisal is not going to be attached to your next job application. It's for your private use only. Do you see how this kind of unvarnished self-assessment can be enlightening? Yes, I know, the other person in the conversation may be a jerk. But is it possible that anything you said (or failed to say) could trigger jerk behavior? Is it even remotely possible—now work with me on this—that *you* might have behaved in a way that the other person could have interpreted as insensitive or arrogant (jerk behavior on your part)?

There's nothing at all wrong about having a left-hand column. We all have them, whether we're aware or oblivious. The point here is that as we become more mindfully conscious and honest about what's going on in our left-hand columns we're better able to recognize the shaky ladder of inference than can cause embarrassing

> **Wisdom is the reward you get for a lifetime of listening when you'd have preferred to talk.**
> **Doug Larson**

and even dangerous stumbles. Then we can use that information to make our attempts at true dialogue more successful than ever.

To help lubricate the flow of inquiry, consider asking questions like these of the other participant(s):

- "That's an interesting perspective. Can you help me understand how you reached that conclusion?"
- "Could you give me some examples of how that idea (process, procedure, protocol, system, etc.) has worked in organizations similar to ours?"
- "You've apparently put a lot of thought into this. Would you please walk me down the path that you've followed in forming that view?"
- "Any of us can have blind spots. Would you please help me understand any point I might be missing?"

Naturally, all of your inquiry should be motivated by genuine curiosity. Behavior can be very elastic. It's easy to snap back into previous patterns. Because of past experiences, you may be "scripted" to be curious only briefly before returning to the "Gotcha!" game. Consciously resist that temptation. Remember, your purpose with inquiry is to discover and learn, not to entrap or rebut.

Then, to double check your own orientation toward dialogue, ask questions like this of yourself:

- "What is my real intention? To win, to be right, to sell, to persuade?"

- "Do I really want to understand, or am I simply looking for chinks in the other guy's armor so I can defeat his position?"
- "Am I sincerely curious, or am I just 'playing the game' so I can get my way?"
- "Am I willing to be influenced by the other person, or do I expect influence to be a one-way street going from me to him?"

Again, the link between listening with empathy and inquiring to discover should be based on a genuine desire to learn. Conversely, our debate culture is based on judgment and criticism. The question, *"What's wrong with this picture?"* creates an orientation toward critical evaluation of what another person is saying or doing. Inherent in the debate culture is a focus on whether we agree or disagree with someone, whether we like or dislike him and what he says, and if his opinion is right or wrong, smart or stupid.

True dialogue is conversation with a center, not sides.

Advocate with Respect

Phil was general manager in the marketing division of a major consumer products company. With the professed purpose of discussing a new promotion campaign, he called a meeting of his staff. These were smart, seasoned people. They knew the industry, knew the product, knew the competition, and knew the target audience.

> *"A lamentable consequence of our debate culture is that we're usually more adept at advocating than inquiring."*

But after only a few perfunctory questions and nothing even approaching real dialogue, Phil announced his own plan for a multi-million-dollar campaign. He prided himself on recruiting and hiring "the best and the brightest," then he dumbed them down by denying the opportunity to engage in meaningful give-and-take.

A lamentable consequence of our debate culture is that we're usually more adept at advocating than inquiring. And the "advocating" we see is often done more as leadership-by-announcement than as part of a true dialogue environment. We have plenty of public models of this. The programming at Fox News, CNN, MSNBC and the other cable networks is heavily weighted with loud and overbearing people whose purpose in life is to ram their views down someone else's throat.

Don't get me wrong. I'm not suggesting that good leadership requires gathering endless reams of "input" before a decision is reached. Neither am I suggesting that decisions must always be preceded by a dialogue session. If the building you're in catches fire, you wouldn't expect the fire marshal to tiptoe into your meeting and launch into timid inquiry: "Excuse me, folks. May I ask, how do you feel about smoke inhalation?" You would want him to say something like, "Please stay calm. There's a fire in the building. Leave this room immediately and proceed to the nearest exit."

> *The birds are molting. If only man could molt also—his mind once a year its errors; his heart once a year its useless passions.*
> **James Allen**

Advocacy is making a statement or expressing a view about your own position. *Inquiry* is using Talk-Friendly questions to explore and discover the views of others. To a great extent, the quality of the dialogue is determined by the spirit with which you state your views and inquire into the others' perspectives. That's where *respect* plays an indispensable role. Even experienced hostage negotiators will tell you that respect for the other party is a critical determinant of their success.

High quality inquiry genuinely explores the panorama of alternative views and encourages challenge of your own views. You'll often hear good practitioners of dialogue say things like, "Oh, you see it differently. Help me understand how you reached that conclusion." Their tone is welcoming and exploratory, not accusing or cynical. Their desire to learn is real, and their willingness to be influenced is a key to the door of collaboration.

High quality advocacy is a clear and understandable presentation of your viewpoint. High quality advocacy is delivered with such precision and focus that the chance of misinterpretation is greatly diminished. We should advocate so clearly that not only is it easy to understand us, but it's difficult to *mis*understand us. And it should be done with a good balance of humility, confidence, and respect. *Humility* because we don't know everything, *confidence* because our position should be based on a reasonable interpretation of available data, and *respect* because the other parties also have valuable contributions and may in fact be able to disabuse us of our position.

There's a big difference between saying, "This change initiative will never get off dead center" and "I'm concerned about sponsorship. I heard the general manager say he thought this was another flavor-of-the-month deal. Without his active support and reinforcement, I don't see how this roll out can be successful. Do others place the same importance on Mike's role, or do you see it differently?"

With advocacy, it's helpful if others can clearly see the data you've selected, the meaning you've attached to the data, and the reasonableness of your conclusion. Make your ladder of inference visible.

A fairly simple way to strengthen the credibility of your advocacy is to offer an example. By illustrating your perspective you metaphorically step down the ladder of inference. The most productive conversations occur on the lower rungs of the ladder, down in the territory of concrete information rather than general and vague concepts. Also, because they're observable and verifiable, concrete examples are easier to confirm or refute. Claiming that "performance accountability is a joke" in the organization is a conclusion that could be debated, but citing a recent company survey that shows only 12% of respondents believe "people who fail to pull their fair share of the load are promptly held accountable" is directly accessible and observable.

> *"True dialogue is suffocated when advocacy takes on the qualities of lecturing or debate."*

Of course not every example enhances the credibility of your advocacy. A lengthy, convoluted illustration may lose your listener in a maze of details. A particular piece of data may be a good illustration of one point, but totally unsuitable in illustrating another. So in selecting an example to serve your needs, be sure to ask yourself:

> ***Does this example describe a pattern or trend?*** If you use an example that represents only an isolated event, it can be easily dismissed as only marginally relevant or of low importance. We're not necessarily looking for pure statistical validity here, just reasonableness.

Is this example easily accessible and observable by others? If it's not, others will be less likely to connect the dots between your example and your conclusion. Your example must be verifiable. If it's not, you're asking others to rely solely on your word. That's okay if the mutual trust is high, but in cases where you're still establishing trust, verifiable examples are best.

Is the example expressed in understandable terms? If you're talking with someone with a non-technical background, you'll want to use layman's language rather than technical jargon. If your dialogue partners hail from different cultural backgrounds (including subcultures within your own culture), you'll be more likely to connect if you use terms that are widely known and do not require "translation." Be careful with words and phrases that are subject to untended interpretations. (Remember what I said earlier about bypassing.)

Is the example interesting and memorable? When Jim Rainey took over the leadership reins at Farmland Industries, he refused to accept a "free" company car. His executive team used that as a model for the belt-tightening needed to get help the company return to profitability. A hospital administrator tells the story of a young patient whose life was saved by a new emergency room protocol. A flight instructor tells the story of singer John Denver's death in a small airplane he was not qualified to fly. Use an example with which people can personally identify and even in which they might visualize themselves.

True dialogue is suffocated when advocacy takes on the qualities of lecturing or debate. The day our son turned 16 seemed like a good time for one of those father-knows-best chats in which I would dispense all-knowing wisdom. I started the conversation with, "Yeah, I can remember when I was 16. In those days . . ." Then I caught myself and stopped in mid sentence. My son's eyes were starting to glaze over and I imagined (I believe correctly) that in his own left-hand column there was something like, "Here Dad goes again. He's going to spin some old family yarns for me. I'm the one turning 16, but he wants to talk about his own teenage years." I changed course and said, "It's been a long time since I was 16, and the world is different now. What's it like for *you* to be 16?" I silently counted to five, waiting for *him* to pick up the dialogue. Sensing the respect of my advocacy and inquiry, he talked freely. I learned new things about his feelings, his interests, his hopes. That was more than two decades ago, and the lines of communication are still wide open.

Pool the Meaning

Change-Friendly dialogue balances courage with consideration, confidence with respect. The best form of influence has no taint of manipulation or coercion. It encourages and enables people to "connect the dots" so they can see for themselves the reasonableness of your position. You, in turn, respectfully see the value of their contributions. By relinquishing power, deferring judgment, taming the elephants, listening with empathy, inquiring to discover, and advocating with respect, you make it possible to "pool the meaning." Again, this doesn't necessarily result in agreement. But agreement, if that's what you're hoping for, cannot come unless and until there is genuine understanding. As a change leader, you will sometimes be required to make decisions that are based on your best judgment rather than on universal concurrence. Just be sure that all the affected players feel genuinely heard.

And throughout your practice of dialogue, be sure to stay alert to the four dimensions of sound thinking:

- *Capacity.* Dialogue, as opposed to routine conversation, is more likely to occur when you maintain a mindset of sincere exploration and learning. No matter how confident you may feel about your current perspective, there's always a chance—probability, really—that you can learn something new and helpful from others.
- *Curiosity.* Think-Friendly questions, offered in a spirit of curiosity rather than interrogation, are the fuel of good dialogue. Operating in the learner mode rather than in the judger mode opens the door of understanding.

- *Conclusions.* If Think-Friendly questions are the fuel of good dialogue, deferred judgment is the oxygen. Remember to FIND-IT, which stands for Focus, Inquire, Notice, Discern – Integrate, Translate. Jumping to unwarranted conclusions is one of the fastest ways to snuff out dialogue.

- *Connections.* Just as my grandmother and I solved jigsaw puzzles best when we collaborated, so does each participant's perspective add to the whole in dialogue. Rather than resist resistance, we can benefit from differences of opinion by pooling our meaning into a richer mix of possibilities.

As I said earlier, you are most effective when you talk so other people will listen *and* when you listen so other people will talk. Being Talk-Friendly is not just about being "nice," although there's much to be said for that. It's about being *effective*.

To do that you must put your best voice forward.

TALK-FRIENDLY SELF-ASSESSMENT

Instructions: *Read each statement and decide how accurately it describes your use of the Talk-Friendly behaviors described in this chapter:*

a. Never or rarely engage in this behavior (0 points)

b. Sometimes engage in this behavior (1 point)

c. Regularly engage in this behavior (2 points)

d. Always or almost always engage in this behavior (3 points)

Place the point value of your response choice beside each statement.

_____ I postpone judgment on things until I have sufficient data to proceed with justifiable confidence.

_____ I identify important "undiscussables" (elephants in the room) and make it safe for people to talk about them openly.

_____ I genuinely listen with the intent to learn and understand rather than to judge or to prepare my rebuttal.

_____ When I advocate a position, I do so with a sincere spirit of humility, confidence, and respect.

_____ While having confidence in my own positions, I listen to contrary views in a welcoming, non-defensive manner.

_____ Total Number of Points

Interpreting Your Scores

0-5: You may be coming across as not really that interested in open dialogue with others. That may not be your actual intent, but as the old saying goes, perception is reality.

6-10: You're clearly making an effort to use good dialogue skills, but there's opportunity to get better. As suggested in the previous chapter, be sure to ask a lot of smart questions— always from the perspective of the "learner" rather than from the "judger." This practice not only helps you think better, it helps you talk better.

11-15: Nice work. You seem to be talking so people will listen, and listening so people will talk. Re-read the Talk-Friendly chapter and make note of what you might do even better. You'll like the result.

It's more important to be trusted than to be loved.
David O. McKay

All power is a trust; and we are accountable
for its exercise.
Benjamin Disraeli

Transcendent values like trust and
integrity literally translate into revenue,
profits and prosperity.
Patricia Aburdene, author of *Megatrends 2010*

Ask yourself . . . mercilessly: Do I exude trust?
E-x-u-d-e. Big word. Do I smack of "trust"?
Think about it. Carefully.
Tom Peters

To be persuasive we must be believable.
To be believable we must be credible.
To be credible we must be truthful.
Edward R. Murrow

Chapter

Trust-Friendly:
Make Trust First to Make It Last

Many organizations have it all wrong. They don't need to motivate their people. They need to stop demotivating them.

In many organizational settings, people do the dance of "cordial hypocrisy."

You know what it looks like. Everyone is polite and collegial because polite and collegial are safe, comfortable, and politically correct. They talk about the weekend ballgame. They swap yarns about each other's families. They inquire about a colleague's new boat. They may even talk about work. But when they do, there seems to be a kind of tacit, silent deal among the parties. There's little more than careful tip-toeing around the real issues of expectations, interdependency, and accountability. Everyone knows there's an elephant in the room (missed deadlines, broken promises, blame shifting, fear of the unknown, etc.), but nobody steps forward to help name and tame the elephant. This "cordial hypocrisy" masquerades for real dialogue.

It's a waste of time.
It chokes engagement.
It thwarts performance.
It's fake work.

THE LANGUAGE OF TRUST

To enhance our success with the Talk-Friendly dialogue skills outlined in the previous chapter, we can learn to communicate in the *language of trust.*

The language of trust is both verbal and non-verbal. It's both words and behaviors. It is not subtle. When used appropriately, the language of trust is deliberate and explicit, and it makes all the difference in every kind of relationship.

My son speaks six languages. It's clearly a gift. I once asked him, "At what point do you realize that you've become truly proficient in a new language?" "When I dream in that language," he said.

Genuine trust is much like that. Most anyone can "say the words" of trust. But when "trust" becomes our default, knee-jerk behavior, when we "dream in trust," then we reap the real benefits of trust.

At this time of economic upheaval and political transition, *trust* is an issue that's front and center more than ever.

Everybody's in favor of trust. We all know it's important. But a lot of people seem to regard trust as soft and intangible, a social virtue that's nice to have but impossible to quantify.

> *"Most anyone can 'say the words' of trust. But when 'trust' becomes our default, knee-jerk behavior, when we 'dream in trust,' then we reap the real benefits of trust."*

Yet trust is much more than that. Trust is a hard-edged economic driver. Yes, trust is indeed a character trait. Trust is also a competency that can be *taught*, and *learned*, and *improved*.

My friend Stephen M.R. Covey has written a best-selling book on the subject. It's called *The Speed of Trust.*

So what's the big idea? The big idea is simply this: Low trust is a tax. High trust is a dividend. It's true in a relationship. It's true on a team. It's true with a client or customer. It's true with every kind of stakeholder.

When trust is low, you pay a "tax"—because everything requires more time to accomplish and everything costs you more. When trust is high, you receive a "dividend"—because you're able to get things done faster and at a lower cost.

This dividend is real. It's not just a feel-good factor. It's an actual economic dividend. And the data on it are overwhelming.

For example, a Watson Wyatt study showed that high-trust organizations outperformed low-trust organizations by 286%—that's nearly three times—in total return to shareholders.

Every year *Fortune* magazine—in conjunction with the Great Place to Work Institute—publishes a list of "The 100 Best Companies to Work for in America."

"The number one most expensive thing that can happen is for their smart and capable people to quit and stay."

Trust is the primary defining characteristic required to get on that list: trust between management and employees, trust between and among work teams. Trust factors comprise more than half of the criteria.

So, how do these high-trust organizations do? They outperform the S&P 500 by 416% in terms of their economic return.

A similar phenomenon occurs in education. We all know there's a correlation between learning and the relationship between student and teacher. And as you'd expect, trust is an important component of that relationship. A national study shows that students in high-trust schools are three-and-a-half times more likely to increase their test scores than are students in low-trust schools.

Regardless of the industry, the research data is compelling: The low-trust tax is real. The high-trust dividend is real.

I frequently tell my clients that the second most expensive thing that can happen with regard to their employees is for smart and capable people to quit and leave. But the number one most expensive thing that can happen is for their smart and capable people to quit and *stay*.

Disengaged employees are enormously expensive. Engagement flows out of trust, and trust flows out of engagement. They are mutually reinforcing.

As mentioned earlier, studies by the Gallup organization show that 96% of engaged employees trust their leaders, while only 46% of *dis*engaged employees trust their leaders. Gallup puts a conservative price tag of $300 billion per year on disengagement in the U.S. alone.

So which comes first—the distrust or the disengagement? Both. And that's the point. Trust affects everything.

Consider something like innovation. *The Financial Times* studied the 100 top companies on their list. They compared the top 20 innovators to the bottom 20 innovators. High trust was the number one differentiating factor.

Think about it. Innovation flourishes and thrives in an environment of high trust. Try innovating in a low-trust culture. People clamor for credit. They point fingers of blame. They tell each other a lot of victim, villain, and helpless stories. They engage in the time- and resource-wasting behaviors of the Saints, the Ain'ts, and the Complaints (see Chapter 4). Because low-trust environments are not safe, it's hard to make strides with innovation. You want more traction with innovation? Increase the trust.

Consider teamwork. Our entire global economy – from the factory floor to relationships between nations—is based on collaboration. Genuine collaboration thrives or dies based upon trust. Without trust it's impossible to collaborate. You might be able to *coordinate* or you may *cooperate*. But genuine collaboration requires trust.

What about partnering? Partnering is an absolutely critical element in most every kind of business. Partnering can take many forms, from loose confederations of like-minded people to strategic alliances between global companies or even nations.

What about outsourcing? A study by the Warwick Business School in the UK focused on outsourcing contracts over a ten-year period. They found that companies that manage their outsourcing relationships based on trust—as opposed to relying on the fine print of service contracts—outperform low-trust organizations by 40%. They call it the 40% dividend.

> *Good leadership is all about credibility, walking the talk.*
> **Anne Mulcahy**

Studies in every industry validate the notion that trust is king. Whether you're talking about execution, loyalty, sales, accelerating growth, or any other metric—high trust is a dividend. Everything —all the execution strategy, all the innovation, all the partnering, all the collaboration, all the growth and performance improvement —all of these things are tied to *trust*.

Now, let's dig deeper into this idea of trust being a competency.

When we begin to grasp the true importance of trust we experience a paradigm shift. We start to *see* things differently. We begin to view the world through our "trust lenses" that bring clarity and focus to the way we manage our relationships. When we begin to *speak* the language of trust, it signals to others that we are committed to earning the dividends of trust. When we *behave* in ways that build trust we actually earn those dividends and minimize the trust taxes we may have been paying.

> *"All of this may seem like a blinding flash of the obvious. Unfortunately, common sense is often not common practice. And in the case of trust, the common practice is often distrust."*

It is *then* that we're best able to achieve the sustainable high results we want.

Now, all of this may seem like a blinding flash of the obvious. Unfortunately, as we all know, common sense is often not common practice. And in the case of trust, the common practice is often distrust.

Distrust is reflected in the silo mentality we frequently see in organizations. The surface relationships may be cordial, but right underneath the top veneer there's often doubt or outright suspicion (more of that "cordial hypocrisy" mentioned earlier).

Fragile trust is often reflected in relationships between management and union members, between companies and suppliers, between supervisors and direct reports, and even among peers. Even when many of the other performance metrics seem to be okay, fragile trust can be a hidden variable—lurking beneath the surface as it slows down processes and drives up costs.

Why does this occur? I suppose there are many reasons. And I believe a primary reason is that most people still regard trust as just a nice-to-have social virtue and don't yet understand trust as an issue they can do something about explicitly, deliberately, and quantitatively.

At one time, most of us didn't understand the effects of cholesterol. But now there's plenty of information available and we can make informed choices about our eating and exercise behaviors. There's also plenty of quantitative information available on the effects of trust.

So let's consider some of the informed choices we can make to earn trust, to maintain trust, and to extend trust. Acting on these informed choices can make a huge difference in your efforts to engage people's heads, hearts, and hopes.

Trust Busters

Tasty though it may be, the marbled fat in a ribeye steak clogs our arteries. A soft drink may produce a temporary lift, but the caffeine can lead to sleep disorders, depression, anxiety, high blood pressure, headaches, cramps, dehydration, and a range of other side effects.

Common human behaviors may produce temporary—though illusory—benefit, but then the reality sets in and the actual result is not at all what we bargained for. That's certainly the case with what I call Trust Busters: common behaviors that undermine confidence and engagement.

Let's consider a few of the more common Trust Busters, along with their fixes, which I call Trust Builders.

Double Talk

A cartoon showed a street scene of the Fine Print Barber Shop. On the sidewalk was a sign that read: "One haircut FREE." Then in fine print, "$25 to cut the rest of them." The barber's advertisement was technically correct, but it certainly left a misleading impression.

While the cartoon may elicit a chuckle, *double talk* is no laughing matter. Double talk takes many forms, all of which damage or destroy trust:

- *Spin:* Every organization and, to an extent, every individual engages in public relations. We communicate with others by sharing our opinions and championing our causes. That's fair and understandable and a natural part of human interaction. "Spin," on the other hand, is often used as a pejorative term, and rightfully so. "Spin" usually describes a heavily biased portrayal in one's own favor of an event, situation, or topic. Although it's possible to spin information honestly, the term as used here implies disingenuous, deceptive, and even manipulative tactics. An obvious example would be the state-run media in some countries that selectively allow news stories that are favorable to the government while censoring anything deemed critical. A common example closer to home is the blather that tries to pass itself off as helpful information in the annual reports of public companies. When a letter to shareholders begins with "This was a challenging year for our company . . ." it's a pretty safe bet that what follows is the rhetorical equivalent of putting lipstick on a pig—the company's performance nosedived, targets were missed, and it can all be blamed on market conditions and political intrigue beyond the control of management.

- *Cherry picking:* This is a close cousin of spin, and takes the form of selectively presenting facts and quotes to support a particular position. The result is often a false impression. Politicians do it all the time. A member of Congress might highlight a piece of legislation he claims to have co-sponsored. The way he tells the story you'd think he was riding into town on a white horse as the primary champion of the cause. In reality, he fails to mention that the legislation is also co-sponsored by more than a hundred other Congressmen and that his actual involvement amounted to little more than adding his name to the list. When I noticed a huge increase in the annual premium on my homeowners policy, I asked the agent to double check the numbers. He came back with a lower premium, but failed to mention that the "new" policy decreased the protection on my home by several hundred thousand dollars. In the corporate world, cherry picking often occurs when restructuring is announced, when performance initiatives are rolled out, and when organization charts are reshuffled. Trust suffers.

- *Euphemisms:* These are words designed to deflect attention from something considered distasteful or unpleasant. In some families, nobody ever dies, they "pass away." In some social circles, nobody is insulted or disrespected, they are "marginalized." In some companies, people don't get fired or dismissed, they are "outplaced." As one writer said, euphemisms are like secret agents on a delicate mission, they are unpleasant truths wearing diplomatic cologne. The trouble with euphemisms is that despite the cologne they still stink.

- *Jargon and buzzwords:* Jargon, much like slang, is terminology that often develops as a kind of short-hand used by members of a group—like computer people talk about RAM, CPU, URLs, and related things. Acronyms—abbreviations formed from initial letters or a term or phrase – are another kind of jargon. These are not inherently a problem, but they tend to fog up communication when used to excess or with people unfamiliar with the code. Buzzwords are in a class by themselves. These overused terms are common to corporate, technical, administrative, and political environments, but they're evident in other places, too. While jargon (ideally) at least has a defined technical meaning, buzzwords are often used primarily to impress with a pretense of knowledge. Instead, they usually result in opaque sentences with mushy meaning. I saw one organization's so-called mission statement that read something like this: "In a spirit of continuous improvement, it is our responsibility to provide access to low-risk high-yield benefits to our customers and to administrate economically sound policies while promoting personal growth and fulfillment for our associates." My ninth grade English teacher would have kicked me out of class for writing a sentence like that. When used sanely, words like leverage, passion, bandwidth, paradigm, empowerment, framework, and space have a welcome place in our language. But when strung together in a cobweb of obfuscation, the result is bewilderment, not communication; suspicion, not trust.

- *Vague commitments:* When a boy picks up your teenage daughter for a date, you'll likely want some information about what's on the agenda for the evening —things like where they're going, who will be there, what the activity will be, and when you can expect your daughter to return home. You want your daughter to have fun and, above all, you want her to be safe. If the guy gives you no more data than "I'll bring her back," you'll have second thoughts about letting your daughter out the front door. In the business world, vague commitments are no less of a trust buster. Some people pay lip service to clarifying expectations, but then they fail to provide specifics on results, deadlines, budgets, or most anything else about performance. It makes no difference whether this failure is inadvertent or by design. The effect is the same: fragile trust.

Trust Builder #1: Clear the Fog

Honesty and clarity are the best prevention against double talk. Simply don't engage in double talk in the first place. Avoid ambiguous or evasive language. Use simple words. Lay out the whole story, warts and all.

Billionaire Warren Buffett, chairman of Berkshire Hathaway, is a model of straight talk in all his business dealings. It's especially evident in his annual "management letter" to shareholders. Buffett's phenomenal success is something he gladly shares with his vice chairman Charles Unger, his small staff, and the managers of his various companies. He's also quick to shoulder responsibility for the negative. He says things like "If Charlie and I fail, we will have no excuses," and "When Charlie and I make mistakes, they are—in tennis parlance—unforced errors."

Clearing the Fog is not complicated:
- To avoid "spin," be sure that all sides to an issue get a

fair hearing. Remember that a pig with lipstick is still a pig. Play it straight. People appreciate—and trust— plain talk.

- Use examples that are plausible, relevant, and real. People trust illustrations that connect to their world.
- Use language that stands up straight. Words that lurk behind corners or tip-toe around issues are neither credible nor convincing. Political correctness is a particular offender.
- Make specific, realistic commitments. Then honor them.

Pulling Rank

Another common trust buster is pulling rank. Some people try to exert influence by using the power of their position or authority. Maybe their ego gets in the way. Maybe they delight in the role of bully. Maybe they're impatient and just want others to do things their way. Maybe they simply lack confidence and are reluctant to entertain the views of others.

Whatever the reasons, pulling rank is never effective in engaging peoples' heads, hearts, and hopes. In fact, it does just the reverse.

During my years at Campbell Soup Company I worked for two CEOs—Harold Shaub and Gordon McGovern. They were worlds apart in virtually every aspect of leadership. Harold Shaub was an old school executive whose closest colleagues—even those who had worked with him for more than thirty-five years—still called him "Mr." He clearly preferred surrounding himself with "yes men," people who blindly followed his orders with no alternatives offered and no questions asked. He seemed to relish the perks of his office, and was none-too-subtle about reminding people that he was the boss.

> *It is better to trust and sometimes be disappointed than to be forever mistrusting and be right occasionally.*
> **Neal A. Maxwell**

When Harold Shaub retired, he was replaced in the corner office by Gordon McGovern. Gordon was nearly a direct opposite.

He preferred the employee cafeteria over the executive dining room with its silver and china and deferential butlers. Though well-bred and Ivy League educated, Gordon was informal and approachable. He thrived on lively conversation, especially with people who offered opposing views. He was as comfortable chatting with a worker on the plant production line as he was in talking with a member of the board of directors. In fact, *because* Gordon was so approachable, he got some of his best ideas from people who operated at several rungs lower on the organization chart. He seemed totally blind to the issues of rank. Though this seemed to annoy some of the Harold Shaub holdovers in the executive suite, it endeared Gordon to nearly everyone else in the company. He was, by far, more effective than his predecessor in bringing out the best in others.

Chuck is a family friend, one of my brother's Naval Academy classmates. Chuck is relatively small in stature, a steadfastly polite and soft-spoken gentleman. In a crowded room he comes across as the one most likely to teach Sunday School (which, in fact, he does). Chuck is retired General Charles C. Krulak, former Commandant of the United States Marine Corps. In the military, and now in private business, Chuck is known as the kind of leader that people love to follow. Rather than just issuing orders and demanding obedience, he earns respect by listening carefully, by coaching, by encouraging. He engages people's ingenuity and commitment. He never bullies. He never pulls rank. He gets results.

Trust Builder #2: Drop the Pretense

Using one's higher status to compel obedience or obtain privileges is guaranteed to spawn resentment. When a boss pulls rank, people respond more out of compliance than out of commitment. Besides, pulling rank often comes across not as a sign of strength but as a sign of weakness. Pulling rank looks like a last resort, even when used early. After all, the reasoning goes, why would anyone need to pull rank if his viewpoint could stand on its own merits?

Let's get real. Even though you may have position, title, a reserved parking space, and maybe a bigger desk lamp than the guy next door, you're really no smarter than most of the people in your organization. You may have "paid your dues," to get where you are. But that doesn't mean you have more brain cells. So drop the pretense. You're all in this together. And the better you are at exercising *influence* rather than *authority*, the better you'll be at engaging the heads, hearts, and hopes of your colleagues.

Here are five steps to help you Drop the Pretense:

(1) Question your motives. Are you using your position or authority to browbeat people into doing things your way? Are you trying to stifle open discussion? Are you using the leverage of your position just because you can? Do you somehow feel threatened—for example, by someone who offers a view difference from yours? If the roles were reversed and someone tried to pull rank on *you*, how would *you* feel?

(2) Examine your case. Are there leaks in the case you're trying to make for adopting your view? Is pulling rank just a way to camouflage those leaks?

(3) Inspect your language. Are you using words like "It's my way or the highway . . ." or "Remember that I'm the boss . . ."or "Just do what you're told . . ." or "I thought you liked working here"? These are blatant examples of pulling rank, with bullying thrown in.

(4) Consider the desired outcomes. If mutual purpose and mutual respect are what you really want in your relationships, you'll realize that pulling rank introduces a tone that's contrary to mutuality.

(5) Practice your Talk-Friendly skills. Remember that true dialogue cannot occur in an atmosphere where one person tries to exert power over another. Stay on the look-out for communication barriers like allness, hardening of the categories, frozen evaluation, inference-observation confusion, and bypassing. These sometimes influence people to shift gears from collaboration to command-and-control. Listen with empathy. This means listening to understand, not to judge or rebut. Inquire to discover. Advocate with respect. Pool the meaning. All of these dialogue skills reinforce a "we're all in this together" tone and

diminish the temptation to exercise unrighteous dominion by pulling rank.

Playing Favorites

Okay, we all have favorites from time to time. Some people are simply easier to work with, more fun to be around, more reliable. It's natural to prefer their companionship. But when our private favoritism affects—or even appears to affect—our judgment, we have a problem. Harry Stonecipher was forced to resign the presidency of aerospace giant Boeing over a personal relationship with another Boeing executive. World Bank president Paul Wolfowitz had to resign after being accused of arranging a big raise and promotion for a woman with whom he was having a relationship. And as anyone who works in an office knows, trust busting favoritism isn't confined to romance and sex. Family relationships and office friendships can also upset people's sense of propriety and fairness and end up undermining the credibility of the players.

> *"People tend to contribute more to an organization's success— they are more* **engaged**— *when they perceive themselves to be treated fairly."*

People tend to contribute more to an organization's success—they are more *engaged*—when they perceive themselves to be treated fairly.

Relationships include a process of negotiated exchanges between parties. In other words, people use a (mostly unconscious) form of cost-benefit analysis in comparing what they're contributing to a relationship to what they're getting from it. When employees believe they are receiving less benefit (pay, privileges, opportunities, attention, appreciation, etc.) than their performance warrants, they tend to reciprocate the perceived unfairness with counterproductive work behavior. This includes the disengagement we've mentioned in earlier chapters.

When envy enters the mix—for example, a supervisor's perceived preferential treatment of one employee over another—the result is magnified. What would otherwise have been a negative interaction between the neglected party and the organization or his supervisor now becomes interpersonal, involving not only the employee and the organization, but another coworker as well.

Unfairness and envy, the two primary ingredients of favoritism, can trigger a chain of victim, villain, and helpless stories. These, in turn, produce a multiplier effect on negative behavior and poor performance.

Trust Builder #3: Level the Field

Again, the reality is that there are likely those among your associates who are simply more reliable and easier to work with than others. In fact, you should strive to be that kind of person yourself. But when focus on one person is perceived as playing unfair favorites, it becomes a problem.

Most good leaders eventually discover this paradox: There's nothing as unequal as the equal treatment of unequals.

As any parent can tell you, different people—even from the same gene pool—may respond uniquely to the same influence. People simply have different needs. For example, one person may appreciate public acknowledgement of his contribution to a project, while another would be embarrassed by such praise. One person may regard inquiring

> *"There's nothing as unequal as the equal treatment of unequals."*

about his family as a friendly, caring gesture while another could see it as an invasion of privacy. Different strokes for different folks.

The danger of playing favorites— or even its perception—requires a disciplined approach to uniform performance standards.

Here are two key steps to help you Level the Field:

(1) Practice your Talk-Friendly skills with the under-achievers. With people who let you down, talk straight about your expectations for their performance and your hopes for their improvement. Be explicit. Provide specific examples of what you want and need and how they can close the gap between what's expected and what they're delivering. In your best Change-Friendly tones, make it clear that you *want* to be able to rely on them. Don't let them off the hook. Agree on milestones, deadlines or other benchmarks that can be used to calibrate and measure performance. Hold them accountable.

(2) Practice your Talk-Friendly skills with the achievers. With people who consistently meet or exceed your expectations, be sure to keep the lines of communication open. Be explicit in pointing out the contributions they make—the links between their work and the efforts of others. Be specific in expressing your appreciation. Otherwise, ironically, you may actually come across as playing favorites with the under-achievers. A common unintended consequence of over-reliance on the better achievers is that they may feel penalized for their achievement. In other words, when Bob continues to miss deadlines and you start to rely more heavily on Mike because he always gets the job done, you're in a sense penalizing Mike for Bob's lack of performance. You may need to rely more on Mike in the short term, but be sure to maintain focus on helping Bob improve.

Flimsy Feedback

While it's true that self-starting achievers typically don't need a lot of strokes, giving too little feedback is a common trust buster. I once heard a so-called leader say "My people should just be grateful to have jobs. If they do something wrong, I'll let 'em know. Otherwise, they should just press on. There's too much work to do to take time with a bunch of back-slapping." In that same conversation this guy wondered aloud why his people didn't seem very engaged in the work.

Perhaps the most common form of flimsy feedback is the mistake of allowing stories to masquerade as facts. Let's say you're talking with Phil about his job performance and you deliver a speech that goes something like this: "Okay, Phil. As you know, we're raising the bar around here. We need to get more out of you this coming year. It seems like you're not really stretching, and

> *"Perhaps the most common form of flimsy feedback is the mistake of allowing stories to masquerade as facts."*

we need you to stretch. You're definitely in the 'Needs Improvement' category, and we need you to step up to the 'Meets Expectations' slot. So get out there and show us what you can do."

That little speech may sound like something from a Saturday Night Live skit, but it's virtually verbatim from the kind of drivel that some people try to pass off as helpful feedback. If you're the Phil in that scenario you'll go home and tell your wife: "I don't know what those people expect of me. I'm already working my tail off and all they tell me is that I need to 'stretch.' What's that supposed to mean?"

Flimsy feedback is often another form of the double talk we discussed earlier. Mind-numbing business jargon can render a well-intended conversation or meeting meaningless. Think about it. How often have you heard (or said) something like this: "Listen up, folks. We're here to touch base, circle the wagons, get our ducks in a row, and get everyone working on the same page. Let's make sure we pick the low-hanging fruit now so we can leverage everyone's bandwidth. We're going to beat the competition only if we become game-changing paradigm-shifters and go to the next level." Okay, that may be a bit of an exaggeration (or maybe not). But you get the idea. People are not inspired by double talk. They are not motivated by long strings of clichés bereft of meaning or substance. They need specifics. They need examples. They need concrete models and illustrations.

> *Relationships of trust depend on our willingness to look not only to our own interests, but also the interests of others.*
> **Peter Farquharson**

Trust Builder #4: Coach With Clarity

First, make sure you focus on facts, verifiable data. If you believe Phil needs to "stretch" in his performance, give him specific examples of what you've observed. In last quarter's product roll-out, did he miss an opportunity to provide additional information that might have helped the marketing team? If so, point it out as an example of what you mean by "stretch" and discuss the impact that kind of effort can have on the overall enterprise. What about upcoming opportunities? In the near future, what kind of behaviors from Phil would you regard as "stretch" behaviors? Be specific. Give examples. Solicit ideas from Phil. Involve him in the brainstorming. What you want is collaborative dialogue, not two competing monologues.

Second, jettison the double talk. If you want people to "be on the same page," tell them specifically what that means. If you mean it only as some vague description of "team agreement," you'd better be ready to define how that actually translates into observable behavior. If you mean it more as an indicator of unified adherence to operational protocols, say so. Be specific. Talking in clichés does not build trust.

Finally, remember to be explicit when you point out the good things people are doing. It's nice to tell Jane that she did a good job on her presentation. But it's even nicer—and more helpful—if you tell her specifically what it is that impressed you about her presentation. Was it the way she introduced the problem before suggesting solutions? Was it the way she connected her presentation to the other items on the meeting agenda? Was it the way she engaged the participants in discussing the solution options? Again, specificity saves the day. The best coaches and colleagues provide explicit feedback that needs no interpretation.

It builds trust.

Fake Work

In virtually every organization on the planet, people are doing fake work. I'm not talking about the laggards who deliberately invest more energy in getting out of work than in performing meaningful service. I'm talking about earnest and honest people who work very hard at well-intended things that don't really contribute to strategic purpose. This includes a lot of the meetings, reports, briefings, procedures and other activities that consume people's time on the job. A couple of my colleagues have even written a book on the subject. It's called *Fake Work: Why People Are Working Harder Than Ever But Accomplishing Less, and How to Fix the Problem.*

In our years of research on the subject, here's some of what we've found:

- 73% of workers say their organization's goals are not translated into specific work tasks they can execute.
- 70% of workers do not connect the dots (planning) in supporting organizational goals with specific work tasks.

- 59% of workers do not clearly understand their organization's most important goals.
- 81% of workers do not feel a strong commitment to their organization's strategies and goals.

Oh, you say, that may be true of many organizations but not of yours? Don't be too quick to plead innocence. Fake work can be both subtle and seductive. Let me illustrate. One of our clients is a leading performer in an industry that's known for its rigorous standards and meticulous performance metrics. The chief executive assured us that in our assessment of his company's culture we would find that people throughout the organization were "on board with the strategy" and "working on the same page." We'd heard that before, and our pre-survey interviews suggested there were huge gaps between assumption and reality.

> *"Fake work can be both subtle and seductive."*

In a comprehensive survey with more than 1,000 respondents, here's what we found:
- Only 22% agreed that the organization avoids unnecessary layers of red tape.
- Only 42% agreed that senior managers know where the most critical problems are.
- Only 37% believed senior managers know how to translate "vision" into plans and systems that help people do their work.
- Only 37% said they ever discuss the linkage between strategic goals and the work they actually perform.
- Only 42% said that when a major change or initiative is announced the business rationale is clearly explained.
- Only 22% said members of their work team can even state the organization's strategic goals.

Clearly, the strategy-alignment-execution model wasn't working at all the way the chief executive assumed it was. In fact, there were significant—even dangerous—gaps between the strategy discussed in the boardroom and the actual work executed throughout the company. In addition to missed opportunities for great performance, the gaps between strategic intent and actual execution resulted in fragile trust. After all, how can you trust leaders who impose layers of unnecessary red tape? How can you trust leaders who are perceived to be out of touch with what's really going on in the organization? How can you trust leaders who fail to translate "vision" into plans and systems that help real people do real work? How can you trust leaders who condone and even reward fake work? How can you trust leaders who insist that trust is not an issue when everyone else knows it is?

One of the most common causes of fake work is the unchallenged assumption. Here are two examples.

A major public utility company held a bi-weekly "leadership council" meeting of key managers. I was invited to observe one of the meetings. It was a sweltering summer day and the meeting was in a windowless room with little ventilation. About 30 people crowded around a huge table. An ancient projector was at the end of the table, its fan throwing off enough heat to melt a glacier. Over a three-hour period we endured several death-by-PowerPoint presentations. Only six or eight of the people in the room ever uttered a word. The folks in the room—none of whom looked ready to do a Bowflex infomercial, if you know what I mean— mostly seemed determined to sip their Diet Cokes and shift in their chairs in an

> *The glue that holds all relationships together – including the relationship between the leader and the led – is trust, and trust is based on integrity.*
> **Brian Tracy**

effort to stay awake. At the end of this marathon I asked the senior executive, "What's the purpose of this meeting?" It was apparently a question he hadn't considered. "Oh, uh, to keep people informed?" he responded, with a question mark of his own. I asked what he meant by that and he said the idea was for the meeting attendees to take what they learned back to their people so everyone would "be on the same page." (There's that double talk again.) I told him my observation was that the meeting has no such effect at all. In fact, in my interviews with many people in the company I'd received basically two responses when I asked what goes on in that bi-weekly leadership council meeting: (1) "I don't have any idea, but my boss is gone for three hours and that's a good thing," or (2) "I don't have any idea, but my boss is gone for three hours and we really need him here with us."

Thirty managers times three hours each times twice a month for many years. You do the math. With no specific strategic purpose for the meeting, with no measures of desired outcomes, with no real protocols for follow up, it was nothing but trust busting fake work.

In another example of fake work, one of my Canadian clients proudly produced what was called the QBR—Quarterly Business Review. The expressed purpose of this massive report (several hundred pages of charts and graphs and meticulous descriptions of operating results) was to "keep people informed" and, you guessed it, "on the same page." I did some digging, and here's what I found. No fewer than 35 people worked virtually full time gathering information from disparate sources and stitching it all together into a patch quilt of mind numbing data. The report was distributed to several dozen people, but only six of them—only six—told me they ever even looked at the report. And all six of those readers said they looked at only a small portion of the report—which contained information they could easily access elsewhere.

> **If you trust Google more than your doctor then maybe it's time to switch doctors.**
> **Jadelr and Cristina Cordova**

When I reported this Canadian version of the Abilene Paradox to senior management they were incredulous. The QBR had been produced for years and nobody had ever complained (certainly not the 35 editors who were gainfully employed doing fake work). Only after further interviews and verification did the senior management team agree to disband the QBR in favor of a much simpler and more useful reporting system.

Again, most fake work is the result of unchallenged assumptions, not the deliberate behavior of someone who merely pretends to be busy. Most fake work is done by honest people who simply have not connected the dots between the work they do and the strategic goals of the causes they serve. And when that fake work is implicitly endorsed (or directed) by people in leadership roles, trust is busted.

Trust Builder #5: Connect the Dots

Because the primary sign of fake work is a lack of connection between strategic intent and actual performance, the steps to connecting those dots are fairly simple (not necessarily easy, but simple):

(1) Clarify, translate, and define strategies. This does not mean that senior managers just announce the strategies like Moses from the mountaintop. To one extent or another, people at all levels in the organization should be involved in strategy development. (How do you like being held responsible for executing a strategy in which you had absolutely no voice?)

(2) Collaborate in defining critical tasks. When people genuinely understand the strategy, you may be pleasantly surprised by their ingenuity in defining specific tasks that make execution successful. Typically, people closest to the work are also very good at identifying tasks that are—well, fake work.

(3) Prioritize and refine critical tasks. Not all tasks, even the important ones, are created equally. Engage your people to ensure that the most critical tasks get the required resources.

(4) Work on alignment. Make sure critical tasks assigned to different players are performed in a mutually reinforcing, cohesive way.

(5) Plan the work and work the plan. Ensure that every worker operates with a personal work plan that explicitly aligns critical tasks with organizational strategy.

(6) Monitor. Measure. Calibrate. Adjust. Get better.

(7) Hold each other accountable.

These simple steps go a long way to ferret out fake work. They help produce change-friendly real work. They replace suspicion and doubt with confidence and engagement. They build trust.

To help you practice Trust Builders, use the dimensions of sound thinking discussed in Chapter 4.

- *Capacity.* Maintain a mindset that it's not only possible—it's imperative—that you constantly expand your ability to earn the trust of others. You do this through both language and behavior. And even if you already enjoy a high level of trust, you can and must constantly nourish that priceless reputation.

- *Curiosity*. Always operate in the learner mode. Ask other people what you can do to earn and maintain their trust. You can probably guess some of the things that are important to them—like honoring your commitments—but don't assume you know everything that's important to them. Ask. Listen. Then behave accordingly.

- *Conclusions*. Remember to FIND-IT, which stands for Focus, Inquire, Notice, Discern – Integrate, Translate. Focus to define and clarify the situation so you can best manage the dynamics in the most trust-building way. Inquire into the needs of the other parties. Notice the nuances (your first impressions may be incomplete, or even wrong). Discern the differences between people's styles, personalities, and needs for information. Integrate your message (both words and actions) into the interdependent pieces of the environment. Translate your meaning into terms that can be easily understood by others. Double check your assumptions. Challenge your stories.

- *Connections*. As you work to build and maintain high levels of trust, constantly ask yourself a series of questions: What are your *known knowns*? What things are you absolutely certain about in the dynamics of the relationship? What are the *known unknowns*? What information is missing and how important is it for you to obtain it? What are the *unknown unknowns*? This is tricky, but it's a pertinent question because it causes us to challenge our own (and others') thinking and consider a broader range of possibilities. And finally, what are the *unknown knowns*? These are things we already know but perhaps have not given due consideration.

In practicing Trust Builders, it becomes obvious that they involve both character and competence. In addition to their moral and ethical qualities, they involve skill. Fortunately, moral and ethical qualities can be taught and learned. So can skills.

This character-competency combination suggests a special challenge for people who want to establish and maintain high trust relationships. It's possible, for example, to *want* for all of the right reasons—honesty, fairness, openness, etc.—to practice a trust building behavior but be relatively incompetent in doing so.

Here's the good news. Practice matters. Repetition matters. Experience matters.

Consider the Listen With Empathy behavior we discussed in the previous chapter. In addition to being a critical Talk-Friendly skill, listening with empathy builds trust. But genuinely listening with empathy is harder than it may sound. Trustworthy people listen not just with their ears, but

> *If you don't know jewelry, know the jeweler.*
> **Warren Buffett**

also with their eyes and their hearts. They're very cautious about making assumptions. They don't presume to have all the answers, or even all the questions.

Another thing to remember about the character-competency combination is that behaviors come in various shades and tones. As we all know from experience, some people are pretty good at playing behavioral shell games. Stephen M.R. Covey refers to these behaviors as "counterfeits." The various forms of double talk discussed earlier are counterfeits of the straight talk that people want and need. A counterfeit of listening with empathy would be to merely pretend to listen, just waiting for your turn to speak, or looking for holes in the other person's position so you can attack theirs and bolster yours. That's not dialogue. That's debate. That's not empathy. That's an ambush. That's a trust busting counterfeit.

Finally, an important way to earn and maintain trust is to *extend* trust.

Trustworthy people have a propensity to trust others. We're not talking about blind trust or gullibility. We're talking here about "smart trust" that's based on a reasonable assessment of risk. Trustworthy people tend to extend trust abundantly to those who have earned it.

They extend trust conditionally to those who are still earning it. But their first inclination is to trust.

A counterfeit behavior is to extend "fake trust." This often comes in the form of giving people responsibility for results but withholding the authority or resources needed to achieve the results. In other words, giving someone a job but then "snoopervising" or hovering over them. Micromanaging is perhaps the most common form of "fake trust."

> *One of the most important ways to manifest integrity is to be loyal to those who are not present. In doing so, we build the trust of those who are present.*
> **Stephen R. Covey**

People tend to behave the way they're treated. If you want people to trust you, extend trust to them. Otherwise, you simply contribute to the downward spiral of distrust and suspicion that imposes low-trust taxes and pushes aside the opportunity for high-trust dividends.

The big idea here is that even if the superficial relationships in an organization are cordial and friendly, fragile trust under the surface can impose a number of expensive, low-trust taxes on overall performance.

Conversely, organizations that appreciate the real, economic effects of trust—and that explicitly and deliberately teach trust behaviors and build cultures of trust—enjoy the benefits of high-trust dividends.

Engaging people's heads, hearts, and hopes is all about relationships of mutual purpose, mutual respect, and mutual trust.

Our repertoire of trust behaviors must be the most explicit of our actions. Yes, we must talk the language of trust. But most importantly, we must clearly and deliberately walk the talk. In the absence of trust, all ambiguous behavior is viewed with suspicion and then, by definition, all behavior is ambiguous. Conversely, a trustworthy leader can enjoy a sort of halo effect. Even when people are unsure of the leader's plan, they are willing to cross the bridge. That's the power of trust. Earn it. Honor it.

TRUST – Both Character and Competence

My son-in-law Luke teaches at a major university, one that takes trust and honor very seriously. But even in this principle-centered environment, some students cheat. As a professor, Luke believes his role is to teach the whole person, not just course content. He's not interested in playing ethics cop. He simply wants to teach his students to engage in trustworthy behavior because it's the right thing to do.

At the beginning of each semester, Luke rolls out the curriculum for the entire term. This includes assigning term papers on a wide range of topics. These are not the typical "research" papers. These personal essays are intended to help develop the students' analytical skills—in short, teach them how to think for themselves.

Because many students are relatively untutored in such skills, there's a temptation to "borrow" someone else's thinking. In this Internet age, some ethics deficient websites actually sell and resell term papers to students who are either too timid or too lazy to do their own thinking. It's easier than ever to take short cuts. But most students who "take short cuts" don't actually buy someone else's work. They "borrow" someone else's work, sometimes in small, addictive doses. A question, of course, is where's the line between inadvertent plagiarism and deliberate thievery?

Luke uses a high-tech tool called Turnitin (see www.turnitin. com) that quickly identifies plagiarism. This compares student work against three massive, continuously updated databases of content: billions of web pages, plus more than 80,000 major newspapers, periodicals, journals, and books, plus more than 100 million student papers from around the world.

Luke's students submit their papers electronically. Then, before he even reads them, the papers are instantly analyzed for—shall we say—attribution problems. On Luke's computer screen appears an "originality report" that highlights matches and shows sources side-by-side. He may see, for example, that a paragraph from a student paper is a 53% match with a Wikipedia article, or a 47% match with an obscure journal, or a 64% match with a paper submitted by another student three years earlier at another university across the country.

Again, Luke is a professor of the fine arts, not a plagiarism cop playing a game of "Gotcha!" In his professor role he can expound with world class authority on a wide range of subjects. And, yes, he wants to teach his students about proper source citation in their term papers.

But he believes, and I agree, that his most important job is to mentor his students in the fine art of *trust*.

He does it by showing them that relying on their own thinking is not only honest, but their own thinking is often better that someone else's anyway.

He teaches them that "trust" is more than just a word in the school's honor code.

He teaches them that trust is one of the most important lessons they can ever learn, and the most valuable attribute they can ever cultivate.

He does it by appealing to their heads and hearts and hopes. Then his young charges come to realize that with confidence comes competence, and then competence begets more confidence.

Yes, trust can be taught.

TRUST-FRIENDLY SELF-ASSESSMENT

Instructions: *Read each statement and decide how accurately it describes your use of the **Trust-Friendly** behaviors described in this chapter:*

    a. Never or rarely engage in this behavior (0 points)

    b. Sometimes engage in this behavior (1 point)

    c. Regularly engage in this behavior (2 points)

    d. Always or almost always engage in this behavior (3 points)

Place the point value of your response choice beside each statement.

_____ I use "the language of trust" by being explicit about my commitments to others and being very clear about what I expect of them.

_____ I am very careful to treat people respectfully, regardless of their position or title.

_____ I honestly question my own motives to ensure that I'm doing the right thing(s) for the right reason(s).

_____ I give people feedback that is honest, specific, fair, and actionable.

_____ When I ask someone to do something (attend a meeting, produce a report, etc.), I make sure the task is not "fake work" —that it is explicitly linked to a clear strategy.

_____ Total Number of Points

Interpreting Your Scores

0-5: You may be paying some low-trust "taxes" that make your work more costly and more time-consuming than it needs to be. Remember: You can be regarded as personally "honest" (a character trait), yet still have considerable room to improve on the competencies associated with high trust.

6-10: You no doubt understand that trust has both character and competency components. Become even more aware of the power of language as you interact with people. Talk the "language of trust" by explicitly discussing how trust is important to you and what you're trying to do to earn and maintain the trust of others. Pay special attention to the Trust Builders.

11-15: Excellent. When it comes to trust issues, you apparently "get it." But take nothing for granted. While a reputation for high trust can take years to establish, that reputation can be shattered by a single act or by one moment of inattention.

Never doubt that a small group of thoughtful,
committed people can change the world.
Indeed, it is the only thing that ever has.
Margaret Mead

Individually, we are one drop. Together, we are
an ocean.
Ryunosuke Satoro

It's amazing how much people get done if they
do not worry about who gets the credit.
Ronald Reagan

A group is a bunch of people in an elevator. A
team is also a bunch of people in an elevator, but
the elevator is broken!
Bonnie Edelstein

Wild ducks make a lot of noise, but they also have
the good sense to fly in formation.
Maxwell Monroe Stone

Chapter

Team-Friendly: Finding Strength in Unity

We are most effective as a team when we compliment each other without embarrassment and disagree without fear.

No doubt about it, teamwork is more common as a buzzword than as an actual practice.

Without benefit of nuance, teamwork is one of those catch-all terms often extended as the magic elixir for the moment's most pressing execution issue. In a bid to boost performance, teamwork is touted in corporate vision statements, on wall posters, T-shirts, key chains, and coffee mugs. Teamwork is the subject of banal pep talks by goofy managers in TV sitcoms. Teamwork has been given a bad name by a world of bad practitioners.

But when we're strategic about putting both the team and the work into teamwork, beautiful things can happen.

The suspension bridge is one of the most impressive accomplishments of modern engineering. It begins as individual wires not much stronger than the ones you'd use to hang pictures on your living room wall. Spun together, these individual wires become strands. Then several of the larger strands are combined into a giant wire rope or cable that can bear thousands of tons of weight and safely cross enormous obstacles like canyons and rivers.

This same principle is part of the marvelous results that can be produced by genuine teamwork. Ordinary people can achieve extraordinary things when they discover strength in unity.

> *Interdependent people combine their own efforts with the efforts of others to achieve their greatest success.*
> **Stephen R. Covey**

In broaching the idea of unity I don't mean to imply that everyone must agree on every issue. In fact, civil *dis*agreement is often a hallmark of an outstanding team effort. But when smart people learn to think, talk, and trust in an environment of common purpose, it is truly amazing what they can accomplish.

Let's consider some ways to make this happen.

CREATING A TEAM-FRIENDLY ENVIRONMENT

Regardless of their composition, teams don't function in a vacuum. To help ensure success, it's critical to establish and maintain the right environment.

A team is most likely to be effective when five conditions exist:

(1) It's a *real team,* not just a team in name only,

(2) It has a *compelling purpose* that kindles the enthusiasm of its members,

(3) It has a *reinforcing framework* that promotes and enables rather than inhibits team achievement,

(4) It enjoys a *nurturing context,* not just lip service support, and

(5) Team members have ready access, individually and collectively, to *skillful coaching* on teamwork issues.

These five conditions are not simply nice-to-have ingredients. Just as a balanced diet, regular exercise, fresh air, and adequate rest are essential to good health, these conditions are imperative for team effectiveness.

Notice that the emphasis here is on *conditions* rather than on the leadership of a single individual. Leadership is of course important. But in the realm of teams, the primary responsibility of leaders is to create and maintain these five enabling conditions. These conditions, in turn, increase the likelihood that a team will conduct its work effectively and achieve its mission.

REAL TEAM

A collection of people is not necessarily a team. In our context, "team" is used to describe a carefully selected group of individuals who work interdependently, who are mutually supportive, and who bring out the best in each other as they strive to accomplish a set of specific goals.

With a real team, in other words, the whole is greater than the sum of the individual parts.

Even groups with individual superstars can miss their goals when they fail to work as a team. A 1986 headline in the *New York Times* read: "Jordan Scores 63 Points in Loss." This was an interesting sporting event, but the small print of the game statistics told the real story. In this NBA playoff game between the Chicago Bulls and the Boston Celtics, six Celtics players scored ten or more points, while only one Bulls player besides Michael Jordan scored more than ten. Clearly, this was an example of how a talented *team* outperformed an individual star.

"In the realm of teams, the primary responsibility of leaders is to create and maintain five enabling conditions."

Years ago in a New York recording studio I observed the music production for a television commercial. The first track recorded was of the keyboard specialist who laid down the basic structure and rhythm of the tune. Next came the guitarist. While listening to the keyboard track in his earphones, he added a rich bass underlay. Then the string musicians fleshed out the melody with violin and cello tones. The fourth track recorded was of the brass instruments that complemented the keyboard, guitar, and strings with just the right punctuation. Finally the percussionist enhanced it all with his combination of drums, cymbals, and delicate chimes. Then, within what seemed like only a few minutes, the sound editor combined all the elements into a cohesive whole. The award-winning finished product was a testament to teamwork. And what was especially amazing to me is that none of the musicians had been in the studio at the same time.

What made that accomplishment possible? Yes, each of the participants clearly had remarkable talent. But so did Michael Jordan's basketball pals in the earlier example. The difference in this instance is that all the musicians played like a real team. No individual outshone the others. Every player complemented and brought out the best in the others. No player dominated because all players contributed their important parts—no more and no less.

> *No member of a crew is praised for the rugged individuality of his rowing.*
> **Ralph Waldo Emerson**

Synergy is the key. It comes from the Greek *syn-ergos,* meaning working together. Again, the idea is to ensure that the whole is greater than the sum of the individual parts.

Composition makes a difference. People who assemble teams should keep in mind three important principles:

(1) *More is not necessarily better.* In a world of political correctness and related mindsets, a desire for inclusion often leads to the mistake of putting too many people on a team. Quality is more important than quantity. Assembling a smaller team with the right mix of capabilities is better than assembling a larger team just for the sake of satisfying various stakeholder groups. A large utility company was behind schedule on a major maintenance and repair outage. So management brought in busloads of "supplemental workers" in the hope of getting back on schedule. The project fell even further behind. The problem was not a lack of people. The real problem was that the work teams were poorly composed. In this case, assuming that more is automatically better was just as faulty as assuming that a

baby can be produced more quickly by assigning nine women to be pregnant for one month each. Overstaffing can have its own set of unintended consequences. Adding manpower to a late project may simply make it more late.

(2) *Mixing is often better than matching.* Some teams fail because their membership is too homogeneous. Selection of team members should focus on complementary skills and backgrounds, not on lock-step similarities that inevitably result in a shared view of reality and bland groupthink. I had the pleasure of serving on an advisory council in an organization that serves the global nuclear power industry. Our team included renowned scientists, corporate executives, specialists in safety issues, a senior director from a major investment firm, and me, a social scientist. We worked together beautifully, not because we had the same views, but because we had *different* views. We complemented each other. We added value to each other's perspectives. The whole was definitely more effective than the sum of the individual parts.

(3) *Interpersonal skills really do matter.* We've all met the guy who's great with a spreadsheet but who has the conversation skills of a hammer. Or the woman who's clearly an expert on some area of content but whose impatience with contrary views has earned her a reputation as someone to sidestep. The last thing you want is for team members to feel obliged to do "workarounds" to avoid uncomfortable confrontations. This is not to say that all team members must be candidates for the congeniality award.

> *"Assuming that more is automatically better was just as faulty as assuming that a baby can be produced more quickly by assigning nine women to be pregnant for one month each."*

Yes, we want friendliness and professionalism. Most of all, we want the collaboration and synergy that come from open and honest communication and challenging the status quo. This suggests use of the Think-Friendly, Talk-Friendly, and Trust-Friendly behaviors discussed earlier.

Context makes a difference. Teams have a greater chance for success when they operate in a context with three key features:

(1) *Clear tasks.* Some tasks are more suited to individual contribution than team collaboration. For example, drafting a mission statement is best done by an individual who understands the organization, its strategic function, and its relationship with important stakeholders. Assigning that task to a team produces the throw-in-every-buzzword-ever-imagined kind of double-talk that we've all seen in such documents. Tasks assigned to a team should clearly be tasks best undertaken by that particular team. And the tasks should be articulated and framed in a way that invites the most productive collaboration by team members (see the SMART Goals sidebar, on the Doctor Duncan website. Refer to page 179).

(2) *Clear boundaries.* Team members should know who is on the team and they should understand the role of each member. In addition, they should understand which activities are—and are not—within the purview of their work. This may seem obvious, but it's surprising how often that clarity is missing. Lack of clarity around team boundaries can lead to frustration, wasted effort, and disengagement.

> *"Lack of clarity around team boundaries can lead to frustration, wasted effort, and disengagement."*

(3) *Clear authority.* From the very beginning, team members should understand both the authority of their team sponsor(s) and the authority that they can exert themselves. Ambiguity on some things can actually help a team. For example, providing plenty of flexibility in the *how* of accomplishing certain tasks can help unleash creativity and ingenuity. But in the realm of

exercising authority, ambiguity should be avoided. Because accountability comes with authority, some team members may feel a bit of angst and timidity at first. But this usually subsides with time. An important thing is for team sponsors to support team decisions and to be extremely slow to withdraw authority once it's delegated. The last thing you want is to dampen enthusiasm and initiative. I, for one, much prefer to tame a tiger than motivate a turtle.

COMPELLING PURPOSE

Engaging people's heads, hearts, and hopes is all about rallying around a compelling purpose. The purpose must have meaning. The purpose must connect to values and principles that are important to the participants. The purpose must energize. And the purpose must be articulated in a way that clearly connects the dots between people's efforts and their accomplishment of worthy objectives.

Team Charter. The positive atmosphere surrounding the early days of a team's formation can fade quickly, so it's important to draft a *team charter*. This is a written document that clarifies the team's mission, the scope of its operations, its objectives, time frames, and consequences. Some charters are drafted by senior management and presented to (or imposed on) teams. In other cases, teams may create their own charters (beware the perils of writing by committee) and then present them for management approval. Either way, management's unwavering endorsement of a team's charter is a critical factor in providing the team the direction—and explicit protection and support—it needs to succeed. Team members need to know what management expects of them. Just as important, non-team members need to know what management expects of the team. A team charter can be regarded as a hunting license granted by the appropriate level of management. Occasionally, the team may need to show its license to *non*-team members, especially

"A team charter can be regarded as a hunting license granted by the appropriate level of management."

middle managers. That way, it's clear that the team has management's approval and authority to conduct its work.

This need not be—in fact, *should not be*—a complicated thing. Here are the main ingredients of a good team charter.

General Description

This is a brief and concise statement of the team's purpose. What problem is being addressed? Why is it important? What difference does it make? It should be articulated in clear terms. For instance, reduce operating cost. Or increase the effectiveness of a particular process. Or decrease the number of lost time accidents. Or make safety consciousness a more explicit part of employee behavior. Or improve the quality of pre-job briefings and other meetings to reinforce desired behaviors. Or increase market penetration of an existing product while successfully launching a new product. Or reduce the number of unwanted teen pregnancies in the community. Or involve more parents in activities of the local schools. Whatever the team's purpose, it should be something that is important enough to earn the interest and commitment of team members.

Background

Summarize the program or project the team is supporting or undertaking. How does the team fit into the organization? Who are the team's key stakeholders? What budget is available to the team and how will it be administered? What is the expected life cycle of the team?

Expected Results

In very specific, quantifiable terms, what is the team charged with accomplishing? (See the SMART Goals sidebar, accessible on the Doctor Duncan website. Refer to page 179.)

Team Composition

Exactly who will serve on the team? If not specified by name, team members should at least be described by position, role in the organization, or other pertinent demographics. If members will be rotated on and off the team, the rationale and protocol for those periodic changes should be specified.

Team Characteristics

This is where political correctness can get in the way. Rather than specify that the team should have a token member from every imaginable subset in the organization (blue-eyed, right-handed, Republican Volvo drivers), it's best to indicate the general profile of people who can contribute the most. For instance, these characteristics might include willingness to deal with big picture perspectives, credibility in challenging the status quo, skill in working as a team member, experience with a particular process, or ability to translate complicated elements into easy-to-understand terms. No team member is likely to have every single one of the ideal characteristics, but each person should possess several of those characteristics.

Boundaries

This section may be as simple as specifying that team members are expected to exemplify the organization's stated values and desired behaviors.

Team Empowerment

The team's authority should be clearly specified. If it is to operate only in an advisory capacity, that should be stated. If the team is authorized to spend resources and make and implement decisions that directly impact stakeholders, that should also be made clear. In this case, ambiguity is the enemy of effectiveness. Weasel words ("The team will carry out its own decisions unless instructed otherwise by senior management") guarantee execution paralysis.

Team Performance Assessment

Document key performance metrics needed to assess the team's success. How will that success be measured? Against what current metrics will the desired outcome be compared? People tend to treasure what they measure, so it's important to be very clear about what success "looks like" and how performance will be assessed.

Milestones and Schedules

These are important because they help team members calibrate their efforts. Milestones also help stakeholders maintain a realistic perspective on deliverables.

Statement of Sponsorship

As we'll explore in a later chapter, there are two basic kinds of sponsors—*authorizing* sponsor and *reinforcing* sponsor. Although they may in some cases be one and the same person, these are complementary but separate roles. The authorizing sponsor provides "permission" and resources (budget, time, equipment, etc.). The reinforcing sponsor provides

> *"A good charter explicitly describes management's support and commitment to the team."*

ongoing official sanction, explicit encouragement, and even cover fire when people outside the team take pot shots at the team's work. A good charter contains a section that explicitly describes management's support and commitment to the team. This is important because some team members may feel they are taking personal risk by joining the team. It's also an indication of the team's "hunting license" mentioned earlier.

Signature page

Each sponsor and each team member should sign the charter, agreeing to the contents and accepting accountability for the commitments laid out.

Means and Ends. Effective teams *are* effective because they navigate well. The first step of that navigation process is an explicit team charter. Another step is the use of SMART goals to focus the team's efforts. In addition, the team must have absolute clarity on means and ends.

Clear *direction* is an imperative component of a team's Compelling Purpose. But, one might ask, should direction be primarily about the team's ultimate purposes, or should direction also include specificity regarding the means available to the team in advancing those purposes? Conversely, should team direction be primarily about means, on the presumption that with the right resources a good team is bound to make good things happen?

> *To succeed as a team is to hold all of the members accountable for their expertise.*
> **Mitchell Caplan**

Consider the graphic below. In a simple way it helps answer those questions by illustrating the implications of specifying means and ends in various combinations.

Neither Ends nor Means. Specifying neither means nor ends is a one-way ticket to chaos and disorder. Why even form a team if the team has no goals and no way to accomplish them even if it did? On the surface, this may sound so silly that you're sure no one would ever launch a team without a sail, without a rudder, and without a destination. Yet many organizations have teams with that precise profile. That's a main cause behind so many window dressing "committees" that seem to result in no meaningful action

SPECIFIC ENDS?

	NO	YES
NO	Chaos, Disorder	Real Work, Engagement
YES	Boredom, Disengagement	Fake Work, Waste

SPECIFIC MEANS?

or deliverables. If a neither-ends-nor-means team does eventually decide on something to do, it's usually so bland that no team member could possibly be offended—or engaged. In your heart of hearts, ask yourself if that's going on in your organization.

Means but not Ends. Specifying means without specifying ends will guarantee boredom and disengagement. When my colleagues and I begin culture assessment work in an organization, one of the first things we request is a "passport" to wander freely around the premises to talk with people at random. For one thing, this helps ensure that our observations are not programmed by an overzealous manager who hopes to skew our conclusions. But most of all, random conversations can be very revealing.

> *"The stone mason who chips mindlessly at blocks of granite will never be as engaged in his work as the one who realizes he's building a great cathedral."*

We usually find people busy with work. After a brief introduction and exchange of pleasantries, we'll ask a person to explain to us how his activity relates to people down the hallway, across the shop floor, in other departments, or the ultimate end user. The extent to which people can articulate the precise linkage between their work and the desired outcomes or ends of their team can reveal volumes about team effectiveness. The stone mason who chips mindlessly at blocks of granite will never be as engaged in his work as the one who realizes he's building a great cathedral.

Both Ends and Means. Teams that operate in this quadrant can of course perform well. With a clear vision of the desired end state and a standardized check list of procedures, they can clip along nicely. But what happens when something goes wrong? What about some unexpected event that's way outside the imagination of the procedure writers? What then? The situation can quickly degenerate into something resembling the "I Love Lucy" scene where Lucy and her friend Ethel were working in a chocolate candy factory. All was going well until the conveyor belt suddenly accelerated. At first, Lucy and Ethel simply worked faster. But soon they were stuffing chocolates into their pockets, into their mouths, and inside their uniforms to prevent their supervisor from discovering they couldn't keep up.

This was a classic example of unintended consequences.

So, you might ask, what about teamwork situations where errors have the potential for catastrophic consequences? For example, wouldn't we want the team in a nuclear power plant control room to adhere inflexibly to both ends and means? Wouldn't we want the pilots in charge of our cross-country flight to stick rigidly to the procedure book?

Well, yes and no. First, remember that no set of procedures can anticipate every possible contingency.

A tank rupture forced the Apollo 13 mission to be aborted. Three astronauts found themselves 200,000 miles from earth, with limited ability to control their spacecraft, and with a rapidly depleting supply of oxygen. Only the ingenuity of the crew, flight controllers, and support personnel enabled the astronauts to return home safely. Most of that ingenuity was "off the books," not part of any standardized procedure.

When a flock of geese shut down the engines on a US Airways flight taking off from New York's LaGuardia Airport, pilot "Sully" Sullenberger didn't have the luxury of time to peruse all the procedure manuals. Calling upon his experience as a glider pilot, he safely landed his 67-ton airliner in the middle of the Hudson River.

Don't misunderstand. I'm not suggesting that people who operate nuclear power plants and airliners should be encouraged to "freelance" if they simply tire of following procedures. I'm merely saying that in addition to complying with the rules (which, after all, are written by human beings) it's sometimes necessary to respond in the moment with ingenuity and creativity. Too rigid adherence to a tight both-ends-and-means protocol can result in fake work and waste. Or in extreme cases, death.

> *"Too rigid adherence to a tight both-ends-and-means protocol can result in fake work and waste. Or in extreme cases, death."*

Ends but not Means. Stewardship delegation—conveying trust and accountability for a particular result—is ideally exercised with an ends-but-not-means approach. When ends are specified but means are not, team members are implicitly encouraged to draw upon their full repertoire of knowledge, experience, skill, and resourcefulness in brainstorming and executing solutions. Like the Apollo 13 support personnel—memorialized in the true-to-life Hollywood movie—team members operating with a clear end but an open-ended set of means can engage in mindful processing to create a workable solution.

Fortunately, the teamwork in which most of us are called on to participate is not nearly as urgent, danger-filled, and adrenaline-pumping as Apollo 13. Most of our teamwork involves such relatively mundane activities as corporate mergers and acquisitions, enhancing organizational culture, boosting performance, replacing software systems, or encouraging people to change their behavior. But the principle is the same. Most teams perform best when a compelling purpose (end) is specified and embraced while the methods (means) of addressing the purpose is left relatively open. Of course merely articulating a compelling purpose and then leaving team members entirely alone is not good leadership. As we will see in later chapters, there's much that leaders can and should do to support work teams along the way.

> *No man is an island, entire of itself; every man is a piece of the continent.*
>
> **John Donne**

REINFORCING FRAMEWORK

A dozen years ago, my wife and I built a beautiful family home near Kansas City, Missouri. Well, we didn't actually build it ourselves. We dreamed the dream and earned the money, then paid others to do the work. We bought a piece of heavily-wooded land in an upscale neighborhood. We drew up plans for our dream home, specifying everything from basic layout to details like lighting treatments, appliances, and electronics to accommodate current and future technology. We hired a home builder with a great reputation for quality. He, in turn, managed all the subcontractors. When our home was finished 18 months later, we invited all the subcontractors and their families to an open house. The excavation crew. The foundation crew. Frame carpenters. Plumbers. Electricians. Roofers. Drywallers. Trim carpenters. Cabinet makers. Painters. Stone masons. Landscapers. Our little move-in party reminded us of two important teamwork principles: (1) People really appreciate seeing the results of their efforts, and they especially like to understand how those results relate to the efforts of others in achieving a larger whole. (2) People work best in a framework—a "structure"—that clarifies and reinforces expected behaviors and, therefore, enables top performance and desired outcomes.

On the pages of this book, both of these principles may seem too obvious to mention. But in actual practice, they are often ignored. Explicitly showing appreciation for good work (during as well as after the work is accomplished) is more than social decency. It's a key to getting more of the same good performance. And helping people understand the context of their work—how it "fits" with other people's work and how it contributes to a bigger picture—is critical to engaging their heads, hearts, and hopes. The second principle may seem just as obvious but it's equally critical to performance success. People need structure. They need a reinforcing framework.

Our home builder runs a very tight ship. He is crystal clear about the quality he expects of his subcontractors. His standards are exacting. He honors budgets and operates on a rigorous schedule. He expects people to be where they say they will be at precisely the time they promise. He expects them to complete their work at the

> *He who wishes to secure the good of others, has already secured his own.*
> **Confucius**

highest quality and with no shortcuts. In return, he is steadfastly fair, he honors every commitment he makes, he keeps his workers busy, and he pays well and on time. Everyone wins—the builder, the subcontractors, and the home owner. It sounds like a simple enough formula. But, amazingly, many organizations try to achieve good results within operational frameworks that are ambiguous or bureaucratic or both.

Teamwork evolves in stages. Psychologist Bruce Tuckman uses the words *Forming, Storming, Norming,* and *Performing* to describe the developmental sequence of high performance that many teams follow. (He later added a fifth stage called *Adjourning.*) It's helpful to consider these phases of a team's development in the context of framework. Just as the conditions of a caterpillar's metamorphosis affect the butterfly's ability to fly, the conditions of a team's evolution affect its ability to produce desired results.

Forming

This is an orientation period when the team is assembled and the tasks are outlined. At this stage, team members tend to behave independently. Although goodwill may exist, they don't know each other well enough to trust each other unconditionally. At this stage people are typically polite and positive. (No one has offended anyone yet.) Both interpersonal and task boundaries are tested. Interdependencies between and among group members and pre-existing standards are explored. Some members may be anxious because it's still a bit unclear exactly what the team is expected to do. Other team members may be frustrated because they simply want to get on with the work. In fact, some members may be so impatient that they want to move directly to the Performing stage without passing through the first three stages. (This should be discouraged, and an explicit explanation of the need for the succeeding stages can be helpful at this point.) The Forming stage may be relatively short, perhaps only a single meeting at which people are introduced to one another and the team charter discussed.

> *"Just as the conditions of a caterpillar's metamorphosis affect the butterfly's ability to fly, the conditions of a team's evolution affect its ability to produce desired results."*

Storming

This is the stage when reality starts to set in. Roles are still getting clarified and there may be some conflict and polarization. The leader's authority may be challenged as others jockey for position. Some team members may feel overwhelmed by how much there is to do, or uncomfortable with the approach being taken. Some may question the team's goals. This is the stage when many teams fail. Even those who stick with it may feel they are on an emotional roller coaster as they try to focus on the task(s) at hand without the support of established processes or relationships with their usual group of colleagues. This is called the Storming stage for good reason. Some team members may resist the work itself. They may resist quality improvement approaches suggested by other members. They may argue even when they agree on the real issues. Behaviors may include defensiveness, competition, and choosing sides. There may be signs of disunity, tension, and jealousy. This is a time when your Talk-Friendly and Trust-Friendly skills can be extremely useful. This stage sometimes requires two or three meetings. But it must be done before the team is ready for the Norming stage.

Norming

As team members get to know and understand each other, resistance begins to be replaced by cohesiveness. Team members are ready for the Norming stage. By now, the team is developing a strong commitment to the team goal(s).

> *Coming together is a beginning.*
> *Keeping together is progress.*
> *Working together is success.*
> **Henry Ford**

Progress becomes more apparent. Team members start to agree on which behaviors are acceptable—and unacceptable—in the group. Behavior that is viewed as appropriate by the team is reinforced. Behavior that is seen as unacceptable or inappropriate is sanctioned. By sanctions I don't mean floggings in the company parking lot. A sanction may be no more than a word of caution or a raised eyebrow or head shake. But behavioral expectations should be made explicit. Team norms can be established in any of three ways: (1) they can be "imported" to the team by individual members, (2) they can evolve gradually as members try different behaviors, and (3) they can be deliberately established anew by the team.

> **Players win games.**
> **Teams win championships.**
> **Bill Taylor**

Norms can be about anything, although in practice they tend to focus on behaviors that members regard as especially important to the team's success. For example, if members decide they want a norm that people don't interrupt another person who's talking, or that everyone will arrive at meetings on time, all they need to do is obtain agreement on those norms. Even more important than good manners, however, are norms involving what work is done, how it is done, and how it supports the team's purpose. Otherwise, team members run the risk of investing in activity that, worthy though it may appear on the surface, doesn't really contribute to the accomplishment of strategic objectives. This is called fake work. As fresh

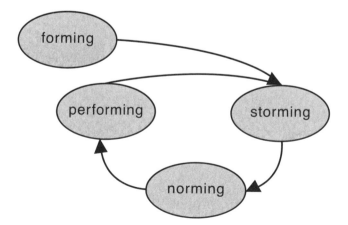

issues emerge, some teams oscillate back and forth between Storming and Norming. As the team matures, regressions become more rare. In the Norming stage, members become more adept at expressing criticism constructively, achieving harmony, and maintaining agree-upon ground rules while pursuing team goals.

Performing

When a team reaches the Performing stage, members are enjoying the benefits of interdependency (what teamwork is all about), and they are less likely to revert to the Storming stage. Roles become more flexible and functional. In the Performing stage, the connection between hard work and progress toward the goal(s) becomes more clear than ever. The team is now an effective, cohesive unit. Group energy is channeled into the task(s). Decision making is collaborative. Dissent is expected and encouraged because team members have developed good levels of mutual trust and respect. Team activity has definite traction. This is clearly a time of high performance.

Adjourning

This final stage of a team's evolution is a good time to celebrate its achievements. After all, you may work with some of these people again. Engagement is much easier with people who view their past experience positively. Therefore, as you work to develop change capacity and change readiness in your organization, it becomes doubly important to ensure that team activity has a clear ending that appropriately connects the team's efforts with outcomes.

> *We must all hang together, or assuredly, we shall all hang separately.*
> **Benjamin Franklin**

Obviously, this teaming process model is not necessarily linear and is not set in concrete. Team members may return to an earlier stage if they experience a significant change. For example, when goals are modified or new members come on board, the team may briefly revisit the Storming and Norming stages. We should be careful not to let a nice turn of phrase lead to laziness on the part of practitioners and trainers. This model is no less and no more than a good metaphor or image to help us make sense of the teaming phenomenon we observe and try to orchestrate.

NURTURING CONTEXT – MORE THAN MERE "PERMISSION"

Teams don't operate in an organizational vacuum. Just as a garden plant requires nurturing soil, water, fresh air, and sunlight, a team requires a context that enables it to thrive and produce. Mere "permission" to form a team is not enough. Appreciation is not enough. Sympathy is not enough. Even encourage-

> *"Even a well-designed team cannot thrive in an unsupportive context."*

ment and cooperation are not enough. A team needs to be defended from the slings and arrows of the naysayers. It needs to be shielded from the grenades lobbed by those who wish to sabotage the team's mission. It needs a safe harbor from the bureaucrats who want to hamstring the team in endless procedures and paperwork. In short, the team needs explicit reinforcement from systems and processes and conspicuous support from credible leaders.

Even a well-designed team cannot thrive in an unsupportive context. Conversely, even the most supportive environment can't enable a fundamentally flawed team to produce good results. This reaffirms the importance of establishing teams with crystal clear purpose, direction, and structure.

Reward System. In later chapters we'll talk more about the importance of meaningful reward systems. But suffice it to say here that teams need recognition and reinforcement explicitly linked to excellent *team* performance. Recognition of good team performance encourages team members to think and behave from a platform of "we," "us," and "ours" rather than "I," "me," and "mine." In addition, team recognition demonstrates that the organization cares enough about the team's performance to invest resources to reward what it accomplishes.

This principle of contingent reward seems fairly simple, but it's amazing how many organizations just don't get it. In a previous chapter I mentioned my consulting work for a national company, a leader in the retail jewelry business. Every meeting I observed in that company featured high testosterone rah rah about the importance of teamwork. Posters and slogans extolling the virtue of teamwork were everywhere, even in the company restrooms. But the reward systems —focused almost exclusively on individual performance—sent a very different message. At the company's annual sales conference, a mammoth extravaganza at Disney World, teamwork was exalted in music, skits, speeches, on shirts, on hats, and on every trinket imaginable. Then it was time to present awards for sales performance. Virtually every presentation was focused on *individual* achievement. Even the awards that purported to acknowledge teamwork were really about individuals because they recognized stores that had two or more outstanding individual performers.

> *The way a team plays as a whole determines its success. You may have the greatest bunch of individual stars in the world, but if they don't play together, the club won't be worth a dime.*
>
> **Babe Ruth**

I tried and tried to point out this mixed message to senior management. But they wouldn't listen. It took a serious hit (literally) to get their attention. One of the company's southern California stores was a leader in overall sales. A couple of its sales people, both perennial top performers, obviously paid no heed to the teamwork mantra because they were rewarded on their individual performance. Teamwork was only the slogan. Fierce competition was the reality. Then one day one of the guys said to the other, "If you step between me and a customer one more time, I'll deck you." It happened. Two well-dressed salesmen punched it out in full view of customers. When both men were fired, I said to the company president, "Who won on that deal? Neither salesman won. The store certainly didn't win. The company didn't win." Only then did my warning about mixed messages get through. The unintended consequence of rewarding individuals while touting teamwork was finally clear.

For the sake of team performance, it's critical that rewards are clearly contingent on what the *team* accomplishes. But while providing rewards that are contingent on desired team performance is important, it's not enough. Team members must clearly understand the outcomes that are wanted and that will be rewarded. They must have confidence in the metrics used to measure performance. They must have genuine influence on the attainment of team goals. And they must believe that their aggregate contributions directly produce the results that trigger the rewards. When these conditions are met, team members see the connection between their collective effort and the available rewards.[1]

Information System. An old joke tells of an airline pilot who gets on the intercom and announces to the passengers: "Ladies and gentlemen, I have bad news and good news. The bad news is that all our instrumentation is out. We don't know how high we are or even what direction we're flying. But the good news is that we have a strong tailwind and we're making very good time." Accurate and timely information is critical to both team planning and team execution.

One summer during my university days I worked in the sliced bacon department of a large meat packing plant. My team worked the night shift. We rarely saw a supervisor. Our job was simple. When the boxes of sliced bacon came down the circular slide from the packaging team upstairs, we stacked the boxes on wooden pallets. Then we used a forklift to take the pallets down the hallway to a refrigerated storage room. This was fairly straightforward and hassle free. Trouble was, we had no way of communicating with the upstairs packaging team. For reasons we never understood, the packagers sent loads of product our way at a totally unpredictable pace. For a period of time, boxes would come down the slide at the very manageable rate of about 15 per minute. Then production would stop unexpectedly, only to lurch back into action at the breakneck speed of 30 to 40 boxes per minute. This

> *We are most effective as a team when we complement each other without embarrassment and disagree without fear.*
> **Unknown**

would inevitably jam the process and damage the product. An "information system" as simple as a bell would have helped, but we had nothing. It made excellent performance virtually impossible.

To produce sustainable top performance, a team needs clear, accurate, and timely information regarding:

(1) Desired outcomes.

(2) Requirements of tasks that will produce the desired outcomes.

(3) Organizational strategies, along with details on how the team "fits" into those strategies and what's expected of it.

(5) Details on interdependencies—how the team is expected to interact and collaborate with other work groups to accomplish organizational goals. (This helps people avoid the silo mentality that plagues so many organizations.)

(5) Metrics for measuring the team's performance. (See the SMART Goals sidebar, accessible on the Doctor Duncan website. Refer to page 179.)

(6) Budgets and other resources (time, space, equipment, staff, etc.) available to the team.

It is absolutely imperative that information available to the team is trustworthy. That includes current data as well as forecasts. And team members should be intimately involved in deciding what information is really needed.

Because information is such a precious and powerful commodity, some short-sighted people tend to hoard it, apparently hoping to parcel it out in carefully calibrated bits to reinforce their own position or stature. Information withholding as a power tool is fatal to good performance, not to mention a violation of every principle of good teamwork. That behavior should be forbidden. Of course information regarding proprietary processes and trade secrets should be held close to prevent discovery by competitors. But most information can be shared with no real risk. Remember the adage: Keep people in the dark, and they'll go where it's light.[2]

> *"It is absolutely imperative that information available to the team is trustworthy."*

The opposite extreme should also be avoided. Too much information can divert attention from the most critical tasks and even result in fake work. As any farmer can tell you, a flood is just as bad as a drought.

Training and Development. In today's high performing organization, competency is no longer defined only in terms of individual capabilities. It also includes the ability to function effectively—indeed, to *thrive*—with other parts of the team.

People need the capacity to solve problems in fresh and creative ways. They need the curiosity that inspires smart questions. They need to challenge their own conclusions so their stories don't masquerade as facts.

> *You don't get harmony when everybody sings the same note.*
> **Doug Floyd**

And they need to connect the dots that outline root causes not previously noticed. That's why we emphasize Think-Friendly skills and behaviors.

People need to challenge the status quo, resolve conflicts, inquire to discover, advocate respectfully, and make it safe for others to speak up in risky situations. That's why we emphasize Talk-Friendly skills and behaviors.

People need to help establish and maintain a working atmosphere in which team members interact openly and honestly, exercise influence rather than authority, coach with clarity, and exchange clear and helpful feedback. That's why we emphasize Trust-Friendly skills and behaviors.

Team-Friendly skills and behaviors deserve to be emphasized, too. In addition to day-to-day reinforcement (see Chapter 13, "Stay on Message"), the skills and behaviors so critical to sustainable change and employee engagement should be accentuated in targeted training and development. As stated earlier, teams (and individuals) don't operate in a vacuum. And targeted training and development must be part of the nurturing context that enables people to produce top results consistently. This can't be the flavor-of-the-month variety. It can't be a let's-throw-stuff-up-against-the-wall-and-see-if-anything-sticks approach. It should be strategically targeted to the needs of the organization and the performance outcomes it's seeking.

Here's an example. South Texas Project (STP) is a world-class nuclear power plant on the Gulf of Mexico near Bay City, Texas. Several years ago the station had a number of performance issues. Many of those issues were related to open and honest communication, especially the ability to challenge a co-worker's performance. Duncan Worldwide introduced a training program emphasizing dialogue skills: how to identify conversations that are at the root of safety issues, how to stay focused on issues that really matter, how to identify the early warning signs that a conversation is headed in a wrong direction, how to make it safe to speak up without fear of retaliation, etc. I delivered some training workshops myself, then I certified more than two dozen internal trainers to take the same training to the remainder of the STP workforce. These certified trainers included several members of the senior management team. One of those was Ed Halpin, STP's president and chief executive officer. Ed didn't make only a brief cameo appearance in the training sessions. He understood the power of modeling leadership behaviors, and he personally facilitated several of the two-day dialogue workshops each year. In addition, STP people reinforce the workshop skills at every opportunity in their day-to-day work—during pre-job briefings, in

> *In teamwork, silence isn't golden, it's deadly.*
> **Mark Sanborn**

newsletters and videos, in special training scenarios in the workplace, at their plan of the day meetings, and in other venues. All of this was designed to ensure that STP people consistently use the skills and behaviors they learned in the workshops. The result? Since rolling out the training, STP has set numerous industry benchmarks for sustained excellence and performance, ranging from top safety records to the highest production reliability measure of any multi-unit nuclear power plant in the United States. Targeted training—and reinforcement—really can help smart people work smarter.

Interdependencies. The "I Love Lucy" chocolate candy factory video mentioned earlier is a funny—though painfully realistic—example of what happens when interdependencies are ignored. In many organizations we see the effects of a silo mentality among the workers. That's when workers in one department fail to connect the dots between their work and that of people in adjoining departments. It doesn't matter if the failure is deliberate or inadvertent. The negative effects are the same: duplication of effort, wasted resources, missed opportunity, fake work.[3]

In a global engineering firm we've seen one department actually bidding against another department for a client project. The competition was clearly not good for the engineering firm, but the client didn't win either. If the two departments had pooled their resources and ingenuity their collaboration would no doubt have produced good synergy and a superior proposal.

At many nuclear power plants we see poor collaboration between maintenance and operations personnel. In consumer products companies we often see poor teamwork between product development and marketing people. Similar fragmentation is common in the health care industry, in financial services, in technology, and in a range of other businesses. The costs are always high, measured in time, money, opportunity, and the psychic energy invested in us-against-them thinking.

Interdependency is not just about "connections," though connections are part of the formula. Interdependency is about mutual reliance and overlapping interests.

Here's an example from nature. On the African savannah, elephants can be seen uprooting and pushing over trees. This may seem destructive, unless one understands the balance, harmony, synergy, and interdependence of the ecosystem:

- In addition to the elephant, the savannah provides habitat for bison, leopards, monkeys, zebra, giraffe, the rhinoceros, many species of birds, and of course the iconic lion.
- Fallen trees provide nourishment for giraffe that can't reach the taller branches, food for other animals that eat the exposed roots, protection for small birds, and shelter for life-sustaining grasses.
- The elephant eats about 300 kilograms (600 pounds) of food each day, some of which comes from the fallen trees.
- Elephant dung is only 40% digested and becomes food for other animals in the ecosystem.

- The tiny dung beetle, one of the less obvious players in this complex food chain, lays its eggs inside the elephant dung. As the dung is rolled across the ground by the beetle, moist seeds are spread along the route.
- The beetle deposits the dung and its eggs in a hole, fertilizing the savannah.
- The result is new growth of trees and other vegetation.

When establishing and developing a team, it's critical that team members consider entire systems rather than just an isolated snapshot of their own operation. Teams should consider swapping members occasionally and benchmarking each other's best practices. They should discuss outputs, compare notes on processes and schedules, and welcome challenging questions about the work they do. Such cross-pollination not only builds camaraderie, but it increases appreciation for the synergy that enables teams to excel in an interdependent environment.

SKILLED COACHING – USING THE GROW MODEL

More than forty years and forty pounds ago I was a high school wrestler. We had an excellent coach, a former Marine drill instructor who knew the importance of conditioning and practice. Most importantly, he understood that wrestling is both an individual and a team effort. If an individual wrestler wins a match, he does it on his own. There's no one else on the mat to take credit or blame for his performance. But the team as a whole succeeds only in proportion to the aggregate individual performances of the team members. So our coach worked us hard to hone our individual skills *and* to enable us to bring out the best in each other. After

> **The nice thing about teamwork is that you always have others on your side.**
> **Margaret Carty**

all, an individual wrestler's success is not just about his six minutes on the mat during a match. His success is mostly a product of endless hours of exhaustingly repetitive practice with his teammates.

In an organizational team setting, an excellent coaching framework is the GROW model popularized by Sir John Whitmore, a race

GOALS
What do you want?

car champion and now a performance coach in the United Kingdom. The version of the model presented here is used by our colleague John Stoker in his breakthrough work with dialogue skills.

Remember: if you're a team leader, your primary responsibility is to help establish and maintain conditions that facilitate team success. If you're a team coach, your responsibility is the same. You'll work with individual performance issues, with a constant focus on ensuring that the whole is greater than the sum of individual efforts.

Here's a quick breakdown of the GROW model.

- Goal – What do you want to accomplish? How will you know if and when you've reached your goal? How will you know the problem has been solved?
- Reality – What is the current situation? What's the effect of that? What's missing? What barriers exist? What's the distance between where you are and where you want to be?
- Options – What ideas, resources, or courses of action are available to you? What are the pros and cons of each option? What alternatives may you consider? What criteria should you use in judging options? What if this or that constraint were removed?
- What's Next? – What are your next steps? When will you start? What will you do to overcome barriers? How will you measure progress?

The value of the GROW model is that it provides a simple, effective, and structured methodology for setting goals and solving problems. Some versions of the model have the 'O' representing Obstacles. Other versions have the 'W' standing for Way Forward or Wrap-up. Nonetheless, the GROW model can be especially helpful as a coaching framework.

A great way to "test drive" the GROW model is using it to address your own challenges and issues. When you're "stuck" with something, use the model to coach yourself. This gives you practical experience in asking helpful questions. Practice with open-ended questions. Asking "What effect did that have?" is more useful than asking "Did that cause a problem?"

> *It is better to have one person working with you than three people working for you.*
> **Dwight D. Eisenhower**

Consider the context of working with a team. As we suggested in the chapter on Think-Friendly skills, asking smart questions helps people expand their problem-solving capacity. Smart questions encourage people to challenge their own and each others' thinking. Smart questions help people make the necessary connections to achieve good results. A good coach can facilitate this with the GROW model.

The GROW model works because it helps ensure that there's nothing lurking at the unconscious level to prevent the team from setting and stretching for its goals. It helps check whether the goals mesh with the team's purpose and capacity, and highlights which behaviors and practices are necessary for success.

Although the GROW model is presented sequentially here, in actual practice it's often a much less linear process. For instance, some teams may wish to begin with the Reality step to gain early clarity around the gap between the current situation and desired outcomes.

It would be helpful here to debunk some common myths about coaching.

Myth #1: Coaches must be subject matter experts. Use the GROW model as a map, just as you would in planning an important journey. The truth about good coaching is that the coach doesn't have to be more expert than the performers (team members) in order to be able to help them. Most performance issues have less to do with the performers not knowing what to do and much more about their doing more consistently what they already know. Many team players already have the knowledge they need, but there's a gap between what they know and what they're doing. A coach can help them see, and then close, the know/do gap.

Myth #2: Coaching is too time-consuming. My grandfather used to say "If you don't have time to do it right, you don't have time to do it over." Thoughtful coaching can help people correct mistakes or even catch them before they happen. Of course the goal is to help people take responsibility for developing solutions themselves. Good coaching does take time, but not nearly as much time as the fake work and inertia that entrap some teams.

Myth #3: Coaching is only for "problem people." The best musicians and athletes in the world have coaches. The same can be said for people in the business world. Coaching is for anyone who seriously wants to do better, go further, have a greater impact.

Myth #4: Coaching is just telling people what they want to hear. In reality, effective coaching is all about getting results. Depending on the situation, a good coach may be "soft," or provocative, or even confrontational. A good coach may offer suggestions, or solicit solutions from the team member(s). The job of a good coach is to nudge people out of their comfort zones toward increasingly improved performance. All of the Think-Friendly, Talk-Friendly, and Trust-Friendly skills discussed earlier are critical ingredients in the coach's behavior.

Effective teamwork is not just a nice-to-have element in change efforts. It's a DBM—a double-barreled must. If you're serious about change, teamwork is not an option. Independence and turf protection are the absolute antithesis of a Change-Friendly environment. As we're reminded in the Japanese proverb, "a single arrow is easily broken, but not ten in a bundle."

TEAM-FRIENDLY SELF-ASSESSMENT

Instructions: *Read each statement and decide how accurately it describes your organization's use of the **Team-Friendly** behaviors described in this chapter:*

     a. We never or rarely engage in this behavior (0 points)
     b. We sometimes engage in this behavior (1 point)
     c. We regularly engage in this behavior (2 points)
     d. We always or almost always engage in this behavior (3 points)

Place the point value of your response choice beside each statement.

_____   The teams in my organization operate with team charters that clearly outline important issues like purpose, tasks, boundaries, tasks, authority, and expected results.

_____   Our teams are organized with an emphasis on needed skills and varied viewpoints rather than just selecting team members on the basis of political correctness (ensuring that every demographic subgroup is "represented").

_____   To achieve specified ends (goals, objectives, targets), our teams are given reasonable flexibility regarding means (how to do it).

_____   In my organization, we emphasize understanding interdependencies—how each team affects and is affected by the efforts of others.

_____   In my organization, we provide coaching that's specifically aimed at improving teamwork.

_____   Total Number of Points

Interpreting Your Scores

0-5:   There's a good chance that the teams in your organization are little more than clusters of people with only minimal direction and influence. This can be worse than having no teams at all because it gives the superficial illusion of teamwork while producing no real results.

6-10: Your organization is headed in the right direction on teamwork issues, but you're still not enjoying the full benefits of synergy. Make sure each team has its own charter that's been mindfully drafted. Make sure your teams have plenty of clarity on both ends and means.

11-15: Excellent. Overall, your organization is doing a good job in its use of teams. Re-read this chapter and make sure your organization is adhering to the key principles and behaviors found in high-performing teams. Also, double check to ensure that the training you offer is specifically designed to strengthen your teams.

---

[1] It should be emphasized that effective "rewards" are not always monetary. For ideas on meaningful non-monetary rewards, see Chapter 12, "Ford the Streams." For excellent insights into positive reinforcement, see the works of Aubrey C. Daniels. Especially note *Bringing Out the Best in People* (New York: McGraw-Hill, 1999); *Other People's Habits* (New York: McGraw-Hill, 2001); and *Oops!* (Atlanta: Performance Management Publications, 2009).

[2] Open-Book Management (OBM) is one of the best communication approaches that organizations can adopt for dramatic improvement of productivity (and trust). Despite being around for many years and being enormously successful in many public and private sector organizations, OBM has not really achieved the popularity it deserves. The OBM concept is simple. Employees are privy to financial objectives and production data, then are trusted to manage the business "by the numbers." In practice, OBM often requires significant changes in the "trust behaviors" displayed in an organization. But it can be done, and it often pays huge dividends in employee engagement and operational results. For more information on OBM, see Jack Stack, *The Great Game of Business* (New York: Broadway Business, 1994); Jack Stack, *A Stake in the Outcome: Building a Culture of Ownership for the Long-Term Success of Your Business* (New York: Broadway Business: 2003); John Case, *Open-Book Experience: Lessons from over 100 Companies Who Successfully Transformed Themselves* (New York: Perseus, 1999); Thomas J. McCoy, *Creating an 'Open-Book' Organization: Where Employees Think & Act Like Business Partners* (New York: Amacom, 1996).

[3] "Silo mentality" is a common phenomenon. But the phrase implies a more benign condition than we sometimes see. "Silo mentality" can conjure up bucolic images of farmers choosing to live independent lives. If left unchecked in an organization, this lack of interdependence can degrade into aggressive politics and turf-protection. An employee in one company we examined put it this way: "Here we have a 'castle mentality.' In defending their castles, people lock the gates, surround themselves with alligator-infested motes, sling rocks and arrows at their enemies, and pour scalding oil over the wall at the invading armies."

Section TWO

BONUS•POINTS

To enrich your use of the Change-Friendly methodology, check out our **Bonus Point** material after reading each section of this book. Additional material is posted on the Doctor Duncan website.

All the material is free to readers of the book (you!), and we'll be adding to it periodically. The Bonus Point material includes thought pieces, White Papers, free diagnostic tools, interviews, videos, and other items.

To access the Bonus Points, simply scan this QR code with your smart phone and let your browser take you directly to the content. Alternatively, go to www.DoctorDuncan.com/BonusPoints

See you there!

◄ Smart Phone Link
DoctorDuncan.com/BonusPoints

Change-Friendly Leadership Model

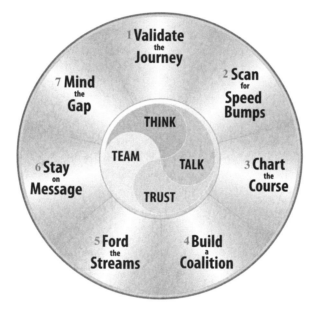

SECTION

THREE

Change Plain and Simple

The problem with many change tools is that they are "schizo-frantic." They involve too many moving parts and make too much noise. They disrupt everything in sight. As weapons of mass distraction, they sometimes scare more than inspire, confuse more than comfort. They can be self-fulfilling prophecies, producing exactly the turmoil that many people associate with change.

This is not to suggest that change is easy or that change processes must be geared to the kindergartner. It's just to say that when change is needed, most people prefer the path to be as straightforward as possible. No academic jargon. No convoluted models. No jumping through unnecessary hoops. Just something that works. Plain and simple, thank you very much.

Managing change does not mean a narrow, lock-step approach that controls all the variables. It means setting boundaries around the chaos, challenging the status quo, and providing a deliberate and proactive process for getting from point A to point B and beyond.

That's where the Change-Friendly protocol can help. Rather than merely responding to change as it hits us in the face, the smartest and most sure way of reaching the future state we desire is to take deliberate leadership over the *dynamics* associated with the change. This must include:

- Assessing the organizational, personal, and cultural barriers to change, transition, and implementation.

- Identifying work-life disruptions that are the consequences of strategic change.
- Developing strategies and tactics to minimize anticipated barriers to change.
- Developing strategies and tactics to leverage key strengths to increase readiness and capacity for change.

The bottom line, of course, is to accelerate the achievement of critical business goals with fewer resources and fewer human casualties. In short, we must save time, save money, and help our people avoid burnout. That requires engaging their heads, hearts, and hopes.

As mentioned in an earlier chapter, it's not so much that people resist change *per se*. It's that we resist the stress that change often produces.

People can learn to welcome change, but the primary emphasis must be on the human dynamics of change. Effective change is not just about spreadsheets and project charts. It's about winning the genuine commitment of real people. Remember: you can rent a person's back and hands, but you must earn his head and heart.

For change to succeed, the emotional and behavioral aspects must be addressed as thoroughly as the operations issues. Change is inherently and inescapably an emotional human process.

Successful promoters of change are carefully attuned to the human elements of their operations. They don't focus only on building a "business case" for action. They also build a strong "psychological case" for action. They clarify the linkages between the needs of their people and the needs of the organization. They provide a sense of psychological ownership. This is not touchy-feely stuff. It's smart business. Besides, aligning people with purpose is a hallmark of great leadership.

Change can be exhilarating and spawn the best work of a lifetime. Organizations that develop a competence for dealing with change have a sustainable competitive advantage. Effective change rarely happens by chance. It's deliberate, it's strategic, and it's carefully orchestrated.

The Change-Friendly protocol provides the framework. Based on the foundational behaviors of the Four Ts discussed in previous chapters, the framework's seven mutually-reinforcing action steps bring order to the tactics required for successful change. It's plain and simple.

The Change-Friendly protocol is *not* intended for use in a rigid, lock-step, no-flexibility-allowed way. That wouldn't be very friendly, would it?

The Change-Friendly protocol *is* designed to help you navigate successfully along the sometimes bumpy road of change.

At the hub of this model are the Four Ts. The way you think, talk, trust, and team should inform everything you do to engage people with the change you champion. The seven steps are presented in a logical order, but this does not mean there's no room for variation. The whole process is rather fluid. For example, before you Validate the Journey doesn't it make sense to at least begin to Scan for Speed Bumps to determine how to make the change appealing? And wouldn't you start to Build a Coalition (including the recruitment of sponsors) from the very beginning? And of course the Stay on Message principles will help you at every step along the way. You get the idea.

The Change-Friendly Leadership Model is your servant, not your master. As your tool, think of it as a combination compass and map.

Glance is the enemy of vision.
Ezra Pound

There is surely nothing quite so useless as doing with great efficiency what should not be done at all.
Peter Drucker

Behold the turtle. He makes progress only when he sticks his neck out.
James Bryant Conant

It is more important to know where you are going than to get there quickly. Do not mistake activity for achievement.
Mabel Newcomber

Chapter

Step 1:
Validate the Journey

Order people around and you probably won't like the result. Appeal to their agenda and you can work wonders.

Stop me if you've heard this one. Phil was general manager of a production plant for a large manufacturing company. He was getting pressure from the home office to boost productivity while lowering costs. So he decided to challenge his troops to increase output by 10% and reduce expenditures by 5%. He thought these were rather modest targets, but he was willing to start out small and then go for bigger targets later. With great fanfare, Phil announced his goals at an all-employee meeting. His assistants passed out T-shirts with the company logo on the front and "10/5, no problem" printed on the back. The slogan soon appeared on posters in the employee cafeteria, as well as on computer screen savers.

Okay, you know exactly where this story is going. That's right, Phil's goals were not met. In fact, despite all the high-testosterone sloganeering, twelve months later production had improved only a percentage point, and costs weren't reduced at all.

It's not that Phil's people weren't capable. And it's not that anyone deliberately sabotaged the effort. It's just that Phil set up the perfect conditions for failure. He tried to practice change-by-announcement. He told people what he wanted, but neglected to involve them in the *what, why, how*, and *when* of the effort. He simply announced his goals, then played the role of cheerleader. His only nod to justification was offering some industry data to illustrate the need to be more efficient to maintain competitiveness. He also mentioned that the big bosses at headquarters wanted it done.

Phil was absolutely well-intentioned. But he was oblivious to the need to engage people's heads, hearts, and hopes. He belly flopped.

When confronted with change, most people tune in to their favorite internal radio station: WIIFM—What's In It For Me? That's not to suggest that most people are selfish. It's simply a fact that *personal context* is usually the first filter we use to evaluate our environment. It's especially true when we're asked to participate in some sort of change.

Change is movement *away* from the Present. Change is movement *through* the Neutral Zone, a place that's neither completely old nor completely new. And change is movement *toward* a Future that promises not just something different but, hopefully, something better.

What we call the Present was never really firm. It was in a constant state of tension between the need to remain stable and the need to respond to the inevitable adjustments of time and circumstance.

Let's say your organization once regarded inventory as a good thing to have around. Your accountants placed inventory in the asset column on the balance sheet. Then, as your business grew, it cost more and more to maintain and store inventory. So

> *"When confronted with change, most people tune in to their favorite internal radio station: WIIFM— What's In It For Me?"*

you figured out a way to buy or produce inventory to ship to your customers "just in time." A change was spawned. Years of relative stability spilled into the chaos of the Neutral Zone.

The Neutral Zone is the transition from the Present to the Future. In the Neutral Zone, people are anything but indifferent. They may feel unsafe, confused, uncertain, or all of the above. This is the price of change. In fact, these very characteristics are the Neutral Zone's primary value. The Neutral Zone can have very wide boundaries, and people need the ability to move freely and creatively within those boundaries. Flexibility enables experimentation, testing, and discovery. Reducing inventory may have produced other changes, from adjustments in work processes to new delivery methods to more efficient billing practices.

> *Let us have integrity and not write checks with our tongues which our conduct cannot cash.*
> **John Adams**

A discrete change rarely occurs in a vacuum. Because the Future is not absolutely firm and fixed (don't delude yourself into assuming otherwise), simply traveling through the Neutral Zone will help alter and redefine the Future.

Change is not what troubles most people. What gives them the greatest heartburn is the *transition* from the Present to the Future. *Change* is situational: the new team roles, the new manager, the new procedure, the new way of operating. *Transition* is the psychological rite of passage during which people come to terms with the new situation (the *change*).

Your challenge is to Validate the Journey.

Every change begins with an ending. People look at the Present and try to compare it to the Future by asking countless questions: What am I losing? Where are we headed? What will the new place look like? How will it be different from what I have now? What about the work flow? Who will be my teammates? What will be the expectations for my contribution? What performance metrics will be used?

In other words, What's In It For Me?

When you ask people to go from where they are to someplace else, your task is to create a vision they can understand and will be willing to embrace. Defining the Future with absolute, irrevocable certainty is rarely possible. But you should try to paint a picture of it with as much clarity as is practical.

Does the change involve creating a new team? Who will be the team leader? Who will be the other team members? What will be the team's tasks and authority?

Does the change involve a new product or service? How will it differ from previous offerings? How will it be positioned with customers? What support will the marketing and distribution people provide?

Does the change involve something amorphous like "better communication"? If so, clarity is especially important. One person may define "better communication" in terms of open and honest dialogue and breaking down inter-departmental silos, while another may think only in terms of getting a new carrier for his cell phone service.

In defining the Future, and the transition(s) required to get there, six steps are especially critical:

(1) Take Off the Blinders. A common ingredient in failed change efforts is that the people advocating the change were blind to any viewpoint other than their own. Be thorough with your due diligence. Ensure that you gather comprehensive data on the change you want to promote. Be careful not to inadvertently (or deliberately) filter out information that contradicts your position. Acknowledging and respecting contrary views will strengthen your credibility. Pretending that contrary views don't exist will make you come across as an ill-informed dunce, or worse.

(2) Tend to the CAST of Characters. Many people in many roles will be affected by and instrumental in the change you're promoting. It's important to tend to their needs throughout the change journey. Here's your CAST of Characters:

- *Champions.* These are people who want the change and work to gain commitment and resources for it.
- *Agents.* They implement the change.
- *Sponsors.* They authorize, legitimize, and demonstrate ownership for the change. Sponsors come in at least two varieties. They possess sufficient organizational power and/or influence to either initiate commitment of resources (Authorizing Sponsor) or they promote the change at the "local" level (Reinforcing Sponsor).
- *Targets.* They are called on to alter their behavior, emotions, and practices. (During the change process, everyone is a Target at one time or another.)

People in different roles have different needs. Staying aware of those roles will help you with your messaging, coalition building, and every other aspect of your change work.

(3) Remember Context. People in the boardroom live in a different world from the folks on the shop floor. That's not at all to suggest that one group is more or less intelligent or valuable than another. It's merely to say that *frame of reference* must always be considered. Senior managers are likely focused on big picture issues like market share and competitive advantage. Mid-level managers and supervisors may focus on the meaning of the change for their budgets and span of control. Line workers will want to know how the change will affect their schedules, their work processes, and the availability of tools and other resources. Some concerns about issues like job opportunity and pay are of course universal. Just remember to package your message in audience-appropriate language, analogies, and examples that allow people to relate.

(4) Use SMART Goals. To the extent possible, use the SMART goals approach mentioned previously. Make sure the Future you define is Specific, Measurable, Attainable, Relevant, and Time-Bound. Not only will this approach help you "position" the desired change, it will help clarify your thinking about it in the first place.

(5) Keep It Simple. No matter how smart the people you're trying to influence may be, take special care not to smother them with too much data. Less really can be more, especially when it's carefully targeted. When the Clinton administration struggled to change the U.S. health care system, the proponents presented mountains of charts, diagrams, lists and other data to support their case. Yet all the Clinton efforts were severely undermined by a series of television commercials that depicted Harry and Louise, a fictional fortysomething middle-class married couple despairing over the bureaucratic problems they saw in the Clinton plan. No amount of economic doubletalk could compete with the persuasive simplicity of the TV spots.

(6) Answer the What, Why, and What If Questions. Even the simplest change effort is likely to meet with at least some resistance. As you Validate the Journey, be sure to have a compelling answer for each of the three most common kinds of questions:

- *What?* What exactly is the change you're advocating? What will it entail? What will it require people to give up? What will be involved in moving from the Present to the Future? What kind of inconvenience or discomfort can people expect to experience in the Neutral Zone?
- *Why?* Why is this change proposed? Why is it necessary for the organization's stability, growth, or survival? Why now? Why not some other change instead?
- *What If?* What if the organization or the team simply sticks with the status quo? What if the proposed change is postponed? What if the change were incremental instead of a clean break with the past? What if we risk death-by-PowerPoint and just study the issue for the next ten years?

Define your change as precisely as you can. Focus on the benefits while respectfully and credibly refuting contrary views. And lay out the consequences of not taking action.

Systems Questions

Most every change involves an adjustment in systems. In this context, I'll define a "system" as any policy, procedure, process, or organizational practice, both formal and informal. Structure or the "organization chart" is also a form of a system because it involves the deployment of people.

To help you think through the change you want to promote, it's imperative that you honestly ask yourself a number of questions. After all, how can you ever Validate the Journey for anyone else unless you are confident in the change yourself?

Ask yourself these questions:

Does the system (or the change you're promoting)	*Yes*	*No*
1. Reinforce the feeling of trust in our organization?	___	___
2. Encourage frank and open communication?	___	___

3. Foster a genuine spirit of camaraderie, teamwork, and synergy? ___ ___

4. Allow each person involved to "win" without doing so at the expense of someone else? ___ ___

5. Instill loyalty and pride in the organization? ___ ___

6. Reflect the organization's professed values? ___ ___

7. Contribute to the organization's mission? ___ ___

8. Bring out the best in our people? ___ ___

And, finally . . .

9. If we were starting all over today, would we introduce this system into our environment? ___ ___

You can no doubt think of additional questions. Just be sure that each question touches on one or more of the Four Ts (*Think-Friendly, Talk-Friendly, Trust-Friendly, Team-Friendly*). If you respond "no" to any question simply because it doesn't seem pertinent to the issue(s) addressed in the system, don't be concerned. But if you respond "no" for any other reasons, you should re-examine the system and consider changing, eliminating, or replacing it.

REMEMBER THE FOUR Ts

As you work to *Validate the Journey*, use the Four Ts.

Think-Friendly

- Make a list of the top ten questions you expect people to ask about the change you're proposing. Be ready to answer each question—not in the spirit of rebuttal, but in the spirit of understanding their concerns. Be sure your answers are backed by sound reasoning and, where possible, credible data.
- Use "systems thinking" to examine the multiplicity of causes and effects. Are you inadvertently filtering out information that contradicts your logic?
- Review the *Think-Friendly* questions in Chapter 4. Which ones can help you anticipate the resistance you will face? Which ones can help you make a psychological case for

action as well as a good business case?

- What stories are you telling yourself about resistance? Do you see resistance as simply the behavior of trouble-making malcontents, or do you see resistance as an opportunity to fine-tune your own thinking? If the former, you're headed for trouble. The latter view will not only help you avoid being blind-sided, but it can lead to fresh insights, unexpected friendships, and helpful alliances.

- Challenge your own conclusions with the **FIND-IT** approach, which stands for Focus, Inquire, Notice, Discern – Integrate, Translate.

Talk-Friendly

- Remember that open dialogue is the lubricant of every good relationship. Engaging people's heads, hearts, and hopes is all about relationships. Use your best dialogue skills at all times.

- Relinquish power. If you have position power, be careful not to pull rank. Listen with empathy to people who will be most affected by the change. Be genuinely open to their concerns. Involve them early and often. To the extent possible, incorporate their suggestions in meaningful ways.

- Put "undiscussables" on the table. Your credibility – and that of your proposed change—is diminished any time you dance around the elephant that everyone knows is in the room.

- Beware the "Abilene Paradox." Make sure you communicate in unmistakable, explicit terms. Invite others to do the same. Allowing people to "go along to get along" may seem convenient in the short term, but in the long term it guarantees problems.

Trust-Friendly

- Beware the most common trust busters. Remember the warning about doubletalk. To avoid "spin," be sure that all sides of the issues get a fair hearing. A pig with lipstick is still a pig. A heavily biased portrayal of your position will doom it to doubt, ridicule, and failure. Talk straight, just as you want people to talk to you.

- Avoid cherry-picking your facts. Make sure your case for action is fair and balanced.
- Resist the temptation to use euphemisms, jargon, and buzzwords. They're often just another form of doubletalk.
- If you make commitments, be prepared to keep them.

Team-Friendly
- As you create a team to help with your change effort (see Build a Coalition, Chapter 11), be sure it's a real team. Recruit the right people. Don't get too hung up on "demographics." Enlist people with the right skills sets, the right attitudes, and the right credibility. Include different perspectives to help ensure that you don't ignore a blind spot.
- Give your team a compelling purpose. Collaborate with team members in creating a team charter that clarifies tasks, boundaries, authority, and other pertinent issues. Nothing smells more like phoniness and fake work than a "team" with no clout.
- Provide your team with a reinforcing framework that clarifies expected behaviors, expected deliverables, and expected outcomes. People appreciate clarity.
- Provide your team with a nurturing context. Team members need more than just permission to operate. They need specific encouragement and appreciation.
- Use **SMART** goals in every phase of your change effort. Make sure that every goal is Specific, Measurable, Attainable, Relevant, and Time-Bound. Anything less guarantees you'll get little traction and no sustainable results.

When planning a trip, it's important to make it appealing to the people you're inviting to get on the bus. Similarly, as you Validate the Journey of your change effort, it's critical that you carefully tend to all the What's In It For Me details for the people affected.

VALIDATE THE JOURNEY SELF-ASSESSMENT

Instructions: *Read each statement and decide how accurately it describes your organization's adherence to the* **Validate the Journey** *principles described in this chapter:*

a. We never or rarely do this (0 points)
b. We sometimes do this (1 point)
c. We regularly do this (2 points)
d. We always or almost always do this (3 points)

Place the point value of your response choice beside each statement.

_____ We ensure that our messages about the intended change explicitly address the WIIFM (What's In It For Me?) questions that most people ask.

_____ We consider the unique needs of each member of the CAST of Characters (Champions, Agents, Sponsors, Targets) in making a case for change.

_____ We pay special attention to the context of the change, making sure that we consider the frame of reference of each stakeholder group.

_____ We position the change by using SMART goals to help clarify what the change will mean for the organization's new Future.

_____ We talk about the change in simple terms to help answer the What, Why, and What If questions that many people likely have about the change.

_____ Total Number of Points

Interpreting Your Scores

0-5: You may be trying to practice change-by-announcement, change-by-slogan, or change-by-executive-decree. To engage the heads, hearts, and hopes of the people you wish to influence, you need to make a strong psychological case for action, not simply a business case for action.

6-10: Your organization is doing a lot of things right, but there's still a lot of room for improvement in terms of connecting with the people whose support you need. Are you conducting active dialogue with your people? Are you genuinely listening to their concerns? Are you accommodating their needs and concerns as you tweak your change plans? Do your people express explicit appreciation for the way you're engaging them? If your response is "no" to any of these questions, that's a clue to what your next steps should be.

11-15: Excellent. You're clearly on the right track as you Validate the Journey. Identify the things you're doing right, and do them some more. Identify the things that could help make both a business case and a strong psychological case for your change, and make sure they are included in your ongoing change efforts. This upfront work pays huge dividends.

We usually see only the things we're looking for—so much so that we sometimes see them where they are not.
Eric Hoffer

The lions may lie down with the lambs, but the lambs won't get much sleep.
Woody Allen

The key to everything is patience. You get the chicken by hatching the egg, not by smashing it.
Arnold Glasow

The bottleneck is often at the top of the bottle.
Maxwell Monroe Stone

Chapter

Step 2:
Scan for Speed Bumps

*If true engagement is what you're after, you
must help people embrace change because they
see the light, not because they feel the heat.*

R esistance is a force that slows movement. It can bring change to
a screeching halt. It comes in a wide variety of forms. In your
organization, resistance will rarely be as conspicuous as the "hell-no-we-
won't-go" rallying cry of anti-war protesters. But resistance will occur.
Count on it.

You may discover resistance in the form of polite silence in meetings, followed by "parking lot vetos" where people commiserate on reasons they think your change is ill-advised. You may see resistance in the
form of naysayer questions after that killer PowerPoint presentation you
hoped would have a Pied Piper effect. Resistance may emerge as mind-
numbing inertia on the part of people whose support you need.

If the change you're promoting fails, it may have nothing to do with
the relative merits of your ideas. Your change may fail because you mis-
handle resistance.

Change never occurs in a vacuum. Neither does resistance. Both occur in the context of real people struggling with real (or imagined) issues that have real (or imagined) consequences. The better you understand that context, the better able you are to behave and lead in a Change-Friendly way.

This step is called Scan for Speed Bumps. Stay alert. Just because it's the second in a seven-step framework doesn't imply that it's only a one-time activity. It's an ongoing, deliberate process.

Consider this analogy: You move carefully through the drive-through lane at your bank because you know it's tight quarters, there are pedestrians nearby, and ignoring the speed bump in the asphalt would rattle your teeth and wreck havoc on your shock absorbers. Once you get out onto the boulevard do you simply delegate the driving responsibility to someone in the backseat? Of course not. You continue to Scan for Speed Bumps (stop signs, other traffic, pot holes in the street, etc.) all the way home. That constant vigilance helps you avoid doing—or receiving—damage. The same principle applies to dealing with change.

A PERSPECTIVE ON RESISTANCE

Some people regard resistance as inherently negative, a noxious intruder that needs to be smothered into silence. In reality, resistance is not necessarily a sign of disloyalty or of "not being a team player." Resistance can actually be a gift because change cannot be improved upon without it. Just as an airplane takes advantage of wind currents (including headwinds), so is tension the energy that propels every change effort. Rather than automatically fighting against resistance, learn to recognize it, respect the source, and see how you can benefit from it. And remember that unexpressed feelings never die, they just come back later in uglier ways.

> *"Resistance can actually be a gift because change cannot be improved upon without it."*

Early Warning Signs

As a very young boy growing up in Oklahoma I became familiar with the term "Tornado Alley." The Sooner State is in the middle of that north-south swath of the United States that has a disproportionately high number of violent tornadoes. I recall times when we had many consecutive days of tornado warnings. A warning was an official alert when a giant funnel cloud was actually sighted. That made for a lot of scurrying to the storm cellar. With the advent of technology like computer modeling and Doppler radar, today's meteorologists are able to provide much more accurate—and timely—information. These early warnings are said to save thousands of lives each year.

As you Scan for Speed Bumps, you will sometimes notice the early warning signs of an impending storm that threatens your change effort. But you have an advantage over the meteorologist: you can actually redirect or even stop the storm. Rather than ducking for cover from resistance, you can meet it head on.

Let's consider some of the common warning signs of resistance.

Confusion

No matter how carefully you've worked to Validate the Journey, some people simply won't get it. It's not that they're deliberately pushing back, and it's not that they're trying to give you a hard time. They just don't yet understand the implications of the change you're proposing. They'll often ask questions like "So, why are we doing this?" "How is this going to impact my budget?" "What will this do to my reporting relationships?" "What will this mean for my current situation?" In other words, "What's In It For Me?"

Don't be troubled by this. Expect it. People have a natural tendency to absorb information that reinforces their current paradigms and filter out data that contradict—or threaten—their current views or situations. Be patient. You'll likely need to explain your change plans over and over and over again.

Silence

You make your presentation and people sit in stone silence. Are they stunned by your brilliance? Do they unanimously agree with you? Are they simply too shy to talk?

Silence can be tough to handle because it's sort of like lassoing a cloud. Never assume that silence means acceptance. Silence *can* mean acceptance, but it can also mean anything from "I don't have a clue what you're talking about" to "I'll do what you're asking only when hell freezes over."

One way to prime the discussion pump is to answer a series of unasked questions—*real* questions that you anticipate people might want to ask but are afraid they'll come across as impertinent or misinformed or just plain stupid.

Easy Agreement

Some people may agree with you without hesitation. That may seem ideal, but you need to be sure they understand the implications of the change you're championing. Don't simply make a presentation and expect people to click their heels and salute. Be sure to engage people in genuine dialogue. Otherwise you risk their swallowing your message whole without fully digesting it, realizing only later that it gave them heartburn.

Denial

The ostrich effect (head in the sand) is a common behavior of people confronted by the need to change. Denial can take many forms: "The foam coming off the wings during launch poses no threat to the space shuttle." "Germs are a myth. Washing my hands between surgeries is a nuisance." "That survey finding doesn't really apply to me and my group."

Malicious Compliance

A couple of Army privates were ordered by an overbearing officer to paint a room "all white." The officer's self-important manner was particularly obnoxious, so the young enlisted men decided to engage in malicious compliance—obeying the order to the absolute letter. They indeed painted the room "all white," including the floor, the ceiling, the window panes, the doors and door knobs, the desk, the chairs, the telephone, and even the light switches. Double-coated, exactly as ordered

Sabotage

Do you remember the "Law of the Hog" story in Chapter 3? Of course not all sabotage is as blatant as tossing perfectly good product into a giant chipping machine. But more subtle forms can be just as damaging: software mysteriously chugs to a halt, messages don't get delivered, documents get lost in the bureaucratic maze, the wrong product is ordered. Watch for it.

Diversion

Many resisters are from the Yeahbut Tribe—"Yeah, but this won't work because …" "Yeah, but you didn't consider …" "Yeah, but the reason I can't do this is …" Diversionary tactics include scapegoating, rehashing the past, and telling victim, villain, and helpless stories. Diversions often occur in meetings where people flit like nervous fleas from one subject to another (see Stay on Message, Chapter 13). Some diversions are no doubt deliberate, but many are unconscious. Unless you recognize them for what they are and address them squarely, they will stall your change into oblivion.

Finding the Bumps

As mentioned earlier, this Scan for Speed Bumps activity is perpet-

"Stay alert for emerging roadblocks all along the way."

ual. Even before you Validate the Journey you need to identify the likely points of resistance. Then you need to stay alert for emerging roadblocks all along the way.

In our work with clients in a wide range of industries and circumstances, we've found that five mutually-reinforcing methods work best in helping Scan for Speed Bumps that can stymie change:

- Conversations
- One-on-one interviews
- Focus group discussions
- Surveys
- 360-degree feedback

Let's consider each of these in turn.

Conversations

In this context, I don't mean just *any* conversation. Chatting about the weather or sports scores won't produce any data on likely points of resistance. I'm talking about the learning-by-walking-around kinds of conversations. Although casual and friendly just like a chat about the weather, these conversations are more targeted. Engage people in conversations about their work. Ask questions that prime the pump for dialogue. What gets in their way? What makes their work fulfilling to them? What concerns do they have? What could make things better for them? At this point you're not at all in the judging mode. You're in the gathering mode. Listen with empathy. Dig. Make it safe for people to express their views.

One-on-one interviews

A good interview is really a conversation with a very specific purpose. In one-on-one interviews it helps to work from a short inventory of pre-planned questions. That way it's easier to compare responses and identify trends and patterns in your findings.

I like to ask a lot of very open-ended questions like "If you could wave a magic wand, what would you change around here?" or "If your best friend applied for a job here, what would you tell him to expect if he got hired?"

Make sure your interviews include a good cross section of your target population. Loading up your interview schedule too heavily with managers and other senior people will virtually guarantee that you'll miss pertinent information from rank-and-file members of the organization.

Focus Group Discussions

A focus group is a qualitative research tool. People are asked about their perceptions, opinions, beliefs, and attitudes regarding specific subjects. It's a method used by manufacturers, advertisers, political candidates, and change practitioners.

Note the word "group." In their zeal for inclusion, some practitioners invite anywhere from 12 to 24 people (or even more) to participate in a focus "group." In my view, a dozen is unwieldy, and 24-plus is a crowd. To help ensure open and comfortable conversation, limit the number of participants to nine or fewer.

Select your participants mindfully. That way you can observe not only individual responses, but the group dynamics as well. For example, to what extent do some group members seem to acquiesce to the opinions of more dominant participants? How open do participants seem to be to thinking that's contrary to their own?

The questions you use to prime the pump in a focus group discussion may be virtually identical to those you'd use in a one-on-one interview. The big difference here is that you are facilitating a discussion among several people. Your role is to keep the discussion on track, not to consume the air time.

Again, listen with empathy, and stay constantly alert for nuances and even tangents that can provide helpful insights.

Surveys

In this age when quick-and-easy survey tools are so readily available, some organizations create survey fatigue among their people. In addition to wearing their people out by asking so many questions so often, they also dilute the utility and impact of the data. Worse yet, they mistake quantity for quality.

As mentioned earlier there are two critical things to remember about surveys. First, ask the *right* questions. That seems axiomatic. But the second thing to remember may not be so obvious: Avoid asking the *wrong* questions. If you ask the wrong questions you'll get plenty of data. But the fancy charts, graphs and tables will lead you to chase the wrong issues. To be effective in managing your change process, you must deal with root causes, not just superficial symptoms. Poor surveying is not just ineffective, it can actually do serious harm.

Avoid the trap of conducting a traditional "employee attitude survey." Bear in mind that "attitudes," as well as behaviors, are driven by underlying *assumptions*. If you examine only behaviors and attitudes without linking them to pertinent assumptions, you can inadvertently head in totally unproductive directions.

The Culture Alignment Profile™ (CAP) methodology developed by Duncan Worldwide helps you successfully navigate the data-gathering phase of your Scan for Speed Bumps work. We'll tell you more about CAP in Chapter 11 (Build a Coalition) and Chapter 12 (Ford the Streams). Our methodology enables us to examine the change bias of an organization. We assess *readiness* to change (do people understand the need for change and do they see the gaps between the Present and the Future?). We assess *willingness* to change (are people sufficiently dissatisfied with the Present to expend the needed effort to reach the Future?). And we assess *ability* to change (do people have the skills and tools needed to bring about the change?) This RWA (Ready-Willing-Able) approach is critical at this stage of information gathering.

For now, suffice it to say that any surveying you do must be very strategic, very focused, and backed by tried-and-true tactics that produce the data you really need.

360-degree Feedback

A common side effect of a culture assessment survey is *denial*—as in "Sure, that kind of stuff goes on around here, but it doesn't apply to me and *my* group!" Another disadvantage of limiting your scanning to the overall organizational landscape is that you might miss the impact of behaviors by particular individuals.

By definition, 360 feedback involves soliciting performance feedback from people most important to an individual's success—his manager, his peers, and if he has any, his direct reports. In addition to alerting an individual to any blind spots he may have and facilitating both coaching and self-improvement, 360 feedback can be of tremendous help to change agents. Access to individual data can provide priceless insights into challenges and opportunities you may have in managing sponsorship for your change.

If individual 360 feedback reports are kept confidential (which is often the case), even aggregate data—trends and patterns in perceived behaviors of demographic sub-groups of people—can be invaluable in your search for potential points of resistance. The Duncan360™ process, which we'll explain later, is a great tool for this purpose.

REMEMBER THE FOUR Ts

As you *Scan for Speed Bumps*, use the Four Ts.

Think-Friendly

- Double check your assumptions about resistance. Learn to regard resistance as an opportunity to clarify your message, fine-tune your approach, and even course correct your direction. Some of your best ideas can come from people who disagree with you.
- Review the *Think-Friendly* questions in Chapter 4. Which ones can help you anticipate resistance and address it productively?

Talk-Friendly
- Use resistance as a springboard to dialogue, not as an evil enemy to be clubbed into submission.
- Pinpoint the source. Is the resistance about the "what" or the "how" of your change? Is the resister sad about losing the old (the present) or apprehensive about the meaning of the new (the future)?
- Make sure that all "undiscussables" are fair game for honest dialogue. To make the point, introduce a pertinent "undiscussable" into the dialogue yourself.

Trust-Friendly
- Be especially careful not to pull rank. If you meet resistance by alluding to position or authority (yours or your sponsor's), you'll drive the resistance underground where it can do more harm.
- Listen with empathy. You may not agree with the resistance, but at least try to understand it. Help people know that they're being heard and, most importantly, respected.

Team-Friendly
- Be sure that your team honestly addresses contrarian views. Rotate the responsibility of playing devil's advocate.
- Does your culture punish people who disagree with "management," or does it explicitly welcome dissent as a sign of the critical thinking that fuels improvement? (After all, *you* are challenging the status quo or you wouldn't be championing change.)

Resistance is covert or overt—concealed or transparent. A critical part of a Change-Friendly environment is getting inevitable resistance out into the open so you can address it. Only when you understand people's concerns can you work to find common ground. Unless and until you make it safe to disagree, you won't have a chance of engaging people's heads, hearts, and hopes.

SCAN FOR SPEED BUMPS SELF-ASSESSMENT

Instructions: *Read each statement and decide how accurately it describes your organization's adherence to the Scan for Speed Bumps principles described in this chapter:*

> a. **We never or rarely do this (0 points)**
> b. **We sometimes do this (1 point)**
> c. **We regularly do this (2 points)**
> d. **We always or almost always do this (3 points)**

Place the point value of your response choice beside each statement.

_____ Our organization treats resistance to change as an opportunity to learn, discover, and clarify rather than as "bad behavior" to be corrected.

_____ To help us Scan for Speed Bumps, we use one-on-one interviews with a broad cross-section of our people.

_____ To help us Scan for Speed Bumps, we conduct focus group interviews with people who are most likely to offer their candid, unvarnished opinions.

_____ To help us Scan for Speed Bumps, we carefully examine our people's underlying assumptions, not just their attitudes and observable behaviors.

_____ To help us Scan for Speed Bumps, we use a 360-degree feedback instrument that's specifically tailored to the issues most pertinent to our organization's change effort.

_____ Total Number of Points

Interpreting Your Scores

0-5: You're running the risk of coming across as not caring about the concerns people may have about your change effort. Moreover, you may be mistaking silence for agreement. Be careful not to make assumptions about how your change plans are being perceived by the people you want to influence. To do so can spell big trouble.

6-10: Your organization is apparently doing some diagnostic work with your target audience. Be sure that the diagnostics are strategic and integrated – that they're all part of a carefully crafted change plan and that the tools you're using (interviews, focus groups, surveys, etc.) are coordinated and mutually-reinforcing. And remember that diagnostics should not be limited to a single iteration. Not all speed bumps (points of resistance) are immediately apparent.

11-15: Excellent. Your organization is listening to the people who can make or break the success of your change initiative. Strengthen your Scan for Speed Bumps efforts by employing a range of listening tools. Respond explicitly to people's concerns and solicit their ideas on how to improve your change plan. With appropriate treatment, some of the most vocal naysayers can become some of your strongest advocates.

*Planning is bringing the future into the
present so you can do something about it now.*
Alan Lakein

*Plans are only good intentions unless they
immediately degenerate into hard work.*
Peter Drucker

*Even Noah got no salary for the first six
months, partly on account of the weather and
partly because he was learning navigation.*
Mark Twain

*A journey of a thousand miles must begin with
a single step.*
Lao Tzu

*One's destination is never a place, but a new
way of seeing things.*
Henry Miller

Chapter

Step 3:
Chart the Course

Good plans shape good decisions. Good decisions produce good results. That's why good planning helps make elusive dreams come true.

"I have an existential map," said comedian Steven Wright. "It has 'You are here' written all over it."

Joking aside, that's exactly what every good change agent needs: a map that shows not only where you've been and where you're going, but keeps you well grounded in the here and now.

After all, part of your role as a change agent is to serve as tour guide.

You make the trip attractive by appealing to the needs of the people you're inviting to travel with you, by invoking their values, and connecting to the things they regard as important. You Validate the Journey.

You carefully examine the landscape, looking for warning signs of resistance to even taking the trip at all, let alone to the destination you promote. You Scan for Speed Bumps.

Now you must plan the trip, with emphasis on the route, the vehicle, and the milestones. You Chart the Course.

Early in this book I asserted that change-by-announcement, change-by-slogan, and certainly change-by-executive-decree are doomed to failure. A mountain of evidence supports that claim.

Effective change requires connecting with people's brains, their feelings, their aspirations. In other words, engaging their heads, hearts, and hopes. This can't be done by merely issuing orders and expecting people to fall in line and mindlessly follow your lead. Of course things like deference to authority may influence people to obey orders. But compliance has its limitations.

For example, would you want your people to adhere to a new safety regulation only because they fear they'll be punished for a violation? Or would you prefer that they adhere to the regulation because they fully understand and support the rationale for it? Do you want them to do only the bare minimum? Or do you want the gift of their discretionary effort? In other words, do you want only their compliance, or do you also want their commitment?

> *All roads lead to accomplishment. You just have to know which direction to turn along the way.*
> **M.C. Duncan**

Effective change efforts often require a dose of compliance. If your company is transitioning from PCs to Apple computers, you'd expect your people to "let go" of their Dell laptops and start using their new MacBook Pros and iMacs. But to make the most of the change, you'd also want your people to "catch the vision" of its purpose. You'd want them to understand the advantages of the change. You'd want them to embrace the change willingly, not begrudgingly. Compliance certainly has it place, but it works best in an atmosphere of commitment.

If you fly from Dallas to New York and don't course correct along the way, you can end up in Nova Scotia. And if you're really not paying attention, welcome to Iceland. Chart the Course. Maps and methods really do matter.

As a tour guide to change, your job is to help people let go of the Present, navigate safely through the Neutral Zone, and arrive at the Future that will then become their new Present.

Exploratory Questions

Asking and answering exploratory questions can help you determine the course that's most likely to produce the change you want.

The Present

- Why do people want to stay in the Present? What's so appealing?
- What rewards (formal and/or informal) does the Present offer?
- What logical things keep people in the Present?
- What illogical things keep people in the Present?
- What is it about the Present that still works okay?
- What is it about the Present that doesn't work so well anymore?
- What's likely to happen if we stay in the Present?

The Neutral Zone

- How might the change produce insecurity? What's uncomfortable?
- How might the change produce a sense of loss?
- How might the change consume time, money, and other resources?
- How might the change produce exhilaration?
- How could the Neutral Zone be made less scary and more appealing?

The Future

- What could influence people to resist the Future?
- What could influence people to desire and even advocate the Future?
- How can you make the Future more attractive than the status quo?
- How can you best position the Future with your CAST of Characters – Champions, Agents, Sponsors, and Targets?

When working with a group that's trying to bring about an important change, I strongly encourage the use of questions like these. One such group was the eCommerce department at American Century, the huge investment firm with tens of thousands of customers around the world. American Century was transitioning from the traditional face-to-face way of doing business to a totally new platform involving heavy reliance on the Internet. The road from analog to digital can be bumpy. This new Future was totally uncharted territory for many of the company's customers, and even some people inside the company were reluctant to give up the old ways of completing transactions. But company leaders made the strategic decision to ride the Internet wave. So the question was no longer "if," but rather "how," to enact the change.

With a dozen or so of the company's smartest people in the room, I facilitated a discussion about the resistance that such a change would meet. Everyone agreed that as important as processes are, this change could never succeed without careful attention to all the "people stuff." The meeting room walls were soon covered with flipchart pages that outlined the Present, the Neutral Zone, and the Future. All along the way we applied the "What's In It For Me?" question to each of the CAST of Characters. As one of the leaders in the room commented, "These questions and their answers provide a path to the change we're after. In fact, this is starting to look like a change strategy."

> *Now is not the end. It is not even the beginning of the end. But it is, perhaps, the end of the beginning.*
> **Winston Churchill,**
> **speaking of a key battle victory**

That's exactly the point. By applying the Change-Friendly framework to their efforts, the eCommerce team enabled the company to make a smoother-than-expected transition. The return on investment was impressive: eCommerce dramatically improved its output while reducing its budget by 45%. As web activity began to skyrocket, the cost per transaction dropped by 74%. This translated into millions of dollars in savings. The department's new slogan of "eBusiness is *the* Business" took on meaning that translated directly to the company's bottom line.

Translate Planning into Implementation

The Chart the Course step is where your planning begins to morph into implementation. To enhance your opportunity for success, it's critical that you mindfully determine the what, when, and where of your beginning. In some cases, several mutually reinforcing methods may be used. In others, a single approach may work best.

Let's consider some of your options:

Conversion by Increment

Work through the changes in one department, division, location, or business unit. Then use your success and lessons learned as a model for others. This is what we did at American Century. The eCommerce department was an early adopter of the analog-to-digital conversion, and other departments quickly jumped on the bandwagon when they saw the success and return on investment. This can work well when operational units see themselves as basically similar. It's a harder sell when silo mentality prevails. An advantage of Conversion by Increment is the opportunity to focus closely on building strong sponsorship.

> *"The Chart the Course step is where your planning begins to morph into implementation."*

Staggered Deployment

Charter one or more "pilots" so you can test drive your change before launching it throughout the entire organization. This approach is helpful if your change involves a new process that can be tested and refined on a small scale. We did this at Campbell Soup Company when we introduced new manufacturing processes. It made a lot of sense to iron out the kinks at one plant before taking the processes to multiple sites. With our Duncan Worldwide clients we often use this approach in rolling out a new training program or a diagnostic process like 360-degree performance feedback. Just be sure there's a common understanding of terms. If you use the word "pilot," you may want to specify that the initial roll-out is an opportunity for refinement, not just a chance for resisters to take pot shots.

Focus on Behavior

Real change, just as real stagnation, occurs one behavior at a time. Rather than painting your change with a broad brush, focus on the individual pixels of behavior. Explicitly define the behaviors that will produce the results you want. All of our nuclear power clients work tirelessly in promoting what they call a safety conscious work environment. Those that are most successful place less emphasis on slogans and posters and more emphasis on teaching—and rewarding—specific behaviors like open and honest dialogue. An advantage of the Focus on Behavior approach is that it reinforces personal accountability for performance.

Copy Cat by Design

This is similar to the Conversion by Increment and Staggered Deployment approaches, but it's different in one very important way. Copy Cat by Design involves using the same people who will help replicate the change in different parts of the organization. These "traveling change agents" become very expert in coaching others in subsequent waves of the implementation. This approach helps accelerate the change because having experts available to show the way shortens the ramp-up time needed to move from the Present, through the Neutral Zone, and into the Future. This approach is especially useful when your change involves replication of a system or process that is mechanical and quantifiable. Transition to a new software program is an example. It can also be useful in promoting behavior changes. In organizations around the world I have certified hundreds of trainers to teach so-called "soft skills" involving communication and trust behaviors. These internal trainers then replicate the change by taking the training to thousands of their colleagues. The ripple effect is very powerful in producing subsequent waves of skilled practitioners.

Make an Example

Bringing in fresh blood can help send a clear signal that "this, too, shall pass" is not an acceptable response to the call for change. With a new sheriff in town, people have a tendency to pay more attention to the local ordinances. That's what happened when Farmland Industries brought in Jim Rainey (mentioned in earlier chapters) as the new CEO. He clearly modeled the values and behaviors needed to create lasting change. The old behaviors were simply no longer in vogue. In fact, the old behaviors became explicitly unacceptable.

Conversely, dismissing a high profile person who's failing to "walk the talk" can be an excellent way to get people's attention. The new CEO of a global engineering firm told his senior team that he expected them to operate in the best interests of the whole company rather than protecting their individual turf. When the head of one division was discovered to be manipulating the financials in favor of his own group to the detriment of others, the CEO fired him. There was no public flogging or humiliation. The man simply got fired. Then the CEO gathered his other team members and told them what he had done. He respectfully catalogued all the good things their former colleague had done over the years, and expressed his appreciation for the man as a friend. Then he told his team about the behavior that got the man fired. That was 14 years ago. Message delivered. The natural consequence of contrary behavior was clarified. Collaboration and transparency have not been a problem since.

> *Hard work spotlights the character of people: some turn up their sleeves, some turn up their noses, and some don't turn up at all.*
> **Sam Ewing**

Use Multiple Influence Levers

How many times have you seen someone who's reluctant to complete a task and you chalked it up to "an attitude problem" or some other personality issue? While it's possible that the person did indeed need an attitude adjustment, it's also possible that he simply didn't know "how" to complete the task.

Stanford psychologist Lee Ross has a term for this tendency to over-value personality-based explanations for observed behaviors while under-valuing situational explanations for the behaviors. He calls it the "fundamental attribution error."

The fundamental attribution error is most often visible when people explain the behavior of others. For example, my neighbor Sarah saw her husband Randy trip over a rock in their garden. Sarah commented that Randy is "clumsy" and frequently bumps into things. Two days later Sarah was working in the garden and tripped over the same rock. This time, however, she blamed the placement of the rock: "That thing shouldn't be there," she said. "It was right in my path. It's no wonder I tripped." Same rock. Same placement. Clumsiness for Randy, just bad luck for Sarah.

Change agents frequently fall into this trap. Faced with resistance, they often assume that the resisters either have bad attitudes

> **We are either doing something or we are not. 'Talking about' is a subset of 'not.'**
> **from "The Office" website**

or need to be motivated. While that may be true, it's often also true that the resisters need training or coaching or some other form of help in actually "doing" what they're asked to do.

This motivation/ability dichotomy should not be viewed as a problem. It is, in fact, a solution. After all, both motivation *and* ability are crucial in every successful change effort.

To use multiple influence levers as you Chart the Course, consider the Want To/Can Do Model illustrated here. Various versions of this model have been postulated by behavioral scientists for decades. Even a kindergartner knows about the Want To/Can Do dichotomy. Trouble is, many (most?) people trying to champion change in their organizations seem to ignore the power (or even the existence) of multiple levers of influence. We'll dive into deeper application of the model in later chapters, but for now let's take a quick look at how it can help us.

The *Individual* level is of course about a person's own motivation and abilities. The *Community* level relates to influences like friends and coworkers. The *Environment*

level involves things like organizational structure, processes, procedures, tools, and even physical factors like room set up and physical space.

Lever 1 – Link to Passions

This is where many people get stuck. In fact, many people seem to think that Lever 1 is the only factor at play. When someone fails to perform to expectation, some managers automatically assume the worker is lazy or uncaring or uncommitted. While any or all of that may be true, it can also be true that the person simply does not know *how* to do the assigned task or that he does not have the appropriate skills. But when the default assumption involves motivation, the manager will likely rely on his own default behavior: pep talks, nagging, or perhaps threats. Even if motivation *is* the most pertinent issue, pep talks, nagging, and threats have only a short-term effect (if any).

The key is to change the *meaning* of a particular expected behavior from negative to positive, from something that's a nuisance to something that's gratifying.

Example: If people regard conducting performance reviews as nothing but bureaucratic paperwork, show them how an effective review is directly linked to clarity of purpose, agreement on expectations, and commitment to improvement. Link the activity to values like personal accomplishment and performance accountability. Discuss how *not* doing a thoughtful performance review violates professed values, while doing it well reinforces professed values and in fact leads to a range of desirable consequences. As the old Alka-Seltzer ad said, "Try it, you'll like it." Appealing to people's intrinsic values—their passions—is an excellent way to reinforce personal accountability. Rather than trying to shame people into compliance, engage them in building commitment on the foundation of what they value.

Lever 2 – Shrink the Know/Do Gap

This helps us escape another dangerous assumption. As most of us have learned, *knowing* is not at all the same as *doing*. I've seen thousands of smart people participate in leadership development workshops. At the end of the training, most of these smart people could pass a written test on the workshop content. But unless and until they mindfully *practice* the skills and behaviors they've been taught, there is negligible improvement in their performance.

To translate knowing into doing, identify and focus on the vital behaviors that produce the results you want.

Example: In my travels I used to stay at Doubletree Hotels. In addition to the comfortable lodging, I liked the fresh (and huge) chocolate chip cookies I received on check-in. While the cookies were delicious, I *knew* they were loaded with empty calories. I *knew* that empty calories did nothing but add inches to my waistline. But

I still ate the cookies. Because I didn't like the result (guilt, tight trousers), I changed my behavior. At first, I simply put the cookies in my briefcase and resolved to take them home to my children. Then either on the way to the airport or on the airplane, I ate the cookies anyway. I was determined to beat my cookie habit, but was getting little traction. Then it finally occurred to me (slow learner?) that the vital behavior I needed to use was simply saying "no thank you" when the cookies were offered. Identifying and then focusing on that particular behavior was the simple solution to my problem. I closed the Know/Do gap.

> *Knowing is not enough; we must apply. Willing is not enough; we must do.*
> **Bruce Lee**

Good solutions are in fact often simple. Many hospitals have dramatically reduced the incidence of infections among patients by requiring that doctors wash their hands before and after each patient examination. Errors in an industrial setting can be dramatically reduced by a skill as simple as three-way communication: Supervisor – "Please start steam pump 219." Operator – "I understand you want me to start steam pump 219." Supervisor – "Correct."

Shrinking the Know/Do gap can also be as simple as clarifying the language we use. One mother was terrified to see her three-year-old playing near the street. "Johnny, I told you to stay away from the intersection!" she shouted. "But Mommy," the little boy said with exasperation. "What's an intersection?"

Lever 3 – Enlist Social Support

This is a key to the success of programs like Weight Watchers and Alcoholics Anonymous. Research clearly validates the advantages of social support in a business setting, too.

In our own work in leadership development and organizational culture, we often ask clients to team up with "learning partners" to hold them accountable for practicing certain skills and embracing particular behaviors. When people are asked to develop action plans based on their 360-degree performance feedback, about 20% will do it on their own. But when you team each recipient with a learning partner (peer or otherwise) and establish a clear protocol of accountability, the follow-through jumps to around 70%. With additional influence levers, nearly 100% will develop action plans and mindfully work on needed improvements.

Lever 4 – Work in Concert

With the proliferation of social networks like Facebook and LinkedIn, millions of people demonstrate their belief in the Beatles' suggestion that we're most likely to succeed when we have "a little help from our friends." As we discussed in our Team-Friendly chapter, synergy is one of the most powerful levers we can use in accomplishing our goals.

In our training sessions with clients, we often use exercises and games to demonstrate the value of constructive collaboration. One approach is to have people work on a problem individually, then work on the same problem with a group to see if the group solution is measurably better. It nearly always is. Why? Because with a little (strategic) help from their friends, most people can produce a result that's superior to what they produce on their own. It's not just a matter of strength in numbers. It's also a function of different brains approaching a problem from different directions.

Lever 4 is also effective in helping establish new group norms. In organizations that employ networks of learning partners, personal accountability is improved, performance is boosted, and other positive change is accelerated.

Lever 5 – Focus on Behaviors

Accountability is all about performance, and performance is all about behaviors. In fact, the overall performance in your organization. . .

- in every conversation
- in every meeting
- in every project
- in every activity of every kind …

. . . is the result of behaviors.

So doesn't it make sense to focus on behaviors?

In organizations where personal accountability for performance is highest, behaviors are not left to chance. In high accountability, high performance organizations, desired behaviors are explicitly defined and explicitly reinforced.

This doesn't have to be stuffy or oppressive. In fact, it can actually be fun.

The key is to be precise about expectations, then promptly close the gap between observed behavior and expected behavior.

The Tennessee Valley Authority is one of my clients. A major department at TVA—it has more than 650 people and serves all of the organization's other 13,000 people—has had challenges with meeting behaviors. So the top managers resolved to model the behaviors they expect in others. They do it with small stuffed animals they bought at a Dollar Store. If someone is behaving like a bully, a colleague will toss a gorilla into his lap. If someone is hogging the time, he'll get a pig in his lap. If someone is throwing out a lot of bull, he gets the cow. If someone needs to speed things up, the rabbit will be his new friend. And the donkey is tossed to anyone who's behaving like, well, you get the idea.

> *Act the way you want to be and soon you'll be the way you act.*
> **George W. Crane**

This is a simple and fun way to keep meeting participants focused on the agreed-upon behaviors that produce effective meetings. And when someone temporarily strays from the standard, he is immediately held accountable by his colleagues.

Just as desired behaviors should be made explicit, so must the behaviors that you *don't* want. Many organizations are pretty good about explaining "here's what we stand for." What's often missing is the second half of the equation: "Here's what we *won't* stand for." A good example of such clarity—and follow through—is the earlier story about the CEO who fired a long-time colleague for violating trust. Accountability works best in an environment of carefully defined—and reinforced—behaviors.

Lever 6 – Make It Easy

Carefully scan your work environment and honestly examine every single system—with "system" defined as a procedure, process, practice, or activity.

As mentioned in an earlier chapter, we give our clients nine simple questions to use in determining if their systems add clear, irrefutable value. If for any reason they respond "no" to any of the questions asked about a particular system, they are encouraged to re-examine the system and consider changing, eliminating, or replacing it.

Unchallenged systems tend to produce fake work. Remove fake

work and you make performance accountability easier.

You can also make accountability easier by providing the necessary tools. In dozens of organizations we've provided training in dialogue skills, trust behaviors, change management techniques, and related areas. When it comes to performance accountability, these skills help "make it easy."

Because implementation is a dynamic, fluid process, your Chart the Course work is never ending. Just as an airplane pilot makes frequent course corrections based on wind conditions and other factors, so must you make adjustments in your change work. That's not to say your intended destination (the Future) will fluctuate. But you should expect to deal with a spectrum of emerging speed bumps along the way. Exploratory questions will help you anticipate, understand, and navigate through (or around) most of the headwinds on your route. And using multiple influence levers will help you engage the heads, hearts, and hopes of the people most critical to the success of your change journey.

Charting the course is all about navigation. The winds are always on the side of the ablest navigators.

REMEMBER THE FOUR Ts

As you work to Chart the Course, use the Four Ts.

Think-Friendly

- Be sure you're considering all the questions that people will likely have about the change you're proposing. Does your change approach take those questions into account?
- Use "systems thinking" as you examine the change approaches available to you. Make sure your plans can stand the tests of reason and logic.
- Challenge your stories. Beware the natural tendency to downplay or even ignore information that contradicts our own views.

Talk-Friendly

- Dialogue with a wide range of people who have interests in the change you champion. Listen especially carefully to those who disagree with you.
- Make it safe to put "undiscussables" on the table for open and honest conversation.
- Be especially attentive as you Listen With Empathy, Inquire to Discover, and Advocate With Respect.

Trust-Friendly

- Consciously use the Language of Trust. Words really do matter.
- Remember throughout the planning process (and at all times thereafter) that your style and demeanor should foster a sense of trust and respect. Carefully avoid trust busters. In this Chart the Course work, Double Talk and Pulling Rank are common temptations.

Team-Friendly

- As you formulate implementation and transition plans, be sure that any teams you establish have clear charters.
- Make sure the organization's teams have SMART goals that are clearly consistent with your change approach and that explicitly support the change strategy you're using.

CHART THE COURSE SELF-ASSESSMENT

Instructions: *Read each statement and decide how accurately it describes your orientation to the* **Chart the Course** *principles in this chapter:*

    a. **Not at all (0 points)**
    b. **Sort of (1 point)**
    c. **With thoughtful intent (2 points)**
    d. **Backed up by strategic action (3 points)**

Place the point value of your response choice beside each statement.

_____ I honestly ask a series of exploratory questions about the Present, the Neutral Zone and the Future.

_____ As planning morphs into implementation, I consider a number of options before deciding on a specific plan.

_____ In deciding on my approach to change, I consider ability issues as well as motivational issues.

_____ In my Change Agent role, I use four or more levers of influence.

_____ I frequently revisit my change approach decision to ensure that the implementation is having its intended effects.

_____ **Total Number of Points**

Interpreting Your Scores

0-5: Your change approach is likely perceived as disorganized and haphazard, earning little confidence from the people you want to influence. At this point, disengagement (or outright resistance) is your biggest roadblock. Unless and until you adopt a more thoughtful approach to planning and implementation, your change efforts will be on the path to failure.

6-10: You are somewhat effective in charting the course for your intended changes. At the same time, you're probably missing some important opportunities to engage people's heads, hearts, and hopes. People are most likely to become—and stay—engaged when they believe the change approach is tailored to their own best interests. Remember the WIIFM (What's In It For Me?) principle.

11-15: You're a Change-Friendly rock star! Your orientation to change is no doubt perceived as thoughtful and respectful. As you continue to be strategic in considering the needs of your change targets, you'll be rewarded by a level of engagement that will keep your efforts on track for success.

Individually we are one drop. Together, we are an ocean.
Ryunosuke Satoro

Coming together is a beginning. Keeping together is progress. Working together is success.
Henry Ford

Nobody can go back and start a new beginning, but anyone can start today and make a new ending.
Maria Robinson

The only man I know who behaves sensibly is my tailor; he takes my measurements anew each time he sees me. The rest go on with their old measurements and expect me to fit them.
George Bernard Shaw

Chapter

Step 4:
Build a Coalition

*Trying to create change with only limited
engagement of the stakeholders is as foolhardy as
a one-man band trying to imitate an orchestra.*

Don't kid yourself. Change does not occur in isolation. No matter how brilliant your ideas may be, no matter how compelling your case for action, no matter how much personal credibility you believe you have, your change will not succeed without the engaged and collaborative involvement of others. Period.

You must Build a Coalition.

My friend Dave, a seasoned change consultant, tells the story of working with a manufacturing firm in Colorado. The CEO/owner had an idea for four minor process changes that he was certain would (1) dramatically improve through-put and productivity, (2) reduce unit cost of the product, and (3) free up time on the production line. At 7:00 o'clock one morning the CEO met with production workers and showed them sketches of his idea, followed by his order to "make it happen."

Later that same day the CEO checked on the line. ***Nothing whatsoever had changed.*** He was dumbstruck. He couldn't believe that a commandment brought down from the mountaintop by the CEO himself did not result in immediate, unquestioned obedience. So he called Dave, the change consultant. Here's the essence of their conversation:

> **Dave**: *How often do your people see you?*
>
> **CEO**: *Four times a year, just like clock work. I have a meeting with the production people. If I can't be there, I send a video.*
>
> **Dave**: *Who do you think has the most influence with your production people—you, or the guys who supervise them every day?*
>
> **CEO**: *This is one of those questions where if I get it wrong you're going to be disappointed in me, aren't you?*

The CEO made the classic mistake of ignoring the necessity of *engaging* people with the desired change rather than merely announcing the change. And if he were really serious about expecting his people to "make it happen," the CEO would have educated himself about the roles people can play in a change scenario.

CAST of Characters

To help clarify the resources available to you, let's review the CAST of Characters introduced in an earlier chapter.

- *Champions* are people who favor the change but lack the power to sanction it. As advocates for the change, Champions must willingly work to gain commitment and resources for it.
- *Agents* are people who plan and execute the implementation of the change. This includes diagnosing potential problems (Scan for Speed Bumps) and addressing the problems strategically.
- *Sponsors* are the people who authorize, legitimize, and demonstrate ownership for the change. As mentioned earlier, you can (and should) have different kinds of Spon-

sors. Authorizing Sponsors have sufficient organizational power and/or influence to initiate commitment of resources. Reinforcing Sponsors help promote the change at the "local" level. Sometimes a single person can fill both of these roles, but successful change efforts usually involve multiple Sponsors. In short, Sponsors are responsible for creating an environment that enables change to occur.

- *Targets* are people whose knowledge, assumptions, attitudes, emotions, and behaviors must be altered for the change to be sustainable. Targets play a critical role in both the short- and long-term success of the change. They must be educated to understand the changes they are expected to accommodate, and they must be appropriately engaged in the implementation of the change.

You'll notice that I frequently use the word "*sustainable.*" That's because in most instances you'll be interested in change that lasts rather than change that produces only a transitory adjustment in direction, behavior, or performance.

It's probably obvious by now that a person can fill multiple roles, even simultaneously. It's common for a Champion of a change to fill the role of change Agent for the same change at the same time — promoting the change while managing the details of execution and implementation. In some instances, that same person may also be a reinforcing Sponsor.

Nearly every member of the CAST of Characters starts out as a Target. Before you can engage someone else as a Sponsor, for example, you must first understand and address his information needs, assumptions, and attitudes. In asking him to accept the role of Sponsor, you must specify the behaviors required for effective sponsorship. You will deal with him as a Target as you negotiate the sponsorship "contract" and reach agreement on mutual expectations. Even after the new role is accepted, you will continue to coach the Target/Sponsor to ensure that you get the support your change effort requires.

"A person can fill multiple roles, even simultaneously."

Avoid the Black Hole

An example of sponsorship failure was seen in the story of the manufacturing company CEO who assumed his unilateral command would automatically produce the change he wanted. This is depicted in the "Black Hole" illustration seen here. The term "black hole" is borrowed from the field of astrophysics where it's used to describe those regions in space from which nothing—not even light—can escape. There's a frustrating equivalent to the black hole in the corporate universe. Management "announces" a change initiative, then all traces of the change vanish in the bureaucracy. Akin to the black hole in space that consumes everything that travels in its vicinity, various players in the middle of the organization either distort or withhold information so it simply disappears. In many organizations, these black holes are a major cause of the "change du jour" mentality.

> *If you want to truly understand something, try to change it.*
> **Kurt Lewin**

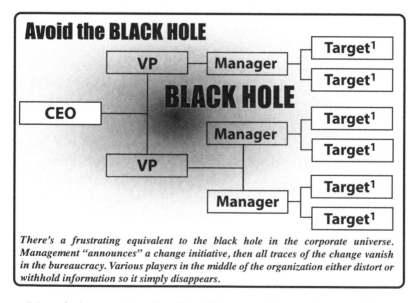

Avoid the BLACK HOLE

CEO — VP — Manager — Target[1] / Target[1]

BLACK HOLE

Manager — Target[1] / Target[1]

VP — Manager — Target[1] / Target[1]

There's a frustrating equivalent to the black hole in the corporate universe. Management "announces" a change initiative, then all traces of the change vanish in the bureaucracy. Various players in the middle of the organization either distort or withhold information so it simply disappears.

Now let's examine the flip side to see how robust and strategic sponsorship can help overcome even the strongest resistance and help produce the change you want.

In 1980 the USS *Saratoga*, one of the U.S. Navy's "super" aircraft carriers, was scheduled to receive the most extensive industrial overhaul ever performed on any Navy ship. The work would take at least 28 months, and would be an economic boon for southern Virginia because the work was slated to be done by the Newport News Shipbuilding company, the largest industrial employer in the state of Virginia. Newport News had had a "lock" on the deal for years. But the members of PENJERDEL—a group of business, government, and academic leaders promoting the mutual interests of Pennsylvania, New Jersey, and Delaware—had another idea. They thought it was in the best interests of the taxpayer (not to mention the PENJERDEL region) for the *Saratoga* work to be done at the Philadelphia Naval Shipyard, a public operation.

At the time, I was a young executive at Campbell Soup Company, headquartered in South Jersey just across the Delaware River from Philadelphia. Campbell's CEO asked me to work with PENJERDEL to "bring the *Saratoga* to Philadelphia." Although I was eager to please the boss, my heart wasn't at all vested in such a mission. First, my own Washington experience suggested it would be a fool's errand to wade through the bureaucratic maze to reverse a long-standing decision on such an expensive and politically-charged issue. Second, my personal political leanings led me to assume that surely such a huge undertaking was in better hands with the private company in Virginia than it would be at a government facility in Philadelphia. I knew that many influential people in our area's business community held similar private-is-better-than-public sentiments.

That's where the CAST of Characters came into play. A man named Thatcher Longstreth would fill a key role in this political theater. Thatcher, a bow-tied businessman with an aristocratic bearing, was founder of PENJERDEL. A former member of the Philadelphia city council, Thatcher was highly respected and well connected with people of every social stratum and political stripe. Thatcher made his case to me. He told me about huge cost overruns at the Virginia com-

> *The bamboo that bends is stronger than the oak that resists.*
> **Japanese Proverb**

pany. He said politics should not trump common sense and that the Philadelphia Naval Shipyard had a markedly superior performance record. Bringing the *Saratoga* to Philadelphia for its overhaul would not only be good for the region, Thatcher said, but it would be the right thing to do for the nation. I could almost hear John Philip Sousa music in the background.

I wanted more dispassionate information, data that could withstand what I knew would be a merciless onslaught from Virginia business leaders and their state's congressional delegation. So we engaged the acclaimed Wharton School of Business to conduct an econometric study to compare the performance of the Newport News Shipbuilding company with the Philadelphia Naval Shipyard. To my surprise and Thatcher's delight, the Wharton study came back with an unqualified recommendation for the Philadelphia facility.

We now had the information needed to make a solid economic case for action. In this instance, though, we needed to make a political case, an emotional case, and even a regional pride case as well.

All that would require engaging the full CAST of Characters.

At first, everyone was a Target: business leaders, politicians, the news media, even the president of Campbell who gave me the assignment in the first place. Armed with the Wharton data, I made presentations at area civic luncheons and club meetings. As they caught the vision of what the *Saratoga* project could mean to the local economy, we quickly turned many of the early *Targets* into enthusiastic *Champions*. Some of these Champions offered resources in the form of loaned employees with skills in government relations, communications, and related disciplines. In turn, these *Agents* helped us build traction with our message. I went to Washington and met one-on-one with key Senators and Congressmen, enlisting *Sponsors* for our bring-the-*Saratoga*-to-Philadelphia effort. The change wouldn't require any legislation, but it certainly would involve some high-powered negotiation at the Pentagon. Meanwhile, of course, there was plenty of resistance in southern Virginia. Civic leaders there were every bit as determined to maintain the status quo (have the aircraft carrier overhauled Virginia) as we were to move the work

> *Time is a dressmaker specializing in alterations.*
> **Faith Baldwin**

to Philadelphia. But we were careful to build a strong coalition that was unified in both message and execution.

The result? The USS *Saratoga* was overhauled in Philadelphia, bringing with it thousands of jobs and tens of millions of dollars in collateral economic benefit to the Delaware Valley. And all of it provided the taxpayer with a better bang for the buck.

Use Cascading Sponsorship

The graphic shown here illustrates how an effective coalition of players can help implement change in a corporate environment. Notice that the *Authorizing* Sponsor avoids the mistake of skipping directly to the people at the lower level of the organization chart. To ensure clear communication along the way and to improve the likelihood of stakeholder engagement, the *Authorizing* Sponsor (likely with the help of Champions and Agents) builds a network of *Reinforcing* Sponsors. This cascading sponsorship is an important key to any successful change effort. It's so critical, in fact, that its absence virtually guarantees failure.

"Take the time to cascade. It's easier to prevent a black hole than to fill one in."

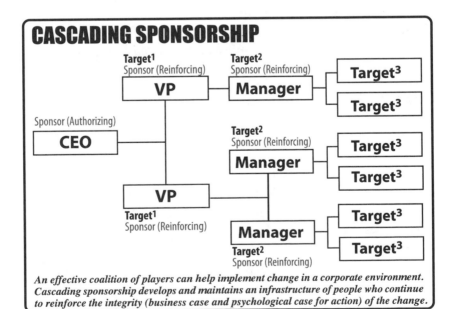

CASCADING SPONSORSHIP

An effective coalition of players can help implement change in a corporate environment. Cascading sponsorship develops and maintains an infrastructure of people who continue to reinforce the integrity (business case and psychological case for action) of the change.

You'll recall several earlier stories about the leadership of Jim Rainey in returning an agribusiness giant to vibrant profitability. Jim would be the first to note that he didn't do it alone. He was very strategic in his use of cascading sponsorship. He first made his case for change to his senior leadership colleagues. Then he dispatched this first layer of Reinforcing Sponsors on "listening tours" throughout the organization's multi-state territory. Good dialogue turned resistance into commitment. The next wave of Reinforcing Sponsors then took the message of change deeper into the organization. People were *engaged*. Jim Rainey understood that voids in the sponsorship chain—black holes—spell disaster.

The primary message here? Cascading sponsorship develops and maintains an infrastructure of people who continue to reinforce the integrity (business case and psychological case for action) of the change.

Take the time to cascade. It's easier to prevent a black hole than to fill one in. Also, remember that black holes can prove fatal to leadership credibility. Any time there's a discrepancy between leadership pronouncements and the reality experienced by your stakeholders, a black hole forms and you lose twice. First, you fail to get the change you want. Second, you teach people to ignore you in the future.

As mentioned before, all along the way you should apply the "What's In It For Me?" question to each of the CAST of Characters. If you did a thorough job in your Scan for Speed Bumps work, you already have a good deal of actionable data.

Key Role Map & Contracting

In your Build a Coalition work I strongly recommend that you literally create a "map" of your coalition showing each of the key members of your CAST of Characters. Because this key role map will change from time to time, you may prefer to create it electronically. Microsoft PowerPoint can do the trick, as well as other software specifically intended for mind mapping. A visual representation of roles and relationships is much easier to work with than a mere list of people. Remember that your coalition must be constantly monitored and *managed*.

> *The key to change is to let go of fear.*
> **Roseanne Cash**

One way to help ensure success with your coalition is to *contract* with the key players. Unclear expectations are a common problem with change efforts. Contracting provides the needed clarity.

I've found it helpful to commit the contracting to writing, literally. Call it a Memorandum of Understanding or anything you wish, but it's still a contract—an explicit agreement on mutual expectations.

Because cascading sponsorship is so critical to every change effort, let's consider how you might contract with a Reinforcing Sponsor.

First, challenge your own assumptions. Just because a person has a relevant title (manager, supervisor, etc.) does not necessarily mean he is ready (or even willing) to provide the sponsorship support you need. So in identifying people to fill the Sponsor role, give yourself honest answers to questions like these:

"Effective sponsorship is about specific behaviors, not about titles or position."

To what extent does this potential Sponsor . . .

- Have credibility with the Targets you want to influence?
- Clearly understand the impact this change will have on targets?
- Communicate in a way that encourages direct feedback?
- Promote collaborative problem solving?
- Demonstrate ownership and personal commitment to the change?
- Walk the talk – personally behave (privately as well as publicly) in ways that are totally consistent with the change message?
- Have good relationships with people who are implementing the change (the Agents)?

You get the idea. Effective sponsorship is about specific behaviors, not about titles or position. Even though your Sponsor authorized the budget or gave a nice kick-off speech, don't assume he will instinctively do and say all the things you need to keep the change effort on track.

When someone agrees to act as a Sponsor for your change effort, it should be no surprise if you say something like "I truly appreciate your willingness to sponsor this change effort. Because your sponsorship is a critical key to our success, could we make sure we have mutual agreement on what we can expect from each other?" That may seem a bit bold, and it is. But it's a request to have the conversation that's absolutely vital to your success.

When you sit down with your Sponsor for the contracting sessions, it's imperative that you're well prepared. I suggest using a specific list of behaviors you need from the Sponsor. This is not the time to tip-toe around. The Sponsor behaviors should be clear and explicit, with no hint of doubletalk.

Your contracting document can begin with something like "Because (name of your change effort) is so important to the future of our organization, (Sponsor) and (You) agree on the following mutual expectations." Then you list—in very explicit terms—the actions you expect from the Sponsor, and the actions the Sponsor can expect from you. Again, it's important that the language be explicit. Also, it's a good idea to talk in terms of SMART goals as discussed in earlier chapters. This contracting document needn't be notarized because that might imply mistrust.

> *Faced with the choice between changing one's mind and proving that there is no need to do so, almost everyone gets busy on the proof.*
> **John Kenneth Galbraith**

But it should be signed by both parties. Simply emphasize that the purpose of the document is to calibrate and align mutual expectations. Drafting this document often requires a second meeting with the Sponsor. That's okay, because it's critical to get this right. You want to be sure that the Sponsor gets no surprises on the requirements of sponsorship, and the Sponsor certainly has a right to have clarity on what to expect from you.

Building a Coalition is not a particularly complicated task. But it is absolutely imperative. You will simplify your life (and probably improve your sleep) if you go about this work strategically. Carefully identify your CAST of Characters. Develop a key role map. Contract with your Sponsors (and others, as necessary). It makes all the difference.

REMEMBER THE FOUR Ts

As you work to Build a Coalition, use the Four Ts.

Think-Friendly

- Be sure you're considering all the questions that people will likely have about the change you're proposing. Actively and continuously engage with your CAST of Characters to ensure that their viewpoints are accommodated in your planning and implementation.
- Use "systems thinking" as you develop your Key Role Map and contract with our Sponsors.
- As always challenge your stories. Beware the natural tendency to downplay or even ignore information that contradicts our own views. Appropriate engagement with your CAST of Characters can provide a good reality check.

Talk-Friendly

- Dialogue early and often with your CAST of Characters. Listen especially carefully to those who disagree with you or who express skepticism about the change you advocate.
- In working with your CAST of Characters, make it safe to put "undiscussables" on the table for open and honest conversation.
- Be especially attentive as you Listen With Empathy, Inquire to Discover, and Advocate With Respect.

Trust-Friendly

- Consciously use the Language of Trust. Deliberately engage in the behaviors of trust. Effective coalitions are fueled by collaboration, which is based on mutual trust.
- Carefully avoid trust busters. In this Build a Coalition work, Double Talk and Pulling Rank are common temptations. Although people play different roles in your change work, remember to treat them as equals. Genuine mutual respect pays huge dividends.

Team-Friendly

- Just as a clear charter is critical to the success of a team, so is an explicit contract vital to the success of your sponsorship. Good sponsorship is all about teamwork.

• Make sure your Sponsors have SMART Goals that are clearly consistent with your change approach and that explicitly support the change strategy you're using.

BUILD A COALITION SELF-ASSESSMENT

Instructions: *Read each statement and decide how accurately it describes your orientation to the **Build a Coalition** principles in this chapter:*
   a. **Never or rarely engage in this behavior (0 points)**
   b. **Sometimes engage in this behavior (1 point)**
   c. **Regularly engage in this behavior (2 points)**
   d. **Always/almost always engage in this behavior (3 points)**

Place the point value of your response choice beside each statement.

_____ I honestly consider the needs of all the CAST of Characters (Champions, Agents, Sponsors, Targets) at every stage of my change work.

_____ Rather than merely solicit support and hope for the best, I specifically *contract* with the Sponsors of the change I'm promoting.

_____ In deciding on my approach to change, I consider ability issues as well as motivational issues.

_____ I use SMART goals to help Sponsors know what's needed and expected from them.

_____ I use cascading sponsorship to help ensure my change work doesn't vanish in a bureaucratic "black hole."

_____ In conversations and other communication, I frequently follow through with my Sponsors to make sure the support they're providing is consistent with what they agreed to do.

_____ **Total Number of Points**

Interpreting Your Scores

0-5:   Your change approach is likely having little real effect in your organization. Without the active, coordinated support of a coalition of people, you cannot expect your efforts to produce the result you want. An active CAST of Characters can help you spot resistance and work to turn it into engagement.

6-10:   You're on the right track to building a coalition. But unless you are mindfully tending to the needs of all of your CAST of Characters, you're probably missing some important opportunities to engage people's heads, hearts, and hopes. Again, remember the WIIFM (What's In It For Me?) principle.

11-15: You clearly "get it" when it comes to appropriate involvement of Champions, Agents, Sponsors, and Targets. By contracting with your Sponsors, you're exponentially increasing the likelihood that your change will succeed. Now, to help make the change sustainable, ensure that your Sponsors understand that they need to continue with the CPR (see "Converse, Practice, Reinforce" in Chapter 3).

Leaders are visionaries with a poorly developed sense of fear and no concept of the odds against them.
Robert Jarvik

When I consider what tremendous consequences come from little things, I'm tempted to think there are no little things.
Bruce Barton

It's a pity to shoot the pianist when the piano is out of tune.
René Coty

I wouldn't give a fig for simplicity this side of complexity but I'd give my right arm for simplicity on the other side of complexity.
Oliver Wendell Holmes

Chapter

Step 5:
Ford the Streams

There is no "right" culture.
There is only the right fit.

Culture eats strategy for breakfast.

What does that mean in our context here? Simply this: When there's a serious conflict between organizational culture and somebody's change effort, culture wins. Always.

So doesn't it make sense to understand your culture? Doesn't it make sense to identify the areas of possible disconnect? And doesn't it make sense to devise—and execute—plans for either changing the culture or lessening the effect of the conflicts?

Smart change agents carefully navigate the currents of organizational change. And when the currents aren't going their way, they Ford the Streams.

In a 2011 study of multiple industries about the globe, Booz & Company concluded that "there may be no more critical source of business success or failure than a company's culture—it trumps strategy and leadership." This isn't to suggest that strategy doesn't matter, the researchers said, "but rather that the particular strategy a company employs will succeed only if it is supported by the appropriate cultural attributes."

Like a lot of other words in modern conversation, "culture" is used to denote a wide range of phenomena. For our purposes here, I'm using "culture" to mean the *patterns* of ways that people interact with each other. Culture includes *values, assumptions, behaviors,* and the *unwritten* rules mentioned in Chapter 3. Culture includes *norms, customs* and *rituals, stories* and *myths.* It includes climate, *metaphors* and *symbols.*

Some people make "culture" more complicated than it needs to be. They devise convoluted systems for exploring and explaining culture, thereby stealing emphasis from the real implementation results they claim to seek. Others make the opposite mistake and try to over-simplify culture with a few catchy slogans and wall posters. Somewhere in between is a more productive approach. I believe the sweet spot in the middle must include sensible diagnostics coupled with a well-conceived and carefully executed plan of action.

And one thing should be emphasized up front. Cultures *evolve.* Don't expect to change yours overnight. Some people make the mistake of assuming that a "new" culture can simply be installed, like you would install a new software program on your computer. Not so. One of my favorite cartoons shows a group of business people at a conference table. On the nearby wall is a large graph, depicting a steep decline in performance. One of the guys at the table says, "What we need here is a good long-term quick fix." If you expect the same, you'll be disappointed. Culture change is a long-term proposition, and there are no quick fixes. You can indeed earn some early wins (the proverbial low-hanging fruit), but genuine culture change requires an extended period of time. (There are exceptions. With thoughtful leadership, it is possible to infuse a culture with a fresh spirit that produces impressive, relatively quick results. An example would be Jim Rainey's turnaround at Farmland Industries, discussed in Chapter 3.)

> *It's easier to act your way into a new way of thinking than to think your way into a new way of acting.*
> **Millard Fuller**

Cultural awareness is critical for leaders. Leaders who fail to become explicitly conscious of the cultures in which they operate have no hope of "managing" their cultures. The cultures will manage the leaders.

Focus on Behaviors

As always, the focus should be on behaviors, because it's behaviors that produce results.

Revisit the questions you asked yourself and others in your Validate the Journey efforts. To what extent does the desired future you described match the present conditions? Be honest with yourself. Be realistic. Don't hedge.

In your Scan for Speed Bumps work, what disconnects do you notice? Where are the incongruities between professed values and actual practice? I earlier described a national company that made a really big deal of promoting teamwork and collaboration. But all of their rewards focused on *individual* performance. I've seen many manufacturing and utility companies that say all the right things about safety, but their actual practices seem to value schedules and budgets over everything else. That sort of disconnect produces the unintended consequence of cynicism and distrust.

"As always, the focus should be on behaviors, because it's behaviors that produce results."

As Yogi Berra famously noted, you can observe a lot by watching. What are the artifacts in your environment that tell you something about the culture? These include things like dress codes, reserved parking spaces, the size of people's offices, and other tangible clues about how values are operationalized.

You can also learn a lot by listening. Listen to the conversations in the hallways and employee cafeteria. Listen to the stories people tell. Listen to the legends perpetuated. The things people talk about —and *how* they talk about them—can shed a lot of light on their culture. (In fact, this talk is itself an important part of the culture.)

In one public utility company I visited one-on-one with 15 randomly-selected employees. My purpose was to get a preliminary feel for the organization's cultural attributes. One of my requests was "Please tell me a story that you believe exemplifies the relationship between senior management and the rest of the workforce." Interestingly, 12 of the 15 people I interviewed told me exactly the same story. About ten years ago, they reported, a senior executive came to the plant to make a presentation in an "all hands" meeting. He subjected the employees to "death by PowerPoint." Then, with his back to the group while he gathered up his notes, the executive perfunctorily asked "Are there any questions?" After a long pause, one employee inquired about a particular point in the presentation. The home office guy slowly turned around and said to the employee: "If you had been listening more carefully you wouldn't ask such an ill-informed question." There was an audible gasp from the group. But the executive wasn't finished. He added to his off-the-chart rudeness with a condescending lecture about how performance would benefit if employees would be less concerned about themselves and more concerned about the company's bottom line.

Unfortunately, variations of that experience are not unusual. But in this case, I found two things especially relevant. First, a dozen people told me precisely the same story about an incident that occurred a full decade earlier. But I was even more amazed when I learned that only four of the 12 even worked at the company ten years before. They had merely heard the story from their workmates. And because the story served as a metaphor for their own experiences and observations, they had adopted it as their own. Those assumptions were having a profound effect on their behavior. Culture really does matter.

> *We cannot become what we need to be by remaining what we are.*
> **Max Dupree**

It's All About Subcultures

Although we're using the word *culture* here in the singular, we should really be talking about *cultures* in the plural. Even the simplest organization has multiple cultures. In my family, for example, my wife and I have been married for 45 years. During that time we have evolved a "marriage culture" in our relationship with each other. When we're with our grown children and their spouses, there's a slightly different (though overlapping) culture at play. And when some of our 11 grandchildren are present, yet another culture can be observed. The "Duncan family culture" is therefore the sum of multiple subcultures. These subcultures have similar characteristics because we have a lot of common experiences and values. But there are some differences, too, and we've learned to accommodate and even treasure those differences.

In a corporate setting we can see a similar dynamic. It's foolhardy to expect a senior executive to have the identical perspective as a new recruit on things like strategic plans, work processes, open communication, performance accountability, and a range of other issues. They might generally agree on the "values" listed in the company's annual report, but they likely have very different views on how those values are (or should be) operationalized in their own versions of the real world.

One CEO was stunned to see survey results showing that 70% of his employees thought the IT department was inept in keeping the company's computer systems up and running. When I inquired about his own personal experience, he said the IT help desk always sent someone to his office immediately when he had a problem. I asked him if he thought that prompt response might have anything to do with his title. Then I told him about the experience of many of his employees who waited up to 72 hours for help. It had never occurred to the CEO that he was viewing the world through his rose-tinted CEO glasses.

In an earlier chapter I mentioned a company president who furiously responded to a survey finding that many of his employees didn't feel free to speak openly and honestly. The elephant in the room was his own bullying style that made candor a dangerous behavior in his organization. This was another case of culture disconnect, an undiscussable with an unintended consequence. He somehow failed to notice that his yelling and name-calling made people reluctant to offer frank and truthful opinions. He hired smart people, but then he dumbed them down.

In your organization, you can likely observe the same kind of cultural differences. This is not to suggest that having differing viewpoints in the workplace is necessarily a bad thing. It's simply reality. In fact—when appropriately appreciated—differing viewpoints can foster vitality and productive energy. Every organization has multi-cultural work teams. I'm not talking about only the most obvious differences such as gender, age, ethnicity, or even nationality. I'm also talking about *occupational* cultures that can be very strong. Take a manufacturing plant as an example. Senior leaders may be preoccupied with things such as planning, budgets, schedules, and output. A maintenance worker, on the other hand, may focus primarily on his workload and whether he has the appropriate tools to complete his tasks. And although "safety" may be sincerely valued by most people in the company, the maintenance worker—because he is most vulnerable to physical injury—likely regards "safety" more as an imperative practice than as an abstract slogan.

In this world of subcultures, doesn't it make sense to Ford the Stream rather than try to re-channel the entire river? In other words, rather than engage in a futile effort to get everyone to walk lockstep along exactly the same path, why not make it acceptable to reach the same goals via multiple paths?

I recommend that you work for cultural alignment rather than absolute cultural integration. In most change efforts, it's much easier to draw on the strengths of the subcultures than to invest what is often fruitless energy in trying to change the subcultures. Again, the focus should be on *behaviors*. If some behaviors are simply unacceptable, focus on altering those behaviors that make the greatest difference. Use appropriate influence levers (see Chapter 10) to make the desired behaviors attractive while rendering the negative behaviors unappealing.

> *I would not waste my life in friction when it could be turned into momentum.*
> **Frances Willard**

Reach Explicit Agreement on Values

A good approach is first to agree on values. This requires some serious work, and involves far more than wall posters and high testosterone coffee mug slogans. Get people from throughout the organization to discuss and agree on definitions of the values they claim to espouse. "Safety," for example is often used in a broad, generic sense to connote physical safety. That's very important, especially in, say, a manufacturing environment or a nuclear power plant. But physical safety cannot be achieved in the best sense unless and until there is psychological safety.

Many organizations operate as a confederation of states without a constitution. What do I mean by that? They have multiple subcultures but no unifying framework to hold them together. They share the same corporate logo, but in reality they operate as a group of separate—and sometimes competing—fiefdoms. The result is redundancy, suspicion, anemic performance, and missed opportunity.

How can a confederation of states (subcultures) create a unifying constitution? It's not about drafting a document, it's more about agreeing upon—and then *practicing*—the behaviors that translate professed values into real results.

I've worked with many organizations that suffered from this challenge. I encourage them to have frank discussions about the values they claim to embrace. I press them to get very specific in defining what those values "look like" in terms of observable behaviors. I teach them to conduct this kind of dialogue with members of different subcultures in their organizations. They are often surprised to discover that people see "values" through different lenses. I teach

> *"Many organizations operate as a confederation of states without a constitution."*

them that one viewpoint is not necessarily more or less valid than another; they're simply different. Once that is acknowledged, the parties are then able to blend their views or to discuss ways to accommodate the differences.

Back to the issue of safety: Many of my clients have dramatically improved their safety records (reducing lost-time injuries and improving similar metrics) simply by learning the skills of open and honest dialogue. When workers learn how to talk so people will listen, and listen so people will talk, all sorts of good things result. One of those good things is that the culture they have evolves into the culture they need.

Diagnostics That Count

Earlier I mentioned the helpfulness of conversations, one-on-one interviews, focus group discussions, surveys, and 360-degree feedback. These are not only useful in identifying speed bumps that interfere with your change efforts, they can also help you understand and deal with culture issues.

Here I will say more about surveys and 360-degree feedback.

When my grandfather taught me to use some of his woodworking tools, he always emphasized safety and utility. First, he didn't want me to harm myself or anyone else. So he carefully demonstrated the proper use of the tools. This sometimes included showing me how *not* to use a particular tool. (Novices often overestimate their abilities.) And he taught me which tools were appropriate for different tasks. A flat-head screwdriver, for example, is not the right tool for scraping paint or applying putty.

This same kind of education can help when we examine culture. Managers like to quantify things. They like to measure things. They like to manipulate things. They like to label things and put them into tidy boxes. So managers' tool of choice is often a survey. They can use a survey to gather data, produce charts and graphs, and draw neat conclusions about their "culture." The problem is that "surveys" can often do more damage than good. That's what can happen when poorly written survey items seem to imply more than one question at a time, thereby rendering meaningful analysis impossible. That's what can happen when novices—even otherwise smart novices—try to practice arts and sciences outside their areas of expertise. Don't kid yourself. Effective surveying is indeed both an art and a science.

My favorite culture assessment tool is an instrument we call the Culture Alignment Profile. It's actually two surveys in one. The first portion invites the respondent to indicate how others in his work group would likely behave in certain situations. This helps us understand the *assumptions* at play in the organization regarding such things as leadership, supervision, psychological ownership, and other issues related to employee engagement and organizational performance. The second part of the survey consists of statements about the organization's operating practices. Respondents are asked to indicate (on a 5-point scale) the extent to which they agree or disagree with each statement. Examples might be "People in our organization seem more interested in accomplishing excellent work than in who gets the credit," or "The values we claim to embrace here are consistently modeled by my supervisor," or "With my supervisor I feel free to voice my honest opinion on any issue." Along with appropriate demographic items, this approach gives us a fairly clear picture of the culture and how it affects outcomes. It also enables us to see the extent to which actual behaviors and practices may be out of sync with professed values and goals.

Why use multiple kinds of items in the same survey? Because the right combination of different question types can flesh out the meaning and help diminish the chance of misinterpretation. For instance, we might ask respondents to tell us the extent to which they agree or disagree with the statement "Our performance appraisal system really helps us do better work." Let's say that 75% of respondents disagree with that statement. A knee-jerk reaction might be, "Oh, my goodness. We need a completely new performance appraisal system." While that may be true, it could also be true that the system itself is not the real issue. It could be that people's *assumptions* about how the system is administered is the more salient issue. If employees are suspicious about the motives and practices of senior executives in general, they are likely to be suspicious about something as otherwise benign as the performance appraisal system. By carefully examining work-

> **It is what we learn after we think we know it all, that counts.**
> **John Wooden**

force assumptions (the first part of the Culture Alignment Profile tool), you're in position to reach more reasonable conclusions about the culture and its impact on behaviors and outcomes.

Just as a good physician gathers diagnostic data on your health condition before prescribing a remedy, so should you collect pertinent data on your culture before introducing adjustments in alignment. There's often more to culture than meets the eye. Solid diagnostics can help you discover and understand what's really going on.

Don't limit your diagnostics to an overall culture assessment. Although such an assessment (with the right tool and skillful analysis) can provide many helpful insights, it can also invite a form of denial. I've seen many people look at culture assessment data and say, in effect: "Yeah, there's a lot of that stuff going on around here. But this doesn't apply to me and my group." I love to be in a position to say, "Oh, yes, but it does. Let me show you exactly how it *does* apply to you and your group."

In addition to an overall culture assessment with appropriate demographic breakouts, I strongly recommend the use of 360-degree performance feedback. A good 360 tool provides individuals with personalized, laser beam specific data. It compares the individual's own views about his behaviors and performance with the views that others have of him. In this instance, the "others" include people who are especially important to the individual's success—his manager, peers, and direct reports. Hence the term "360-degree feedback." My 360 instrument of choice can be customized to address the culture and performance issues that are most relevant in the individual's work environment. The individual's final report consists of about 35 pages of data. Not a single page is boilerplate. Every table and graph and written comment is specifically about the individual being profiled. The report is accompanied by a detailed Action Planning Guide. This helps the individual interpret the findings, then translate them into simple (one page) action plans for improvement. When this process is accompanied by an accountability protocol—for example, asking the individual to discuss his action plans with his immediate supervisor—amazing (and measurable) improvements often result.

> *Cooperation isn't the absence of conflict but a means of managing conflict.*
> **Deborah Tannen**

Whatever diagnostic approach you take, be sure that the diagnostic tools are your servant, not your master. Some people make the mistake of chasing numbers. They focus on simply improving their survey results rather than focusing on the behaviors that produce improvements that are then reflected in survey results. Single-minded focus on desired behaviors is the key to improved performance.

When your computer's operating system isn't working right, even the best software program cannot deliver the results you want. Culture is your organization's operating system. Tend to your culture with tender-loving care and it will help you and your people get the outcomes you're after.

REMEMBER THE FOUR Ts

As you work to *Ford the Streams,* use the Four Ts.

Think-Friendly

- Carefully consider all the nuances in your organization's culture—including the various subcultures. Use the FIND-IT model to challenge the stories you've told yourself. Invite others to challenge their stories, too.
- Use the Systems Questions (Chapter 8) to examine the practices and protocols in your culture. Which ones are really serving you well? Which ones are producing unintended consequences? What are the Unwritten Rules in your organization? What impact do they have on people's behaviors? On trust? On collaboration?
- Identify the Saints, Ain'ts, and Complaints in your workplace. Which ones can be converted to help with the change effort? Which ones will need special attention as you deal with resistance?

Talk-Friendly

- What practices, behaviors, policies, or procedures are the "elephants" that need to be called out and tamed? Who's in the best position to do the taming?
- What seems to be going on in people's Left-Hand Columns? How can a clearer understanding of that phenomenon help your cause? How can it help in the elephant-taming process?
- Be especially attentive as you Listen With Empathy, Inquire to Discover, and Advocate With Respect. These behaviors go a long way in encouraging people to confront undiscussables.

Trust-Friendly

- People are very protective of their subcultures. As you identify and examine those subcultures, consciously use the Language of Trust. Deliberately engage in the behaviors of trust. Be respectful.
- Carefully avoid trust busters. In this Ford the Streams work, Double Talk and Pulling Rank are common temp-

tations. As you solicit honest and meaningful feedback, be sure to reciprocate with feedback to others. Candor goes a long way in building trust.

Team-Friendly

- Is Ferris Bueller on your team? Do any of your people behave like the high school wise guy from the pop movie? Just a couple of characters like that can spell real trouble for your change effort. Some resistance can be expected, but serious trouble-makers should be invited to operate somewhere else.
- To the extent possible, make sure your various groups (subcultures) have team charters. Most importantly, make sure the overall organization has a unifying document that explicitly spells out the professed valued and expected behaviors. (Don't be a confederation of states without a constitution.)
- Be sure that your reward and information systems provide a nurturing context for genuine collaboration between and among your subcultures.

FORD THE STREAMS SELF-ASSESSMENT

Instructions: *Read each statement and decide how accurately it describes your organization's adherence to the Ford the Streams principles in this chapter:*

a. **This never or rarely occurs (0 points)**
b. **This sometimes occurs (1 point)**
c. **This regularly occurs (2 points)**
d. **This always or almost always occurs (3 points)**

Place the point value of your response choice beside each statement.

_____ We use a specific set of metrics to help us understand the effects of culture in our organization.

_____ Our senior leaders clearly "get it" that they operate in a different world from more junior people in the organization.

_____ We appreciate the differences in our organization's subcultures.

_____ We draw on the strengths of our subcultures rather than try to get everyone to see things in exactly the same way.

_____ Our day-to-day behaviors align very closely with the values we profess to embrace.

_____ Total Number of Points

Interpreting Your Scores

0-5: You may be falling into the trap of regarding your organization's culture as one big cohesive collection of people. That's seldom the reality. Most organizational cultures consist of multiple, overlapping subcultures. People may generally agree on a set of stated values (integrity, open communication, safety, quality, etc.), but they often have different assumptions about how those values are operationalized in observable behaviors.

6-10: Your organization is doing some good things in tending to the "culture issue." But there's still room for improvement. Make sure you're using tried-and-true tools for measuring the impact of culture. Make sure you're using clear and meaningful definitions of the values being touted as important. Make sure people at every level are being held accountable for "living" those values in ways that help produce desired outcomes.

11-15: Cultural factors, and their impact on performance, are clearly emphasized in your organization. Be sure to measure "the culture stuff" on a regular basis. Culture can be very elastic. A change in leadership, for example, can influence people to behave in different ways. Be very clear about the behaviors that produce the results you want, then reinforce those behaviors at every opportunity.

*If you can't explain it simply, you don't
understand it well enough.*
Albert Einstein

*We change when the pain to change is less than
the pain to remain as we are.*
Ed Foreman

*Your assumptions are your windows on the world.
Scrub them off every once in a while, or the light
won't come in.*
Alan Alda

*Amateurs practice until they get it right.
Professionals practice until they can't get it wrong.*
Unknown

Chapter

Step 6:
Stay on Message

*It's not what you claim to believe that's most important—
but what you model, encourage, reward, and allow to happen.*

George Bernard Shaw had it right: "The single biggest problem in communication is the illusion that it has taken place."

Too many so-called leaders buy into the myth that simply sending a message will produce the result they want. That single mistake is at the root of most challenges with change efforts.

Do you remember the game called Grapevine? It's also known as Broken Telephone, Whisper Down the Lane, or Pass the Message. It works like this: One person whispers a message to another. The message is then passed through a successive line of several other people until the last player announces the message to the entire group. Errors inevitably accumulate in the retellings. The message announced by the last player differs significantly—often amusingly —from the one conveyed by the first. Children sometimes play this game at parties or on the playground. But the game is often unwittingly played by adults in the workplace, with not-so-funny results. This phenomenon is a metaphor for cumulative error, especially the inaccuracies that emerge as messages (including rumors and gossip) are spread. It's also a reminder of how carefully we must be in managing our communications.

In one company the CEO announced that changes would be made in the performance appraisal system. He didn't specify exactly what the changes would involve. What he *meant* was that the mechanics of administering the performance appraisal system were bureaucratic and cumbersome. What he *meant* was that the system would be simplified to a more user-friendly format. What he *meant* was that senior managers had listened to the troops and were responding to their feedback. But he failed to say any of that. Then, to his chagrin, his initial announcement that "changes will be made in the performance appraisal system" created a firestorm of recrimination throughout the employee population. Because trust was so fragile in the organization, the CEO's message about the performance appraisal system was translated as "we've been too soft on you people so we're going to open your personnel files and lower your performance ratings." Ouch! The employees expected the worst. And in the absence of clarity and appropriate repetition, they heard precisely what they expected. The rest of the story is that the CEO made the situation even worse when, instead of acknowledging his own communication failure, he chastised his employees for being so cynical.

The CAST of Characters

As you manage your communication, recall the CAST of Characters discussed in earlier chapters. Remember that throughout the communication process people may play multiple roles simultaneously. *Champions*, the people who work to gain commitment and resources for the change, must make a good case for the change they advocate. *Agents*, those who implement the change, must maintain open communication with *Champions, Sponsors,* and *Targets. Sponsors,* those who authorize, legitimize, and demonstrate ownership for the change, must constantly reinforce their support. And everyone in the process must address the concerns and needs of the *Targets.* Meanwhile, everyone is a *Target* for someone else. The CEO mentioned above regarded himself only as the transmitter of information and instruction. He failed to recognize that true communication is a continuous send-receive-send-receive loop. His approach came across as "Here's my message, end of discussion."

Manage the Meaning

Change-Friendly leaders—those who transform good intentions into great performance—get very clear on what and how and when they want to communicate. Then they Stay on Message.

Change-Friendly leadership is all about managing *meaning*. And because *meaning* is conveyed in behaviors as well as in words, you'll want to reinforce your intended meaning in multiple ways.

Here are some key points to remember:

Respect the Targets. Effective communication involves adjusting the balance (leaving the present state) in the *Targets'* frame of reference. Will people really understand what you're trying to tell them? They will if you package your messages

> *Listening is a gift you give to others. Be generous.*
> **Unknown**

in *their* language, in *their* analogies, in stories that make sense from *their* perspective, in terms that are meaningful in *their* world.

In the absence of information, a natural tendency is to fill in the blanks with our own assumptions. Pre-empt that by candidly (1) telling people what you know, (2) telling them what you don't know, (3) telling them when you'll know, and (4) telling them when you'll tell them. Most people can sense if you're blowing smoke. So don't.

Employ an integrated systems approach. Your change-friendly leadership tools must include (1) a communication system, (2) a learning system, and (3) a reward and reinforcement system.

Your communication system needn't be complicated, but it certainly needs to include a well-conceived strategy with appropriate tactics. Precisely what is the core message (see Validate the Journey)? Who are the most credible people to communicate the core message? What media are most appropriate to use (face-to-face communication is always the ideal). Typically, Targets do *not* want to hear about change from the HR department. They do want to hear it from their manager, from their manager's manager, and from the head of the organization. They want to bring questions directly to people they know and trust. This way, Targets become part of the communication cascade and are more likely to become partners in the change process. Notice that last word: process. Change is rarely a singular event. It's a *process*. To support it well, your communication must be methodically planned and executed. After the core message is developed and delivered, what supporting messages will be needed? Who should deliver them? When? On what schedule? How will resistance be handled? None of this can be left to chance. Carefully plan your communication system.

Your learning system is especially critical in your change effort. When people are invited to change, they inevitably ask the WIIFM question ("What's In It For Me?"). They also usually ask "Do I *want* to change?" and "Do I *know how* to change?" If your change involves the introduction of a new computer software program, people will need to learn how to use it. If the change involves a new piece of equipment on the production line, people will need to learn how to use the new equipment and understand how it interacts with existing equipment. If the change involves something intangible like behaviors, people will need training on multiple dimensions. They'll need to learn precisely *what* the "new" behaviors are. They'll need to learn *why* the behaviors are relevant to them and their work, and what kind of outcomes they can expect.

> **Education is not filling a bucket, but lighting a fire.**
> **William Butler Yeats**

They'll need to learn *how* to use the behaviors. And they'll need to practice the behaviors in a psychologically comfortable environment that allows for coaching and correction. In the realm of "culture change," which for many people is a nebulous concept anyway, it's especially important to provide very explicit training and practice in the specific behaviors that produce the kind of culture you're after.

With a carefully planned communication system in place, supported by a learning system that fills in the knowledge and skill gap, one might assume that a change is destined to succeed. But not so fast. There's still one more critical piece. To enable your change to succeed, you can't simply talk about it, and you can't just teach people new skills and behaviors. You must implement a thoughtful reinforcement system. In Chapter 3 we introduced the Converse-Practice-Reinforce (CPR) Model. Reinforcement involves deliberate application of affirmation, encouragement, and "rewards" for positive behavior. In addition, effective reinforcement involves specific and deliberate (and friendly) correction of negative behavior. If you can remember the word PICNIC, you'll have a helpful set of

guidelines at your disposal. Reinforcement for new, desired behavior should be Positive, Immediate, and Certain. Reinforcement of old, undesired behavior should be Negative, Immediate, and Certain. If people in your organization have a "this, too, shall pass" mentality about change, the PICNIC approach can help bring them around to the reality that this change is not going away. Remember that your PICs and your NICs must be clear and specific. This is no time for ambiguity. Your Think-Friendly, Talk-Friendly, Trust-Friendly and Team-Friendly skills will serve you well in administering the PICs and NICs. Be sure that you use the language and the frame of reference of your Target(s). Either you reinforce the behaviors of the desired change or you reinforce the behaviors of the status quo. If you fail to do the former, you will by default accomplish the latter.

Positive norms will stick only if the group—not just the leader —puts them into practice over and over again. Clarity is one of the hallmarks of effective groups. When the group is crystal clear about expected behaviors and reaches agreement about mutual accountability, it's easier for group members to practice the desired "new" behaviors and increasingly uncomfortable to practice the previous behaviors. In fact, peer-to-peer accountability is a sign of excellent leadership because people are doing the right things for the right reasons even when the leader is not present.

In all of this, be sure to model the behaviors you expect in others. For example, if one of the "new" behaviors you're trying to promote is about building trust and respect, be sure to exhibit those very values when you hold someone accountable for not practicing the desired behaviors.

And remember that reinforcement includes rewards. Although money is on everyone's list, study after study shows that monetary rewards are not necessarily the most effective. At the other end of the spectrum, don't assume that coffee mugs or company T-shirts will provide the best recognition. The workers at a manufacturing plant in Arizona exceeded the monthly production goal. Managers had the great idea of actually asking the workers what kind of recognition they would most welcome. The majority of the workers were Catholic, Mexican immigrants who were separated from their families for extended periods. To the surprise of their managers, the workers said the reward they would most appreciate would be to have a priest celebrate a special mass on the production floor. Remember to ask. Then listen.

Practice, Practice, Practice

How do these principles look in actual practice? In Chapter 7 you learned about Ed Halpin, the president and CEO at South Texas Project (STP). STP is a world-class nuclear power plant. As you can imagine, the people who work there are very much the no-nonsense type. They take their work very seriously and they have zero patience with anything that doesn't add value. Several years ago the people at STP had, by their own admission, sort of plateaued. They

> *"These Talk-Friendly skills would enable them to step up to risky conversations."*

had improved quite a bit, but then they found themselves stuck on good-but-not-great. So they asked for our help. We introduced them to a training program in dialogue skills. These Talk-Friendly skills would enable them to step up to risky conversations about safety, accountability, and other critical performance issues. I've already told you about Ed Halpin's strong, personal sponsorship of the training. That sponsorship wasn't a short-term, flavor-of-the-month kind of thing. It was and is a long-term commitment. Ed's sponsorship is more than just words. It's reflected in the way he and his colleagues constantly "stay on message" in reinforcing the desired behaviors. The need for improved dialogue skills was not just identified and discussed. Something was done about it. Nearly two thousand STP people participated in the skills training. Much of the training—which continues today—is conducted by managers, not just training personnel. People are held accountable for practicing the skills learned in the training, and they're recognized and rewarded when they make those skills their default behaviors. In STP meetings you'll hear explicit discussion about the skills, with specific reference to how the skills helped in a particular situation or how they could be used even more effectively in the future. Ed Halpin has now moved to another company. But the legacy of excellence remains alive and well at STP. Talk-Friendly skills are definitely not a passing fad there. They have become the go-to behaviors of hundreds of smart people who are now working smarter than ever. But it didn't happen because someone spouted some slogans or put up some posters. It's the result of relentless attention to the details of good communication: Listening. Clarifying. Repeating. Reinforcing.

> *Correction does much, but encouragement does more.*
> **Goethe**

Another great example of staying on message is at Campbell Soup Company. When Douglas Conant took over as Campbell's president and CEO in 2001, the company's stock was trailing the S&P 500 and falling steeply. Of all the major food companies in the world, Campbell was the rock bottom performer. Doug's challenge was to lead the company back to greatness. It looked like a daunting task. In Doug's words, the company had "a very toxic culture." Employees were disheartened, management systems were dysfunctional, trust was low, a lot of people felt and behaved like victims. When Doug first entered the scene, employee engagement was extremely anemic: for every two people actively engaged, one person was looking for a job. "You can't expect a company to perform at high levels unless people are personally engaged," Doug said. "And they won't be personally engaged unless they believe you [the leader] are personally engaged in trying to make their lives better."

Doug said there are two keys to staying on the message of engagement. The first is to "declare yourself." People aren't mind readers. They can't know what you're thinking unless you tell them. Explicitly. By declaring yourself, you might say something like, "Okay, we're going to make it safe to challenge the status quo.

"You must model the new behaviors at every opportunity. You must walk the talk."

We're going to make it safe to offer opinions that run counter to the current thinking. We're going to have a culture that places real value on fresh ideas." Doug said a second step to staying on message is to "deliver on your promises." You must hold yourself accountable to the new standard. You must model the new behaviors at every opportunity. You must walk the talk.

As Campbell's CEO, Doug walked the engagement talk in the most literal way. He wore a pedometer on his belt, and sometime during each day—whether at the headquarters building in New Jersey or at a production plant in Europe or Asia—he put on a pair of walking shoes. His goal was to log 10,000 steps a day (great for the heart!) and to interact meaningfully with as many employees as possible. "This practice showed people I was paying attention, that I was 'all in,'" Doug said. These brief encounters had multiple benefits. They helped Doug stay informed with the goings-on throughout the company, and to connect personally with people at every level. They enabled people to put a human face on the company's strategy and direction. And they enabled Doug to help celebrate the thousands of little successes that add up to big differences.

In addition to putting in lots of steps, Doug did something else that's unusual for a CEO. He hand-wrote up to 20 notes a day to employees celebrating their successes and contributions. "In my line of work I've been trained to find the busted number in a spreadsheet and identify things that are going wrong," he said. "Most cultures don't do a good job of celebrating contributions.

> *"Messages matter. Repetition matters. Clarity matters."*

So I developed the practice of writing notes to our employees. Over ten years, it amounted to more than 30,000 notes, and we had only 20,000 employees. Wherever I'd go in the world, in employee cubicles you'd find my handwritten notes posted on their bulletin boards." Doug's notes were not gratuitous. They celebrated specific contributions. And because the notes were handwritten, they seemed to be treasured more than an email message might be.

What's the primary point here? Messages matter. Repetition matters. Clarity matters. The "personal touch" matters. In fact, Doug Conant has coauthored a bestselling book on the subject. It's entitled *TouchPoints: Creating Powerful Leadership Connections in the Smallest of Moments.*

At a time when the information age has morphed into the interruption age, great leaders like Doug Conant learn to look at daily interactions through a fresh lens. Every interaction—whether it's planned or spontaneous, casual or choreographed, in a conference room or on a factory floor—is an opportunity to exercise change-friendly leadership.

By the way, what measurable effect did this kind of leadership have at Campbell Soup Company? Doug and his team achieved extraordinary results. By 2009 the company was outperforming both the S&P Food Group and the S&P 500. Sales and earnings were on the upswing. Core businesses were flourishing. And employee engagement was at world-class levels—the company now had 17 people who were enthusiastically engaged for every one who was not.

Doug used a simple behavioral model to help operationalize this high engagement philosophy. "Leaders have a bias for action," he said. "When they're listening, it may not feel like they're accomplishing anything. Nothing could be further from the truth. The touch point triad is simple: Listen, Frame, Advance. Asking the question, 'How can I help?' gets you started. Listening intently helps you figure out what is really going on and what

> *The task of the leader is to get people from where they are to where they have not been.*
> **Henry Kissinger**

others need from you. It's a way to demonstrate that you genuinely care. Framing the issue ensures that everyone in the touch point has the same understanding of the issue. Advancing the agenda means deciding what next steps to take and who will take them. As you engage in touch point after touch point, all you need to remember is to master the touch by using listen-frame-advance, listen-frame-advance."

A behavior as simple as the listen-frame-advance triad powerfully changes the communication dynamic from "It's all about me" to "It's all about us because we're in this together." Exclusiveness fosters distance. Inclusiveness fosters engagement. Great leaders know that you must listen with your head and your heart as well as with your ears. If you don't, you can end up solving the wrong problem or addressing a symptom rather than the underlying disease. And the listen-frame-advance model used by Doug Conant and his colleagues provides a great way to Stay on Message.

REMEMBER THE FOUR TS

As you work to *Stay on Message*, use the Four Ts.

Think-Friendly
- Carefully consider the questions that people likely have about the proposed change. Resist the urge to judge the "validity" of their questions. If a question has value for some of your Targets, you should address it openly and respectfully.
- What stories are people telling themselves about the change? What stories are you telling yourself that should be challenged? How can you use stories in your Stay on Message work?
- Who are the Saints, Ain'ts, and Complaints in your workplace? What can you do to convert them to your cause—or at the very least to neutralize the effect of their resistance?

Talk-Friendly
- Stay on the alert for Allness, Hardening of the Categories, Frozen Evaluation, Inference-Observation Confusion, and Bypassing. These communication problems are often very subtle and can sabotage your Stay on Message work.
- Beware the elephant herd. Clearly identify and tame the "elephants"—the uncomfortable issues that need to be confronted and resolved openly.
- Listen with Empathy, Inquire to Discover, and Advocate With Respect. Remember at all times that good communication is a continuous loop, not a simple one-way trajectory.

Trust-Friendly
- Mindfully use the Language of Trust. Deliberately engage in the behaviors of trust. Always—*always*—tell absolutely nothing but the truth.
- Clear the Fog. Drop the Pretense. Level the Field. Coach With Clarity. Connect the dots. Practiced faithfully, these

behaviors help keep your message(s) credible.

- Constantly solicit feedback. Accept it graciously, even when you disagree with it.

Team-Friendly

- Make sure your Sponsors have the information they need to help reinforce the primary change message. Don't be afraid to coach them. They will likely appreciate tips on content, tone, timing, and other important communication elements.
- Help your allies develop carefully integrated SMART Goals. While you want all your fellow communicators to be natural and comfortable, this is no time for freelancing. Help them stay on the same page.
- Ensure that appropriate reinforcement systems are in place. Make the old behaviors unattractive (or impossible). Make the new desired behaviors both attractive and progressively easier.

STAY ON MESSAGE SELF-ASSESSMENT

Instructions: *Read each statement and decide how accurately it describes your organization's adherence to the Stay on Message principles in this chapter:*

Place the point value of your response choice beside each statement.
    a. **This never or rarely occurs (0 points)**
    b. **This sometimes occurs (1 point)**
    c. **This regularly occurs (2 points)**
    d. **This always or almost always occurs (3 points)**

Place the point value of your response choice beside each statement.

_____ In planning and delivering our messages, we carefully consider the different communication needs of our CAST of Characters.

_____ We provide pertinent training to ensure that our people have the skills and tools to achieve the change we want.

_____ We are very explicit in communicating the behaviors that are expected and the behaviors that are unacceptable.

_____ We have clear agreement on the PICNICs we'll use to reinforce the behaviors needed to make our change successful.

_____ We're on the constant look-out for opportunities to celebrate people's successes in adopting our desired change.

_____ **Total Number of Points**

Interpreting Your Scores

0-5: Are you limiting your "messaging" to announcements and instructions? If you truly wish to *engage* people in your change effort (and engagement is really the only way to achieve sustainable change), you must address the communication needs of people in various roles.

6-10: You're doing many things right, but there's still room for improvement. Make sure people are held appropriately accountable for embracing the "new" behaviors. Give them the support they need to make the desired changes. Acknowledge their efforts.

11-15: You're engaging your CAST of Characters. Be sure to course correct frequently as you manage your communication, learning, and reinforcement systems. Ensure that your systems are appropriately integrated.

One of the true tests of leadership is the ability to recognize a problem before it becomes an emergency.
Arnold Glasow

Where performance is measured, performance improves. Where performance is measured and reported, the rate of improvement accelerates.
Thomas S. Monson

There are no traffic jams along the extra mile.
Roger Staubach

It's a funny thing about life: if you refuse to accept anything but the best, you very often get it.
W. Somerset Maugham

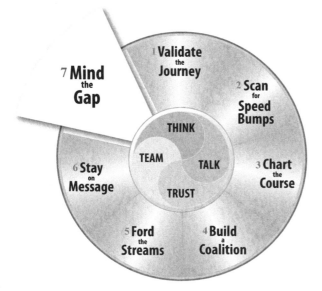

Chapter

Step 7:
Mind the Gap!

*Nobody made a greater mistake than he who
did nothing because he could do so little.*

My young grandson Duncan loves the family trips to England
and Scotland. One of his earliest memories is of riding the
London tube, or underground train system. On his first trip he especially liked the recorded safety message played loudly as passengers
stepped on and off the train: "Mind the gap!"

"Mind the gap!" is also an appropriate safety reminder in managing change. After all, minding the gap is what change is all about.

What's the gap between where we were and where we are?

What's the gap between where we are and where we want and
need to be?

What's the gap between any lingering old behaviors and the desired new behaviors?

What's the gap between messages sent and messages received?

What's the gap between the skills we have and the skills we need?

What's the gap between the good intentions we express and the great performance we seek?

The Change-Friendly Leadership framework, though presented in a linear fashion, is intended for use in a flexible and fluid way. Consider this metaphor: If you were flying a plane cross country or driving a car across town, you'd likely plan a specific route. But when faced with an unexpected headwind or traffic jam, you'd make necessary course corrections. Leading in an atmosphere of change requires course corrections. So you Mind the Gap.

A Case Study

Let's briefly consider a case study to illustrate how **Mind the Gap** work is integrated into the entire framework. Because of confidentiality issues, reporting this particular case study requires a bit of finesse. Rest assured that it's real.

In addition to working with dozens of corporate clients, I provide consulting services to a number of entities in the U.S. government.

> *The person who says it cannot be done should not interrupt the person doing it.*
> **Chinese proverb**

They're all interesting for different reasons, but they all have one thing in common: their reason for being is to serve the best interests of millions of Americans. With billions (sometimes trillions) of taxpayer dollars at stake, I'm of course very eager to help these government clients do their work more efficiently and effectively.

Eric Wilson (not his real name) is head of an organization that I'll simply call AGA (Anonymous Government Agency). Eric and his senior leadership team decided it was time for AGA to "go to the next level" of performance. When they asked for my help, I introduced them to the Change-Friendly Leadership framework. There are some details of the engagement that I can't share, even with fabricated names. But with broad strokes I can report how the framework was used to great advantage:

It was clear at the beginning that some elements of the AGA culture were getting in the way of performance. The need for change was obvious. The big questions were exactly *what* change? *How* do we do it? Everyone seemed to understand the importance of the "What's in it for me?" principle. In addition, it was agreed that necessary change would never happen unless and until we could **Validate the Journey.**

So our **Scan for Speed Bumps** work started with a series of confidential one-on-one interviews. The purpose of the interviews was to identify specific patterns of behaviors associated with undesirable outcomes. We conducted an organization-wide culture assessment using our Culture Alignment Profile instrument. The survey questions were carefully tailored to address the issues identified in the interviews. Then, beginning with the top man himself, we provided 360-degree performance feedback to every single employee in the AGA organization. Again, these were tailored to address issues of special interest in AGA. While the individual 360 reports were made available only to the people who were profiled, we used the aggregate data to cross validate the findings from the culture assessment. We carefully focused on root causes rather than superficial symptoms. With this integrated approach we were able to identify specific skill gaps that were contributing to various communication, trust, and performance challenges in the organization. These findings provided solid qualitative and quantitative evidence to support the needed change. We used the findings to circle back and flesh out our Validate the Journey efforts.

Next, we needed to **Chart the Course.** The evidence showed that well-intended people were not getting the results they needed because many of them lacked specific skills related to dialogue and trust-building. We introduced training that was tailored to the situation. In groups of about 24, every single person in the organization participated in a three-day workshop focused on Talk-Friendly and Trust-Friendly skills. The training included coaching in how to translate findings from 360-degree feedback into specific action plans for personal improvement. Individual accountability is critical in any change effort, and the 360s provided just the data people needed to "work on me first."

> *"Individual accountability is critical in any change effort."*

To enable any change to work, you must **Build a Coalition.** As mentioned earlier, synergy is not created by merely *adding* things together. Synergy comes from *bonding* things together *differently*. AGA already had a natural vehicle for this. It was called the Leadership Council, a group of about a dozen people from various functions and levels of the organization. Although the broad purpose for the Council was noble (represent the needs of all AGA employees), a crisper charter was needed. So, using the Team-Friendly principles outlined here in Chapter 7, the Leadership Council overhauled its charter to clarify its mission and functionality. Because the rotating membership represents all AGA employees, the Leadership Council assumed a high-profile role in monitoring the change efforts in the organization.

Change and/or transition must fit comfortably with the organization's pertinent cultural elements. So it's necessary to **Ford the Streams.** In this instance, some cultural elements—old behaviors that produced unwanted results—needed to be replaced with new behaviors (and skills) to produce desired results. This was not the time for ambiguity. In the most explicit terms possible, undesirable behaviors were identified. Undiscussables were courageously placed on the table for open dialogue. Elephants were rounded up and tamed. As AGA people produced better results with their newfound Talk-Friendly and Trust-Friendly skills, success begat success. As they became more competent in using their new skills, individual and group confidence soared. Performance improvements came right along.

Because the AGA people are serious about creating change that's sustainable, they pay special attention to their **Stay on Message** work. This takes multiple forms. Eric Wilson and other senior leaders conduct day-long follow-up sessions about every other month. These sessions are kept small enough (about 20 participants each) to accommodate plenty of interaction and open discussion (engagement!). Weekly newsletters provide case studies of AGA people practicing the skills they've been taught and reporting on the benefits. If someone stubs his toe (old behaviors), the situation is quietly but explicitly addressed. When people practice the Talk-Friendly and Trust-Friendly skills (new behaviors) they're acknowledged and celebrated. PICNIC skills, mentioned in the previous chapter, are especially helpful with this reinforcement. Each person is asked to meet frequently with a "learning partner." These informal discussions focus on individual progress and performance accountability.

To help **Mind the Gap**, shorter culture surveys are conducted every few months to help AGA people monitor their progress. In the brief survey, respondents are asked to report the extent to which they agree or disagree with explicit statements like "Performance standards are crystal clear, with no 'wiggle room' on what's acceptable and what's not" and "Compared to 12-18 months ago, it now seems more 'safe' to challenge the status quo." Open-ended survey items provide the opportunity to comment on improvements or elaborate on any concerns. Follow-up 360-degree performance feedback profiles are also part of the mix. These enable people to see with great specificity just how much they're improving from the perspective of their circle of colleagues who are important to their success. The Mind the Gap efforts are also supported by the Stay on Message work. For example, in one of the follow-up training sessions each AGA employee was asked to write a six-word autobiography. The assignment was inspired by the challenge once given to novelist Ernest Hemingway. Hemingway, known for his terse prose, was challenged by a friend

> *A dream is just a dream. A goal is a dream with a plan and a deadline.*
> **Harvey Mackay**

to write a short story in only six words. Hemingway complied: "For sale. Baby shoes. Never worn." Writing most anything in only six words is a great exercise in mental gymnastics. It requires laser focus on only the most essential elements. Throughout AGA, employees were given a couple of weeks to think about their six-word autobiographies. They were asked to focus on their specific, personal commitments to make the AGA culture more productive and user-friendly. The resulting "autobiographies" ranged from funny to deeply thought-provoking. In every case, people embraced the "work on me first" principle and emphasized personal accountability for results. They were engaged!

AGA people were already very good. Now their performance is better than ever, and the improvements are clearly quantified in both the culture assessment data as well as the performance metrics they've always monitored. It's all clearly the result good people who are determined to Mind the Gap.

Personal behaviors, and the cultures they produce, tend to be somewhat elastic. It's sometimes easy to snap back into a previous habit or behavior. Even the most attentive performer can have an occasional relapse. Consequently, Mind the Gap work must be both personal and institutional. Individuals must be given systems and processes—such as training and coaching, learning partners, and 360-degree feedback—to help them stay on course. And the organization must provide an atmosphere that constantly reinforces the behaviors that produce the desired outcomes. Culture building is not like installing a new air conditioning system. It requires constant vigilance.

Mind the Gap.

REMEMBER THE FOUR TS

As you work to Mind the Gap, continue to engage in the Four Ts behaviors used in previous steps of the Change-Friendly Leadership framework.

MIND THE GAP SELF-ASSESSMENT

Instructions: *Read each statement and decide how accurately it describes your organization's adherence to the **Mind the Gap** principles in this chapter:*

Place the point value of your response choice beside each statement.

    a. We never or rarely do this (0 points)
    b. We sometimes do this (1 point)
    c. We regularly do this (2 points)
    d. We always or almost always do this (3 points)

Place the point value of your response choice beside each statement.

_____ To determine the progress of our change effort(s), we use quantitative tools (culture surveys, 360-degree feedback, etc.) rather than rely only on anecdotal data.

_____ We stay on the look-out for systems, processes, procedures, and behaviors that get in the way of our change efforts.

_____ We hold people personally accountable for contributing (primarily through their behavior) to the change we need.

_____ When we notice a gap between desired performance and what's actually being delivered, we promptly step in to close the gap.

_____ As part of our Mind the Gap work, we circle back to other steps in the Change-Friendly Leadership framework to ensure appropriate integration of our efforts.

_____ Total Number of Points

Interpreting Your Scores

0-5: Are you relying mostly on informal observation to determine progress with your change? You need reliable metrics on the performance issues that count the most.

6-10: Not bad, but you can do much better. Remember that people have a tendency to treasure what you measure. Ensure that you have systems and protocols in place to quantify performance. Reduce the "wiggle room" in defining desired performance.

11-15: You understand the need for constant vigilance in closing the gap between the current state and the desired future state. Keep on keeping on.

Section

THREE

BONUS•POINTS

To enrich your use of the Change-Friendly methodology, check out our **Bonus Point** material after reading each section of this book. Additional material is posted on the Doctor Duncan website.

All the material is free to readers of the book (you!), and we'll be adding to it periodically. The Bonus Point material includes thought pieces, White Papers, free diagnostic tools, interviews, videos, and other items.

To access the Bonus Points, simply scan this QR code with your smart phone and let your browser take you directly to the content. Alternatively, go to www.DoctorDuncan.com/BonusPoints

See you there!

◄ Smart Phone Link
DoctorDuncan.com/BonusPoints

AFTERWORD

Explore, Discover, Explore

Leadership does not require a title. Many people who provide the uplifting and encouraging influence of true leadership do so without authority or position. Change-Friendly leadership is not about ordering people around. It's about engaging people's heads, hearts, and hopes. Don't diminish the importance of this by calling it "soft stuff." Appropriate engagement of people is absolutely essential to success with all the "hard stuff" of organizational performance. And it must never end. There are brief stopping off points along the way, but it's a journey, not a destination.

We can take inspiration from lines by T.S. Eliot: "We shall not cease from exploration, and the end of all our exploring will be to arrive where we started and know the place for the first time." Although I have offered a framework to make change efforts more manageable, I should underscore a critical point: Change-Friendly leadership is a continuous loop of exploring and discovering. No one has all the answers, or even all the questions, about dealing with change. But we can be certain of one thing. Genuinely engaging other human beings—the "friendly factor" discussed throughout this book—really does work. And as we mindfully apply these ageless principles, we can rediscover the joy of knowing them for the first time.

Acknowledgments

*God gives us 1,440 minutes a day. Shouldn't
we use at least a few of them to say thank you?*

Nearly every worthwhile thing we do in life is a collaborative effort. Producing this book is no exception.

What I've learned about good writing I owe to early teachers and editors who helped me develop my natural love for language and polish my own style of expression. Hundreds of my consulting and coaching clients have provided an ongoing laboratory for applying and validating the Change-Friendly principles you'll read about here. Countless professional colleagues have helped me fine-tune my thinking about leadership, communication, change, and transition.

All that was an excellent start. It got me to the point of envisioning this book. Then there was that little part about actually doing the writing.

Several good friends generously read the manuscript and made helpful comments and suggestions. I particularly appreciate the insights of Dr. Brent D. Peterson, truly worthy of the appellation "guru" in the world of organizational development and leadership. Many others were kind in their endorsements, some of which are published here in the book.

Thanks to Nancy Newland, my friend and graphic designer. Nancy is a huge talent, bursting with joy and great ideas. She has a true gift for translating written words into something that appeals to the eye as comfortably as it entreats the inner ear.

Thanks to my New York team of Eric Kampmann, Margot Atwell, Sarah Lucie and Megan Trank at Midpoint Trade Books. They've been superstars in helping me bring this book through the various stages of production and getting it into the right distribution channels.

Thanks to Jessica Krakoski, Margaret Kingbury, Rusty Shelton, and others at Cave Henricks Communications. Their tireless efforts to generate media attention for *Change-Friendly Leadership* will pay dividends for years to come.

Thanks to Judy O'Beirn and her terrific team at Hasmark Services. They really do put their hearts and souls into book launches, and their careful handling of my "baby" is much appreciated.

Naturally, I'm grateful to Stephen M.R. Covey for his generous foreword to this book. Stephen and his father Stephen R. Covey have been my friends for decades and I deeply appreciate their groundbreaking contributions to the fields of business, organizational effectiveness, principle-centered leadership, and self-improvement.

I humbly acknowledge the tireless encouragement of dear Rean Robbins, my exceptional wife and sweetheart for these past four and a half decades. While I could have retired years ago, Rean patiently stands by (and mostly stays at home) because she knows how much I love my clients and because she appreciates my sense of mission with the principles I teach.

Most of all, I thank God for his goodness and tender mercies. And for the privilege of doing work that really matters.

Dr. Rodger Dean Duncan
Liberty, Missouri
June 2012

ABOUT THE AUTHOR

Dr. Rodger Dean Duncan is widely known for helping individuals and organizations transform good intentions into great performance.

His interest in leadership issues was first sprouted when he was a university undergraduate. That interest blossomed into full-scale passion when he covered business and politics as a young journalist. One of his early editors was Jim Lehrer (later of PBS television fame), who taught him how to connect the dots between what people aspire to and what they actually accomplish.

After reporting for *The Salt Lake Tribune, The Fort Worth Star-Telegram,* and *The Dallas Times Herald,* Rodger was managing editor of two daily newspapers in east Texas. He also wrote a nationally syndicated column and freelanced for many national magazines.

In 1972, Rodger launched a consulting practice focusing on leadership and performance improvement issues. His clients have ranged from cabinet officers in two White House administrations to senior leaders in many of the world's best companies in more than a dozen industries. In addition, he headed communications at Campbell Soup Company, and was vice president of a global energy firm.

Rodger earned his PhD in organizational dynamics at Purdue University. His Internet column reaches opt-in business subscribers in more than 200 countries. Bestselling author Stephen R. Covey calls Rodger's work in leadership "brilliantly insightful and inspiring; profound, yet user friendly; visionary, yet highly practical."

Dr. Duncan is active in many pursuits focused on bringing out the best in people. For example, he served two terms on the Advisory Council of the Institute of Nuclear Power Operations. He was a founding board member of the CAMIE Awards (Character and Morality in Entertainment), an organization celebrating family-friendly productions from Hollywood and network television. And he served as president of Fellowship of the Concerned, an ecumenical group that fosters harmony among people of different ethnic and religious backgrounds.

Rodger and his wife live in Missouri. They are parents of four grown children, and have eleven grandchildren.